IMAGES
of America

HANOVER

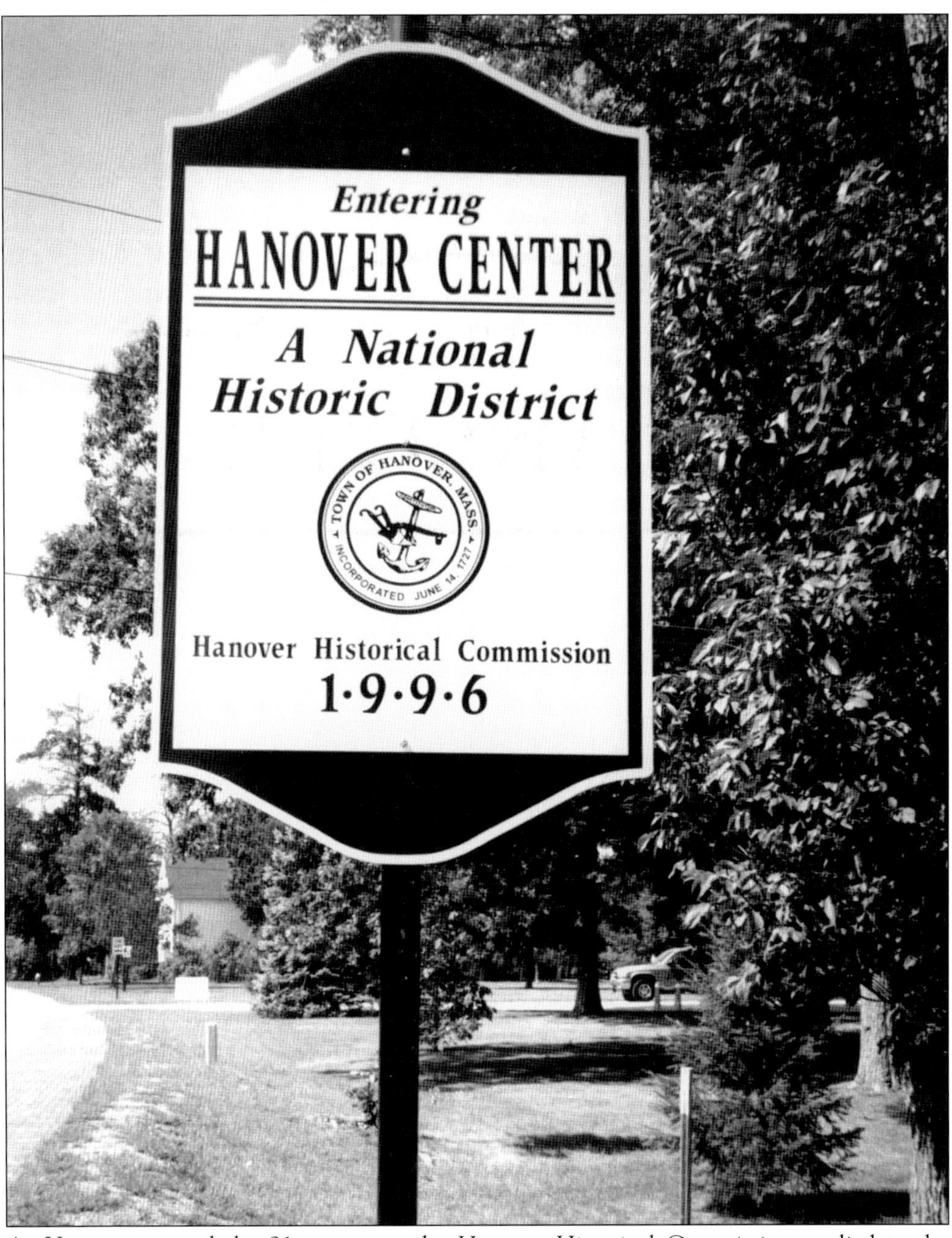

As Hanover entered the 21st century, the Hanover Historical Commission applied to the Massachusetts Historical Commission for nomination of Hanover Center as a National Historic District. The district, marked by brick sidewalks, includes the Sylvester School, the Stetson House, the First Congregational Church, Hanover Center Cemetery, the John Curtis Library, and the town hall. Adjacent is the pastoral atmosphere of Briggs Riding Stable and its pastures.

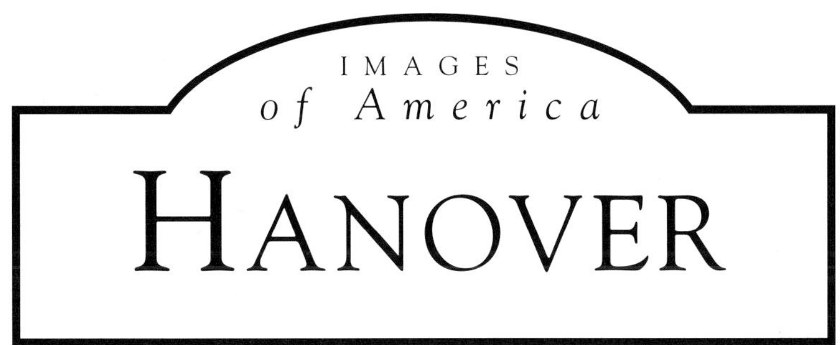

Barbara U. Barker and Leslie J. Molyneaux

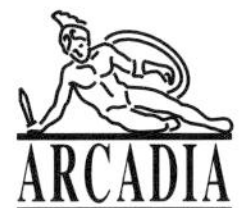

ISBN 0-7385-3690-3

First published 2004

Published by Arcadia Publishing,
Charleston SC, Chicago IL, Portsmouth NH, San Francisco CA

Printed in Great Britain

Library of Congress Catalog Card Number: 2004110292

For all general information, contact Arcadia Publishing:
Telephone 843-853-2070
Fax 843-853-0044
E-mail sales@arcadiapublishing.com
For customer service and orders:
Toll-free 1-888-313-2665

Visit us on the Internet at www.arcadiapublishing.com

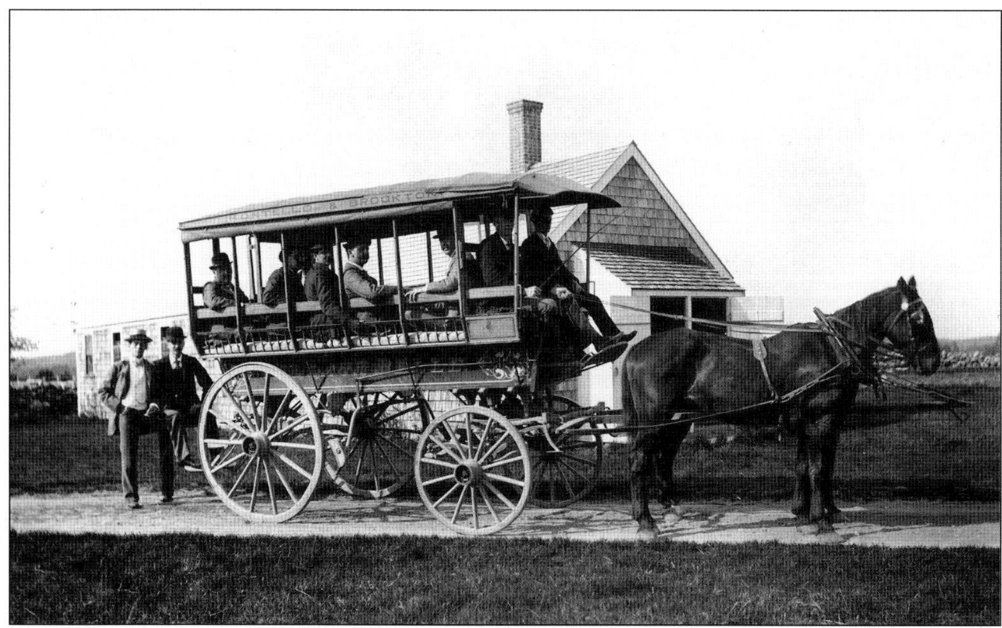

The photographers featured in this volume span the history of photography, and every medium from glass-plate negatives to digital images is featured. The cover image shows Hanover photographer H. R. Sturtevant and associates on an 1896 field excursion to the Ponkapoag area of Milton. The same group is shown here, traveling by horse-drawn carriage from the Brockton and Montello Barge Company.

Contents

ACKNOWLEDGMENTS

Encouraged by Arcadia Publishing, and with the support of the Hanover Historical Society, the authors have endeavored to present a pictorial history of Hanover that will be a useful reference. We would like to acknowledge those who have helped us to collect the images and information presented in the book. We trust that the reader will develop a better understanding of the history of the villages of Hanover and the people who lived there.

Among the many who have assisted us are Tony Acampora, Paul Acampora, Edith Bates, J. David Congalton, the Ellis-Vincent family, Carol Franzosa, Nancy Goldthwait, Kenton Greene, Dorothy Greene, Diane Haigh, Barbara Young Itz, Mark Jacobson, Barbara Matheny, Jean Migre, Elsie Nelson, James Rodriguez, and Albert Sullivan. The historical society will benefit from the proceeds.

INTRODUCTION

The first recorded white man to set foot in Hanover was Phineas Pratt, a resident of Thomas Weston's settlement in Wessagusset, now Weymouth. In the spring of 1622, the Native Americans were intending to attack the Plymouth settlement from the north. Unable to recruit a messenger to warn the colonists in Plymouth, Pratt set out on a perilous journey along the old Native American pathways to alert the settlers, spending his first night camping near the North River and fording it at a rocky place later called Luddam's Ford.

The first settler in the area now known as Hanover was William Barstow, who came with his wife and children up the North River from Scituate in 1649. He built his cabin near the river and the intersection of two paths, in a location known today as the village of Four Corners. Barstow was commissioned to build the first bridge over the North River, the abutments of which are still visible several feet upriver from the present bridge. Barstow acquired the skills of a shipbuilder, as did his sons, and many ships were built on the river's winding banks. Others followed the Barstows, and these early settlers made their homes along the old Native American trails and crossroads, near fertile farmland and water sources for mills. Parcels of land were granted by the Colony Court in the second half of the 17th century for the areas that became the villages of North Hanover, West Hanover, Drinkwater, and South Hanover. Assinippi grew up at the crossroads by Third Herring Brook, known by the Native Americans as "Hassen Ippi," meaning "rocky water."

At the Luddam's Ford area, a dam and bridge were built to power early gristmills and sawmills. Also established there later was an ironworks that claims to have forged the anchor "for that grand old warship *Constitution*." Farther upstream, dams were erected to harness the waterpower, and by 1720, a forge and refinery were established in South Hanover. There was also an early forge on King Street, which later became the site of the National Fireworks Company.

The first town meeting of the citizens of these villages was held in Hanover Center at the home of Drummer Stetson in 1727. The first order of business was to establish the new town of Hanover, raise and collect funds to build a meetinghouse, hire a minister, and engage a schoolmaster. Though the villages were separated by woodlands and streams, the men of each village gathered to raise funds, lay out roads, elect leaders, and discuss other business of the town. Within seven years, the town began to appropriate funds for defense. The first soldiers were sent to battle by 1740.

Seven distinct villages developed, each with its own industry and mills, school, general store and post office, blacksmith shop, and by the early 1900s, fire station. Several villages had a church, and by 1868, railroad tracks had been laid from the main line in Abington, through West Hanover and South Hanover, and ending at Four Corners.

The shoe industry became an important business, and by 1870, many village people were employed in this trade. Clapp Rubber Mill employed 400 hands in that factory at the turn of the 20th century, and Lot Phillips's box factory was a growing business. National Fireworks hired many new immigrants at its factory in the West Hanover-Drinkwater section. Though many Hanover residents were employed in factory work, almost every family was still engaged in agriculture.

World War I and, to a much greater degree, World War II brought rapid change to Hanover. The National Fireworks Company, during World War I, was the first company in the United States to manufacture tracer bullets. During World War II, the National Fireworks Company was one of the largest munitions manufacturers in the world, with many branch plants, and employing as many as 8,000 workers in this area alone.

After World War II, the National Fireworks Company ceased munitions manufacturing, and Hanover again became a quiet country town. Following the Korean War, the need for housing and the improved roadway system led to the residential growth that continues today. Village distinctions have gradually disappeared, as have the district schools, and a sense of unity and community spirit has developed that makes Hanover a highly desirable community in which to live.

Throughout its history, Hanover has been fortunate to be the home of talented and, in some cases, prolific amateur photographers. They recorded the mundane as well as the exceptional events in town. Alpheus Packard, Jared Gardner, Edmund Packard, and L. Vernon Briggs all dabbled in photography, but residents are most indebted to Thomas Drew, L. Herman Sturtevant, and Charles Gleason for their extensive production of images.

Thomas Drew, born in 1845, was a merchant who resided on Broadway in South Hanover. Many of Drew's surviving glass-plate negatives show the South Hanover vicinity, as well as portraits of his relatives and neighbors. Drew took most of the photographs in the 1910 *History of Hanover* (Jedediah Dwelley and John F. Simmons, *History of the Town of Hanover, Massachusetts with Family Genealogies* [Town of Hanover, 1910]). In addition, he published several photographic postcards of the area.

L. Herman Sturtevant, born in 1852, was a member of a camera club. An album in the archives of the Hanover Historical Society shows him and his associates as they took field trips around the South Shore to practice their skills.

Charles Gleason, born in 1880, created numerous photographic scrapbooks containing not only a multitude of local photographs from 1905 to the 1960s, but also detailed descriptions of the people and places shown in his pictures.

Jean Migre, our most prolific contemporary photographer, attends virtually every public event with her camera. Without her efforts, life in Hanover today would be lost to history.

In her book *On Photography*, Susan Sontag wrote, "In America, the photographer is not simply the person who records the past, but the one who invents it." Join us now, as we travel through time from the 1800s to today, stopping here and there to visit in the villages of Hanover.

One
Hanover Center

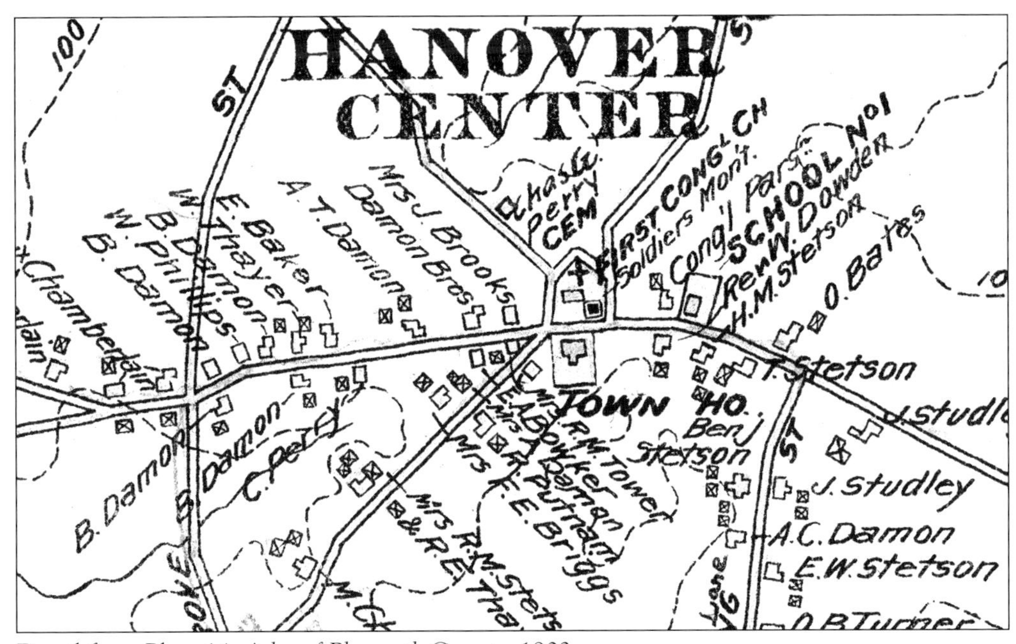

Detail from Plate 14, *Atlas of Plymouth County*, 1903.

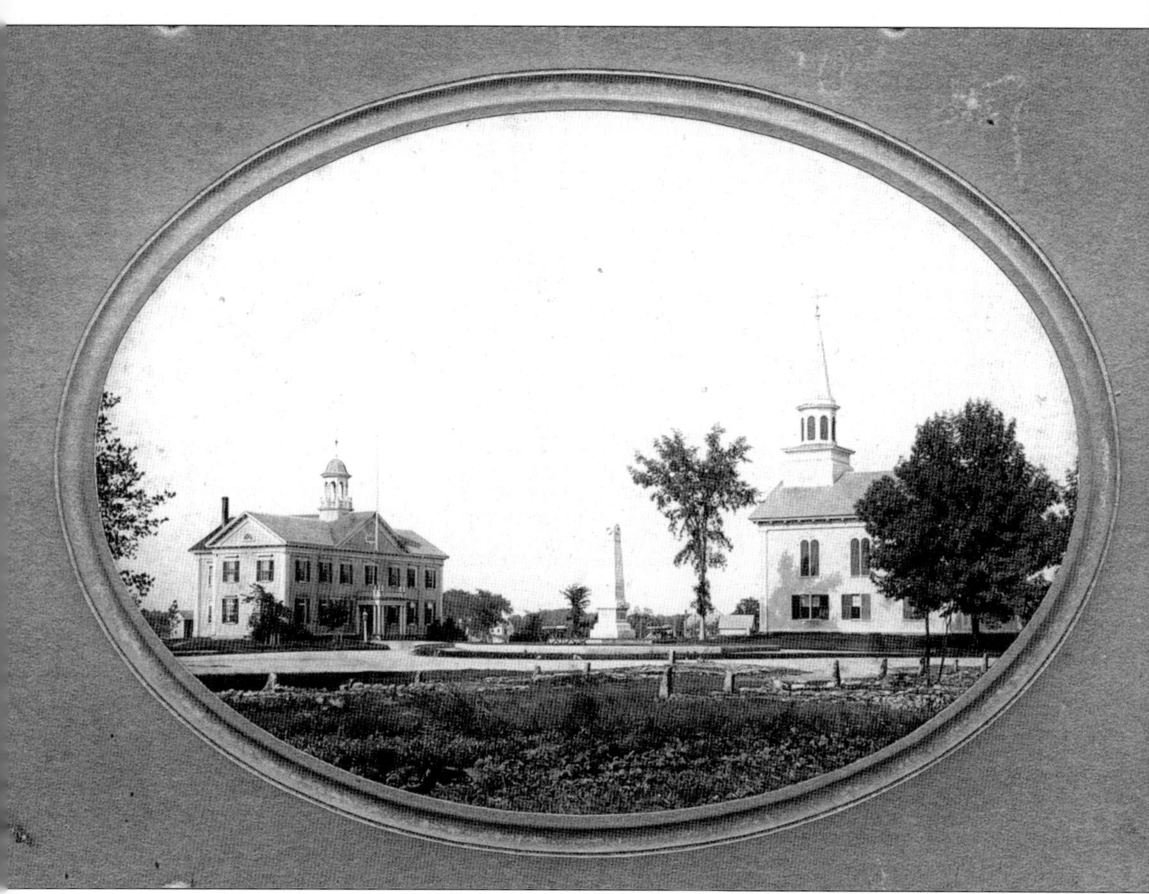

Hanover Center, recognized as a National Historic District, has changed little since 1900. In 1862, a devastating fire destroyed the Third Congregational Church, as well as the town hall, which stood six feet away to the west. In 1863, a new town hall was built (left). The ells were constructed in 1896, so this photograph must have been taken after that date. The church was also rebuilt in 1863. In the foreground are the granite fence posts that bounded the Center District School.

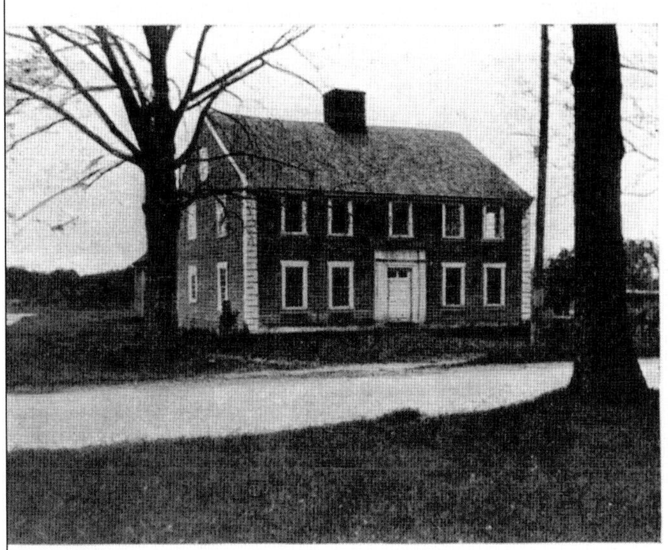

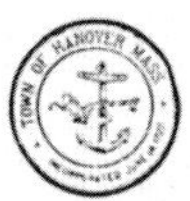

THIS HOUSE was built in 1716 and before the erection of the "First Meeting House" in 1729. The people gathered here regularly for the "Public Worship of God." The historical exhibit is in this house.

200th Anniversary

TOWN OF HANOVER

JUNE 14, 1927

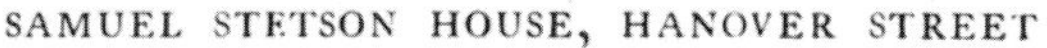

SAMUEL STETSON HOUSE, HANOVER STREET

Postcards, like this one of the Samuel Stetson House, were published for the 200th anniversary of the town of Hanover on June 14, 1927. The house was built *c.* 1716, and served as the gathering place for the town until the first meetinghouse was constructed across the street in 1729. In the 1920s, Dr. L. Vernon Briggs restored the building, which had been the home of four generations of Stetsons. It was purchased by the town in 1978, and is listed on the National Historic Register.

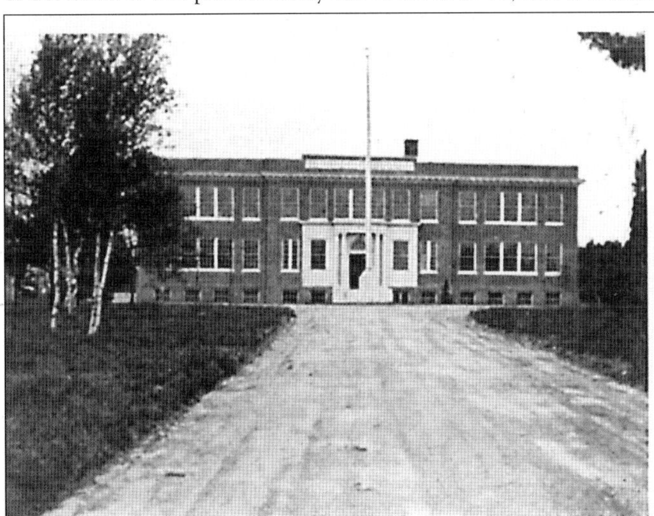

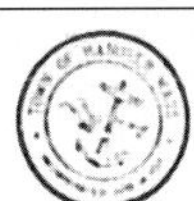

THIS building was constructed 1926 - 27 and named for Edmund Q. Sylvester whose gift of $50,000 made its erection possible. It was dedicated March 11, 1927.

The memorial to the Veterans of the World War in the form of a flag staff with a monumental base has been placed in front of the entrance to this new building and is to be dedicated during the Anniversary Week.

200th Anniversary

TOWN OF HANOVER

JUNE 14, 1927

THE EDMUND Q. SYLVESTER HIGH SCHOOL

The Edmund Q. Sylvester High School is featured on a 1927 postcard. After much discussion at the 1926 town meeting about the need for a new high school, Edmund Q. Sylvester stood up and announced that he would donate $50,000 toward such a purpose. Other donors followed, and the town meeting appropriated the remaining funds. The new school, designed by local architect John Williams Beal, was dedicated March 11, 1927, the year of the town's 200th anniversary.

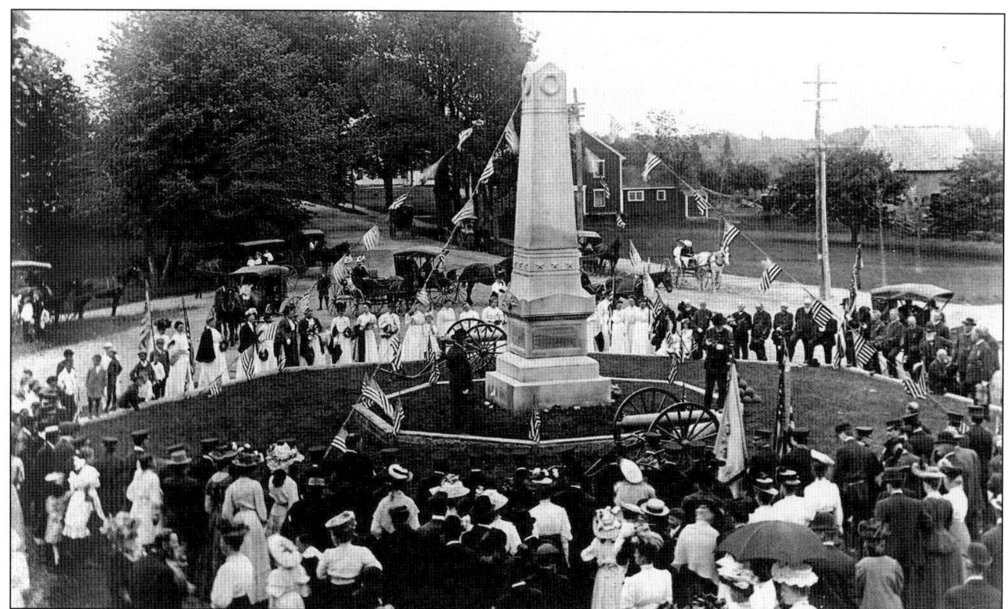

On July 17, 1878, the Hanover Soldiers and Sailors Monument was dedicated. The morning train brought state dignitaries for the daylong festivities, which commenced with breakfast at St. Andrew's Church prior to a parade to Hanover Center. Town officials, GAR post members, members of the Ancient and Honorable Artillery, bands, and local clubs all participated. In the photograph, this later Memorial Day ceremony at the monument, now called the Civil War Monument, recognized the veterans of all wars.

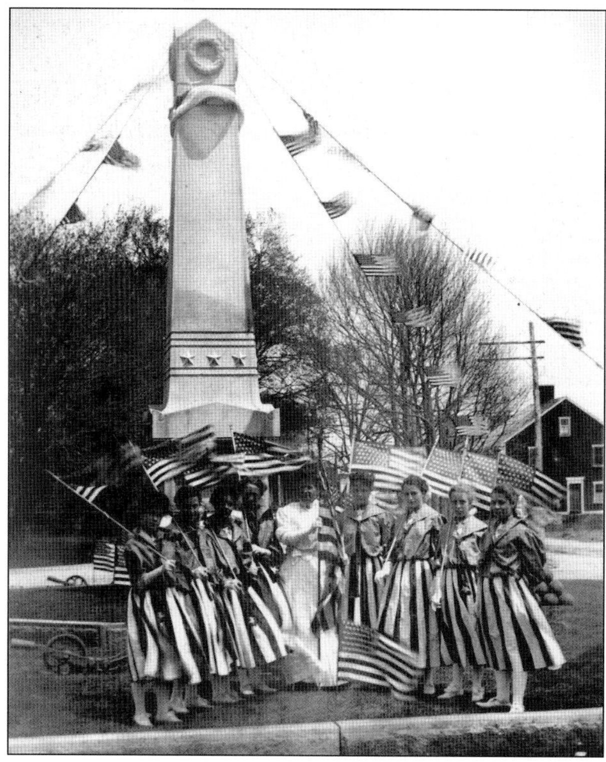

The Civil War Monument in Hanover Center provides the backdrop for this group of young ladies in patriotic dress. The Stetson House can be seen in the back on the right.

John Curtis was born in Hanover in 1817, and attended local schools. Although he made his fortune in Boston and lived in the city, he always came back to Hanover. When leaving funds to build a library, he wrote: "Born and raised in this town, I feel an interest in the welfare of its people. . . . I desire to repay, in part, my obligation . . . to afford better opportunities to present and coming generations of boys and girls of my native town."

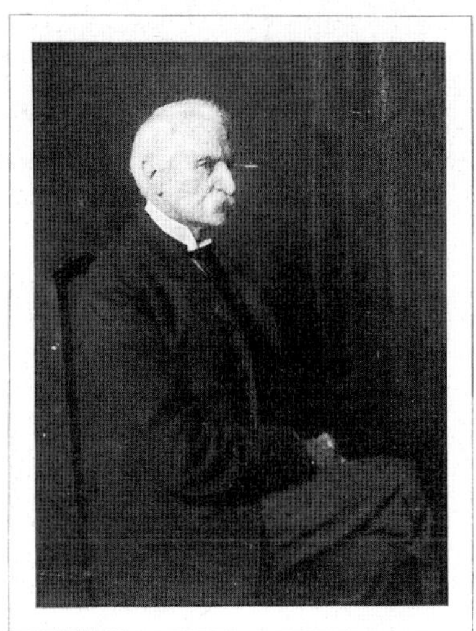

DEDICATION OF
John Curtis Free Library
HANOVER, MASS.
Thursday, Dec. 12, 1907
Souvenir

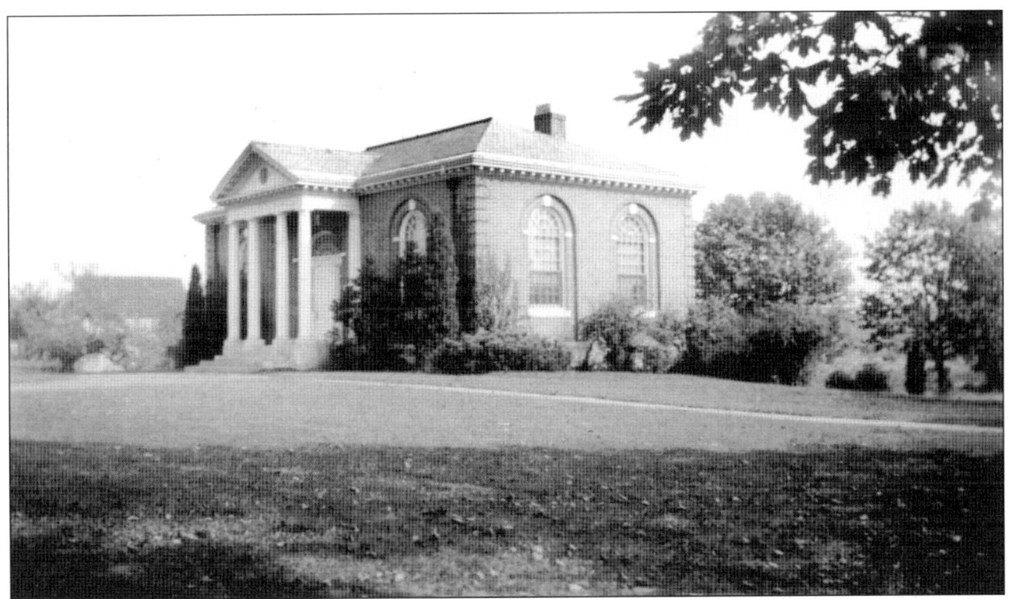

In 1887, John Curtis donated his collection of books to the town to be housed in two rooms of the town hall. Later, in his will, he set aside $15,000 for the building of a new structure to serve as a library. The building, designed by local architect Edmund Q. Sylvester, was constructed in 1907. This photograph by Charles Gleason was taken *c.* 1930. A recent addition has incorporated the original building.

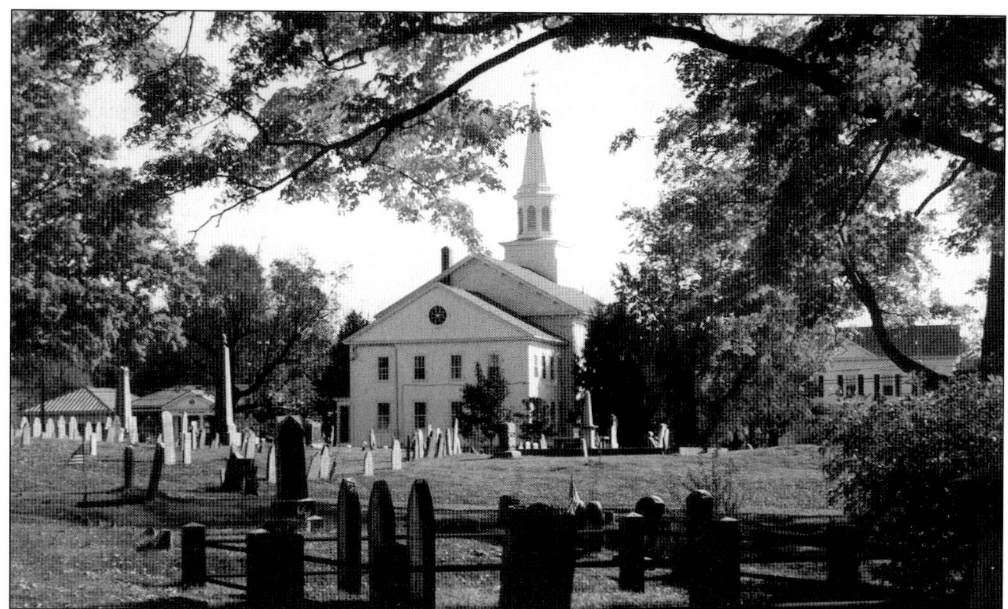

The view from inside the cemetery in Hanover Center has changed little over the past 100 years. Sometimes called "God's Acre," this oldest part of the cemetery, behind the First Congregational Church, is a quiet, pretty spot in which to contemplate the past. The earliest slate headstones in the foreground are from the 1700s and bear designs such as angel faces and weeping willows.

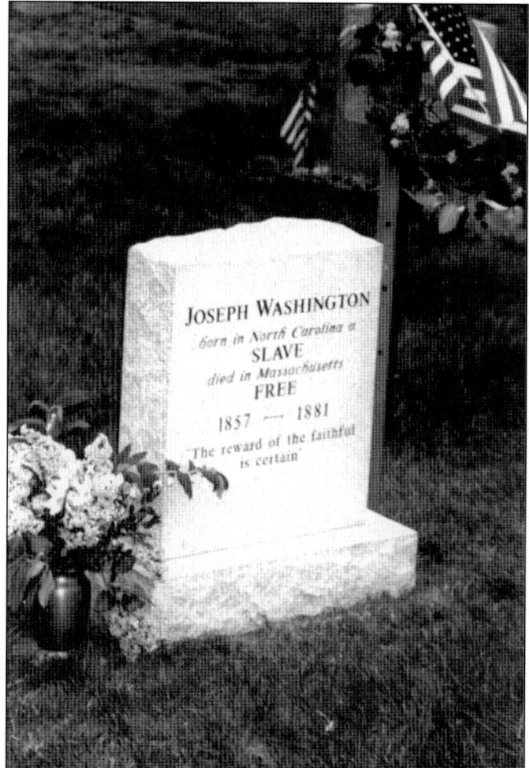

The cemetery is the resting place of Joseph Washington, a former slave brought to Hanover from North Carolina by Joseph Church at the close of the Civil War. Washington, an orphan, became a part of the Church family on King Street. The stone shown here was placed in 2000, following a public subscription. It replaced an older marker but bears the same inscription, "born in North Carolina a SLAVE, died in Massachusetts FREE."

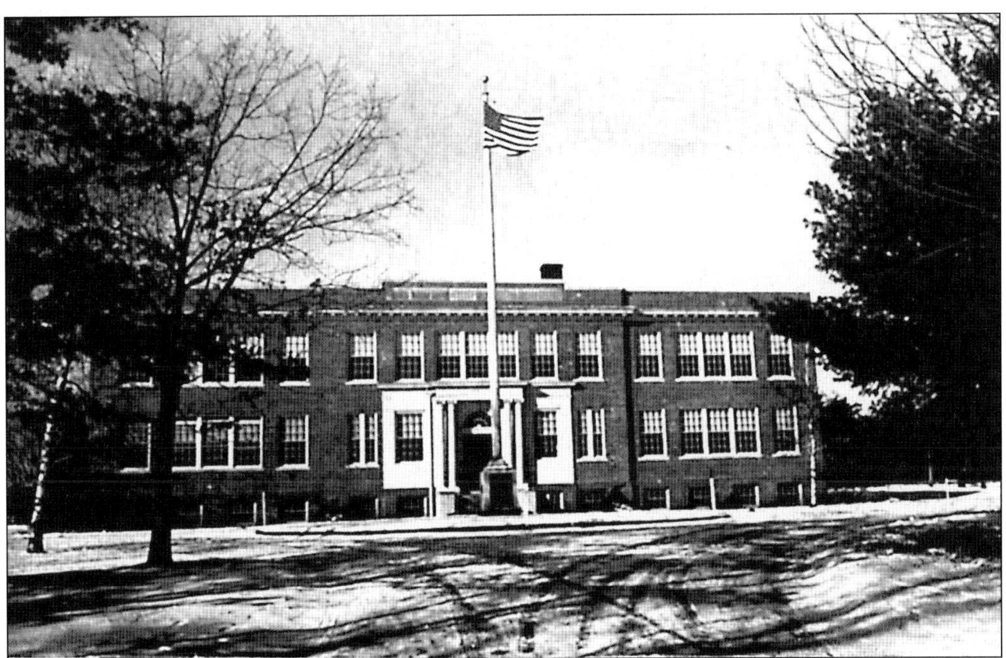

Sylvester High School, built in 1927, is shown in this early postcard image. Located in the Hanover Historic District, the structure is now an elementary school for third- and fourth-graders.

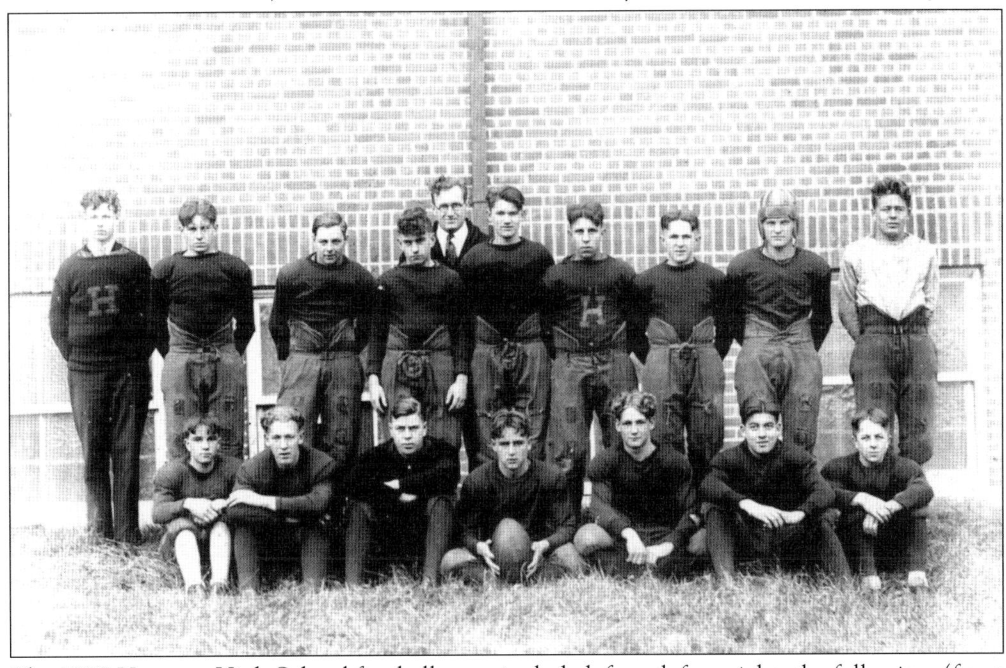

The 1928 Hanover High School football team included, from left to right, the following: (front row) Wilbur "Peewee" Trafton, Earl "Curley" Wells, Edward "Groggy" Leary, Frederic "Jack" Kellow, Stuart "Stew" Studley, Russell "Hendy" Henderson, and Wesley "Spider" Sides; (back row) Kenneth "Ken" Lovell, Gilbert "Gilly" MacDonald, Fred Nelson, Edgar "Ned" Packard, coach Curtis Brooks, Frederic "Freddy" Gleason, Alfred "Stinky" Davis, Joseph Yustavich, Gordon Bray, and John "Johnny" Stetson.

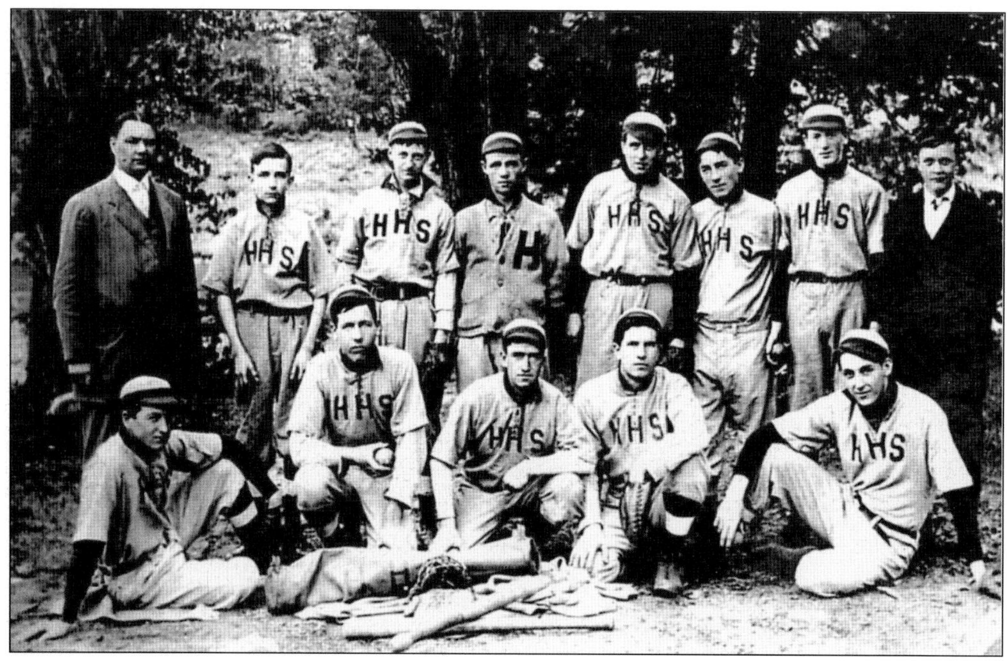

The cut of the cap was a bit different in 1910, but Hanover High School has always fielded competitive baseball teams.

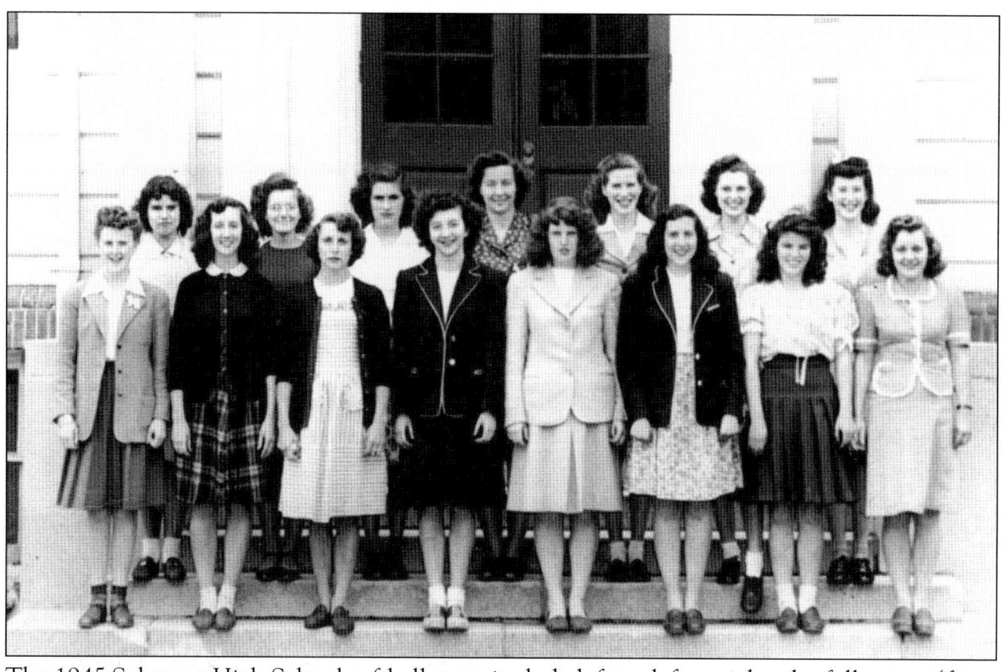

The 1945 Sylvester High School softball team included, from left to right, the following: (front row) Jean Marie Lovell, Eleanor Downing Kimball, Barbara Legg Adams, Lorraine Hennigar, Christine Damon, Shirley Henderson Adams, Joyce Tucker, and Arlene Mahon Hannigan; (back row) Marilyn Pratt, Betty Lloyd, Phyllis Gorrill, Ruth Graves Montgomery, Thelma Wood Smith, Edna MacFadgen Grays, and Marjorie Wood Cleveland.

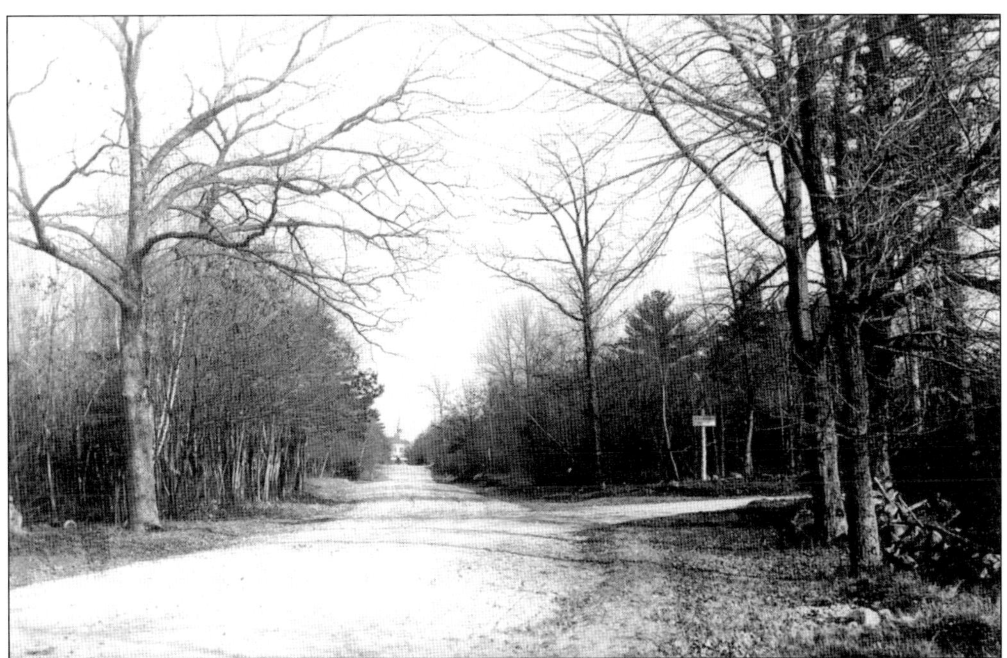

Main Street in Hanover Center was a real country dirt road when this photograph was taken. The signpost on the right marks the entry to Grove Street, and the First Congregational Church can be seen at the far end of Main Street.

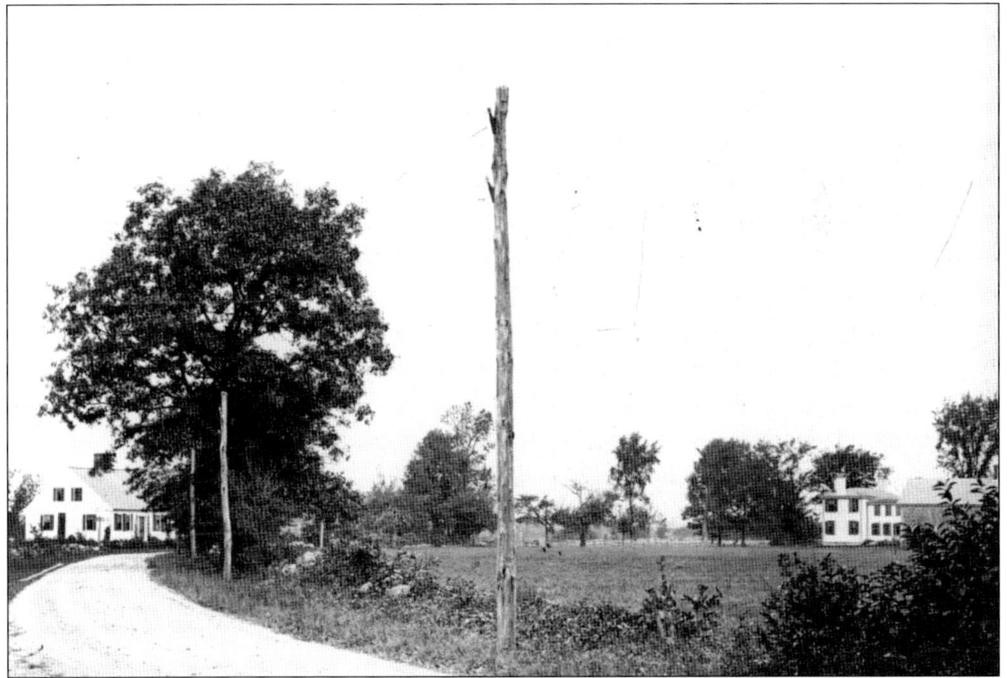

This rare view shows homes located at 402 and 429 Main Street. The Federal Colonial–style house on the right, built by William Stockbridge in 1809, was a farm of about 60 acres. It included land on both sides of Main Street that was part of the original Hatherly grant. Amos Sylvester built the Cape-style house on the left, on the corner of Plain Street, before 1759.

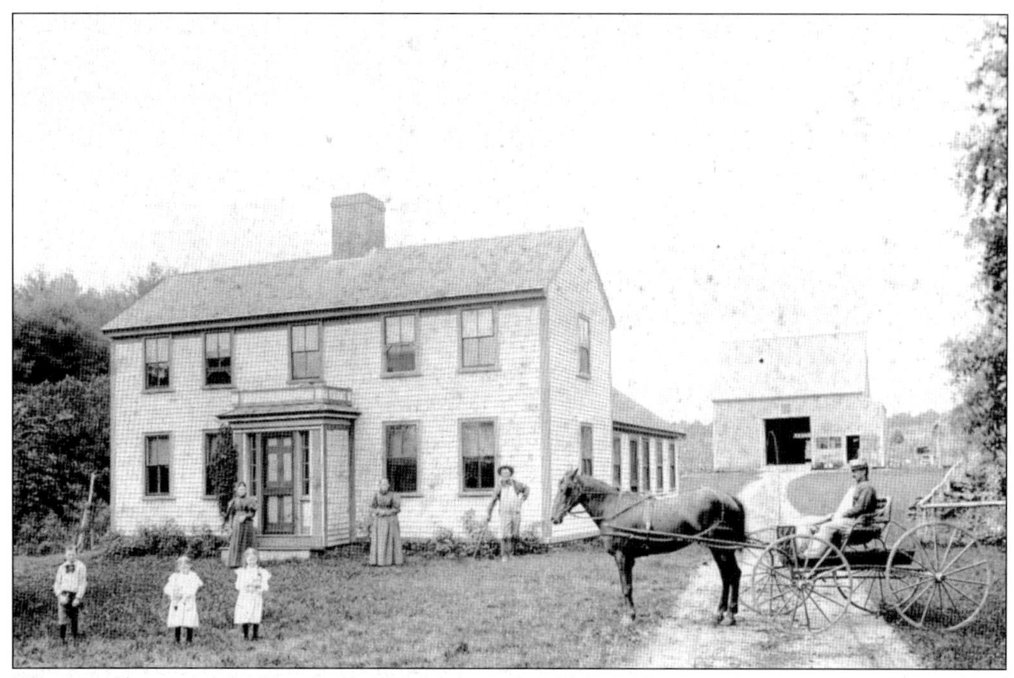

The rear portion of the Bonney homestead, at 184 Old Washington Street, was constructed *c.* 1740. The Bonney twins, Anne and Lucy, and their brother Percy were born in this house. They are shown here (in left foreground) with their mother, father, aunt and uncle. Anne and Lucy both lived more than 100 years and were vital to the preservation of Hanover's history.

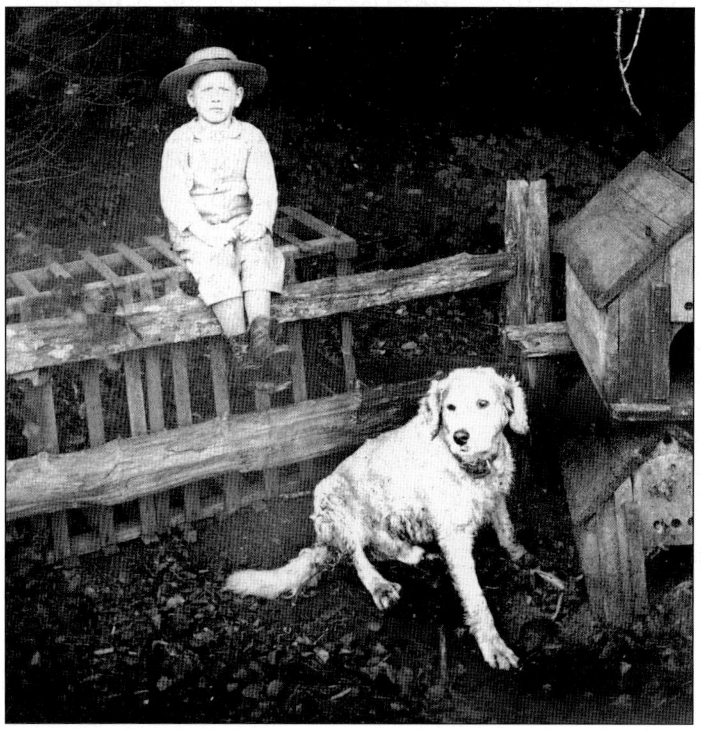

Percy Bonney, the older brother of twins Anne and Lucy, loved the outdoors and exploring the woods with his dog, Carlo. They are seen here in an 1894 photograph. After serving in World War I, Percy became a mechanic and was known to fix anything. He built a school bus and drove many students to school.

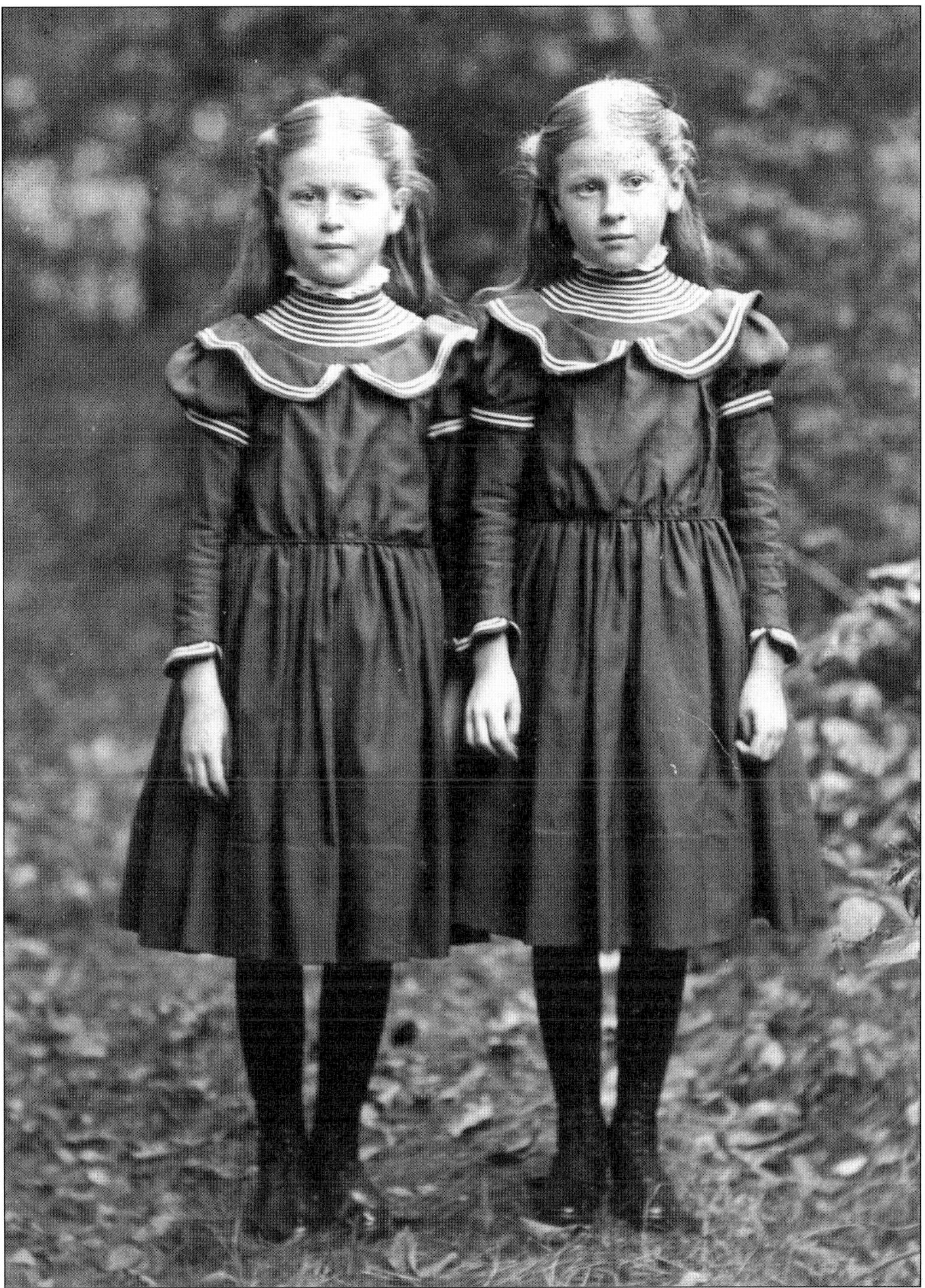

Twins Anne and Lucy Bonney were born in the family homestead on Washington Street, at the foot of the Union Street hill. This H. L. Sturtevant photograph, dated October 12, 1900, shows them at nine years of age. The two graduated from Radcliffe College in 1918, and then taught in Connecticut. Co-authors of *Houses of the Revolution*, the sisters were active historians throughout their long lives.

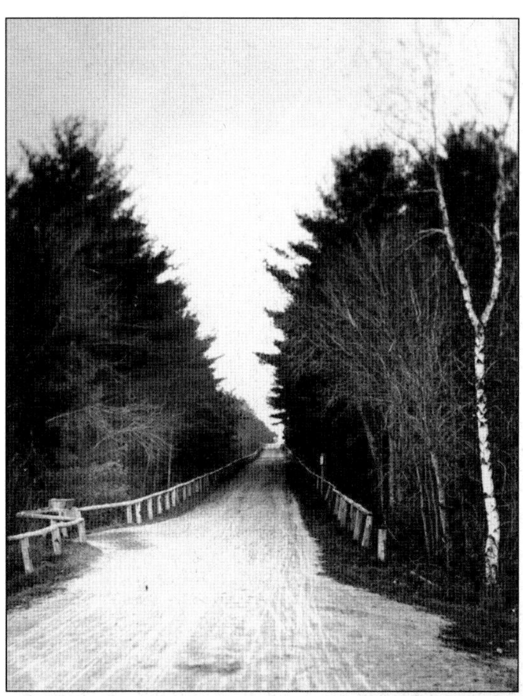

Woodward Hill, also known as Folly Hill, is the long incline from Columbia Road west toward the town hall on Rockland and Hanover Streets. The police station, the transfer station, the post office, and many businesses and homes have replaced the wooded roadside seen in this *c.* 1900 photograph.

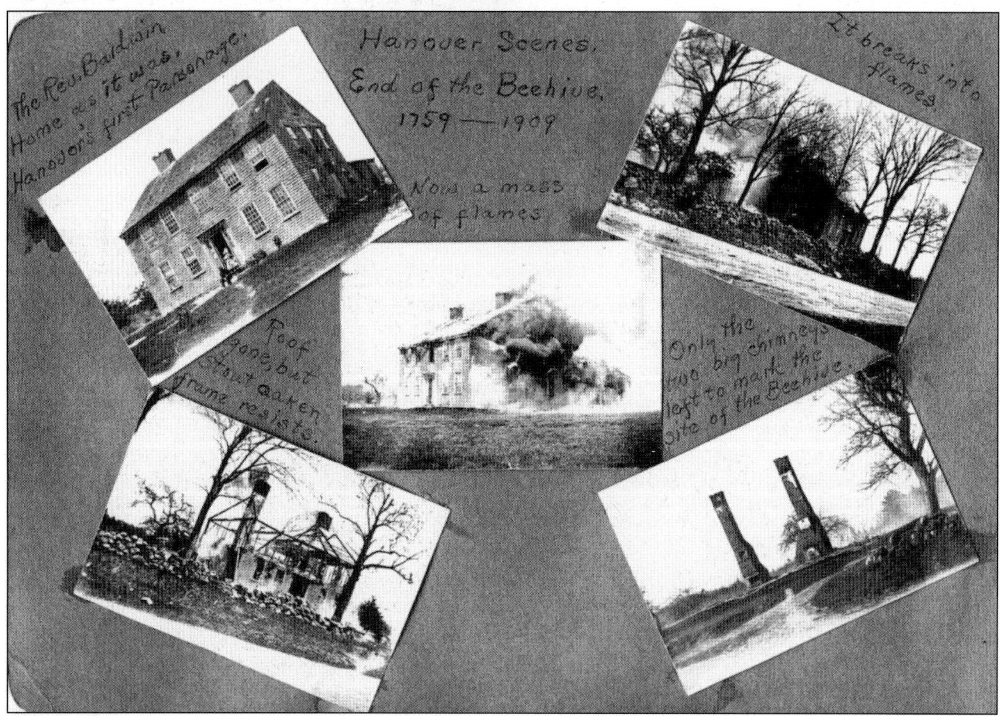

Charles Gleason was on hand to take photographs when Hanover's first parsonage, the Reverend Samuel Baldwin home (built in 1759), was consumed by fire in 1909. This album page, with Gleason's notations, chronicles the before and after of the historic house. His title, "Hanover Scenes, End of the Beehive," refers to the fact that the house had been in use as an apartment building, with large numbers of people coming and going.

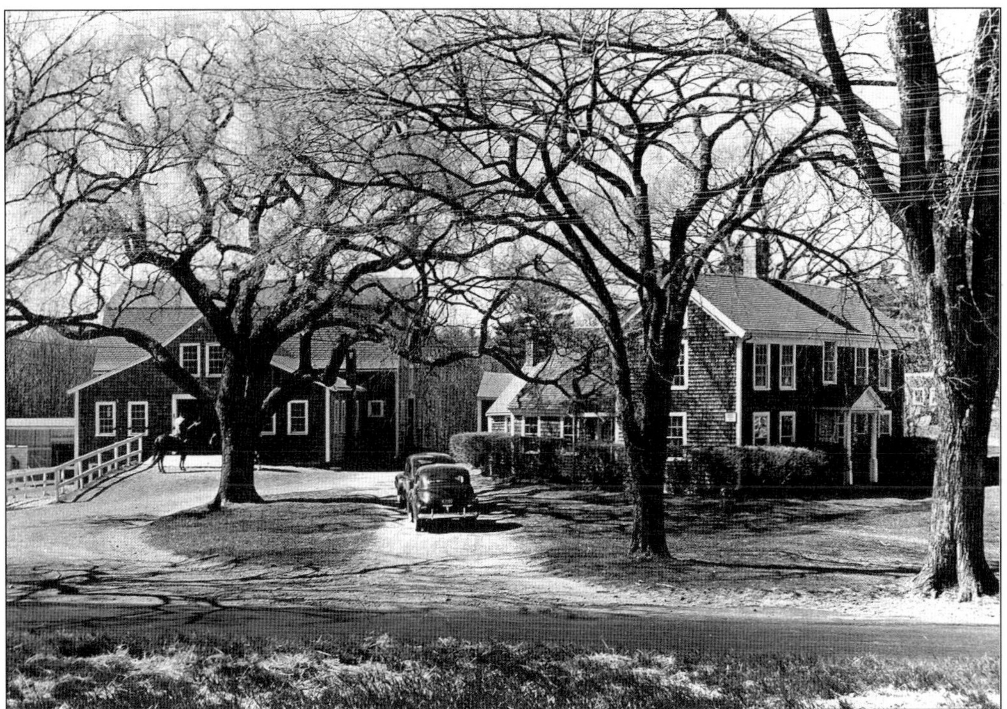

Briggs Riding Stable has been a busy place since it was established by Stanley Briggs in the 1920s. His family has lived in this 1740 house in Hanover Center since 1854. Three generations of the Briggs family have carried on the business to the present time. Each year, the mares with their young foals in the roadside pasture draw admiring spectators; the scene is one of the few remaining vestiges of Hanover's country roots.

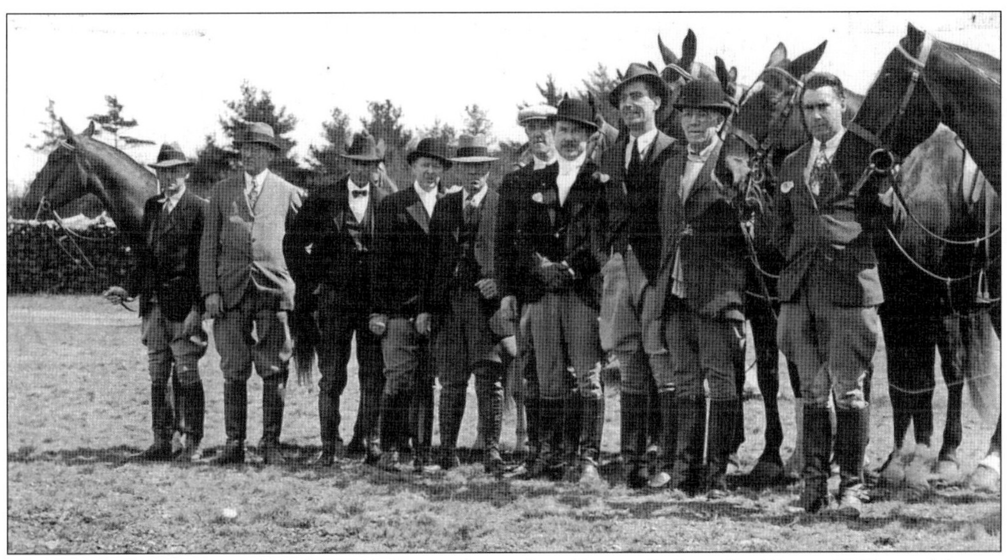

The Hanover Hunt and Riding Club was formed at Briggs Riding Stable in 1933, and horse lovers still come to Hanover from miles around for the horse shows and competitions. Pictured from left to right are Mr. Priggin, Fred Phillips (club president), Dr. Corbert, Ray Mullin, Mr. Lamont, Burt Phillips, Dr. Dwyer, Otis Mann, Mr. Davis, and Stanley Briggs (stable owner).

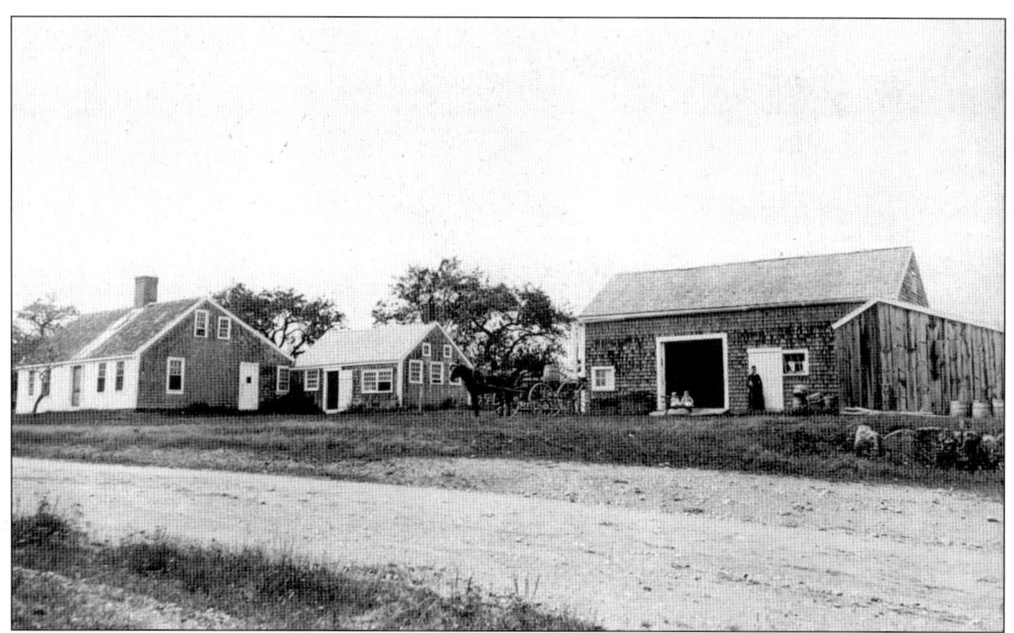

Asa Gurney, a Rockland photographer, took this photograph of 715 Hanover Street in Hanover Center. Edward Briscoe built this low, Cape-style home in 1727 on what was then called Drinkwater Road. The ell was formed from an old fulling mill that was moved from the Curtis Forge. Many old Hanover families have lived here, including the Stetsons, Studleys, Damons, and Halls. The house remains as one of Hanover's oldest.

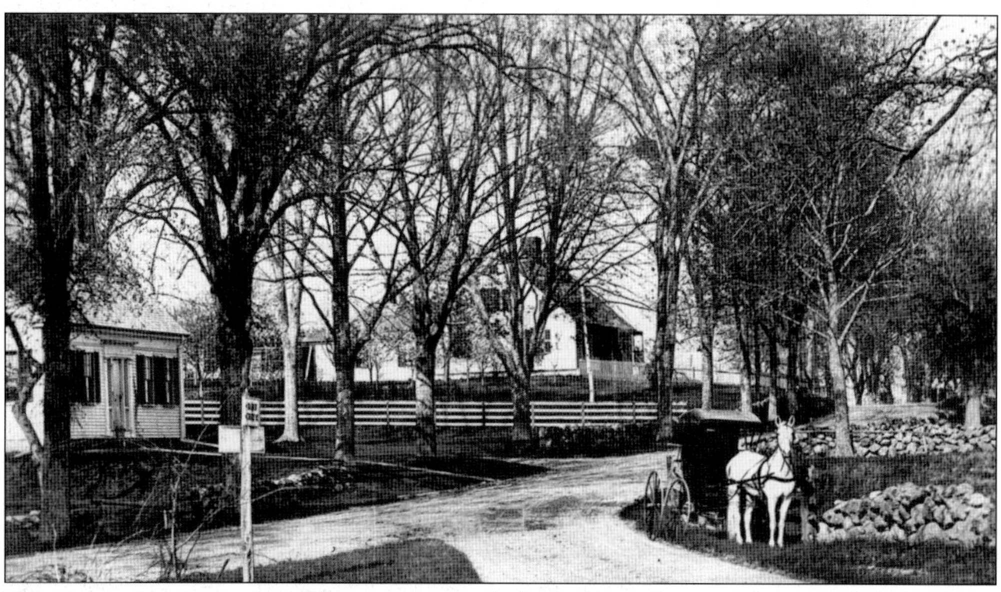

This postcard photograph by Thomas Drew includes highway directional signs to help locate its setting. One sign that points down the roadway to the right, in the direction the horse is facing, says "Circuit Street" and "Hanson," with arrows pointing in the same direction. This would place the site at the east end of Circuit Street, and the homes are on Hanover Street.

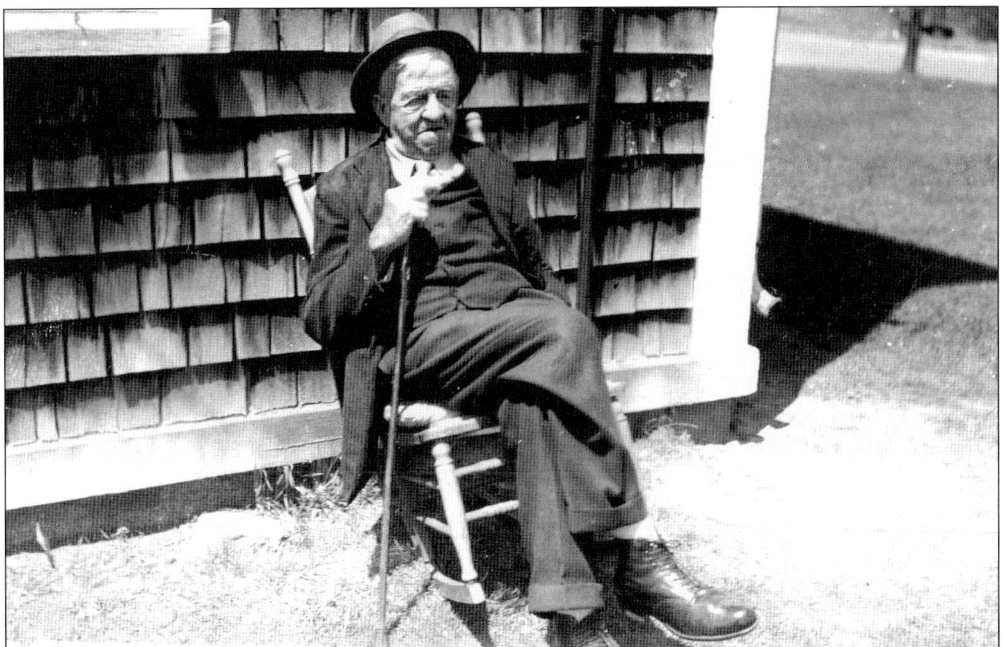

Here sits old Joshua Studley, whose Hanover lineage dates from his 17th-century great-great-great-grandfather, Benoni. The family farm was on Hanover Street, east of Spring Street. Charles Gleason said, "It seems but a few short years ago that we used to see Joshua coming down the road with two very fresh grey horses and a mowing machine."

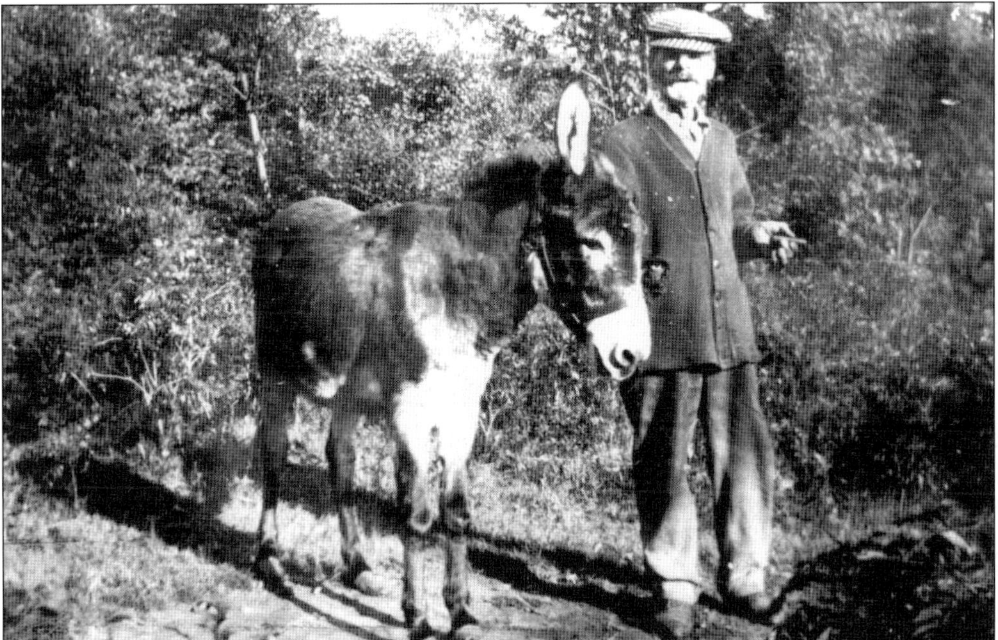

Pegham Clark, a Center Street resident, leads the donkey of neighbor John F. Brooks. This 1923 Charles Gleason snapshot bears the notation that Pegham's wife, Lydia, was "a good pipe smoker." Gleason also wrote, "She could put up a cord [of wood] a day, and her tongue could go a mile a minute."

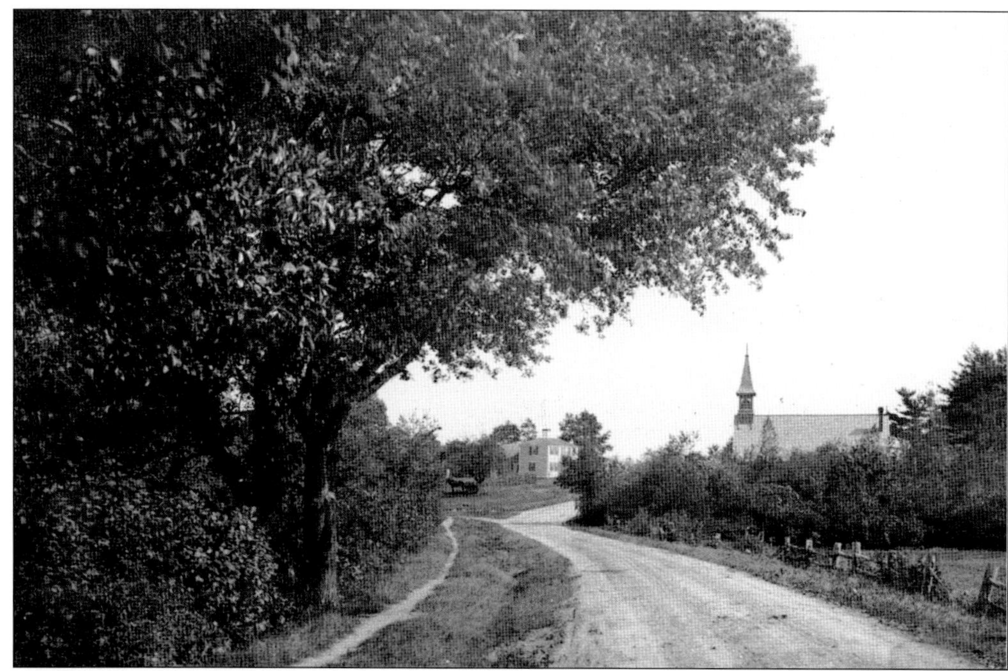

Beneath the spreading maple, many a soul must have paused on the winding path as they made their way to Mass at the Chapel of Our Lady of the Sacred Heart on Broadway. This beautiful little house of worship, opposite the end of Spring Street, was dedicated in 1882 and was used until the current church was built at the other end of Spring Street in 1953. The chapel remains, as a private residence, as does the home also shown in this early 1900s photograph.

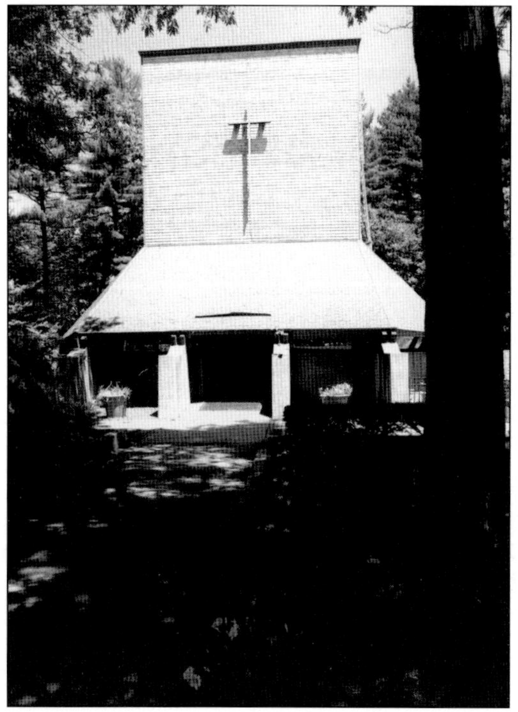

The Lutheran church was built in 1966 on property off Rockland Street in a wooded area at the top of Folly Hill. The congregation has grown steadily over the years and is an addition to Hanover's growing community.

Two
Four Corners

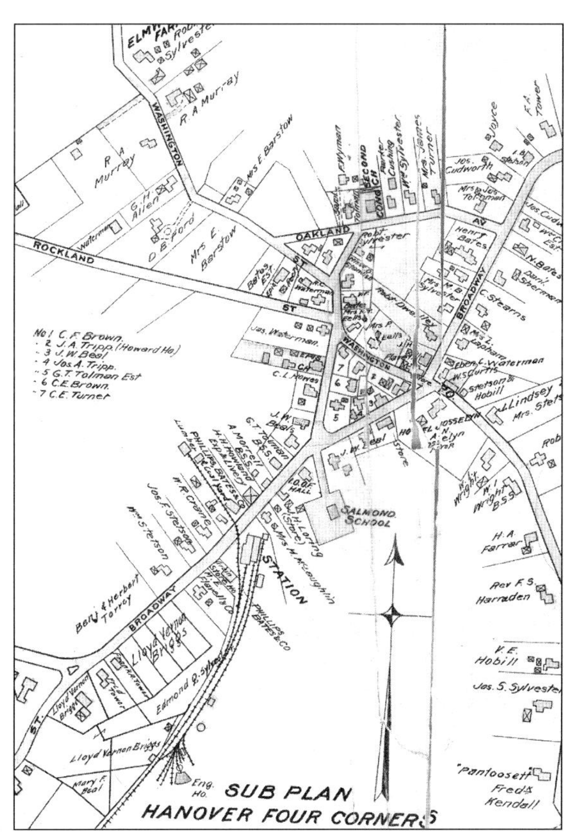

Detail from Plate 14, *Atlas of Plymouth County*, 1903.

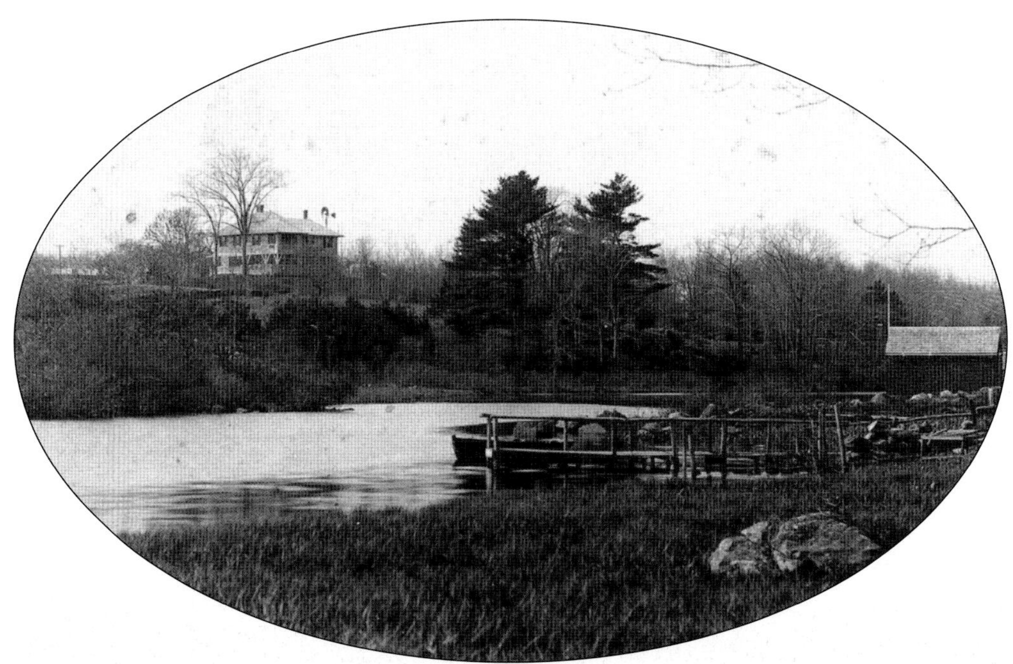

The first shipyard in Hanover occupied the area now covered by the abutments of the present North River Bridge on Washington Street. William Barstow, the first settler, came up the river in 1649 and settled near the present location of Oakland Avenue. Author L. Vernon Briggs, in *Shipbuilding on the North River* (1899), maintains that Barstow probably began shipbuilding in the 1660s. This H. L. Sturtevant photograph of the site of the first shipyard is a view from Hanover toward the Pembroke shore.

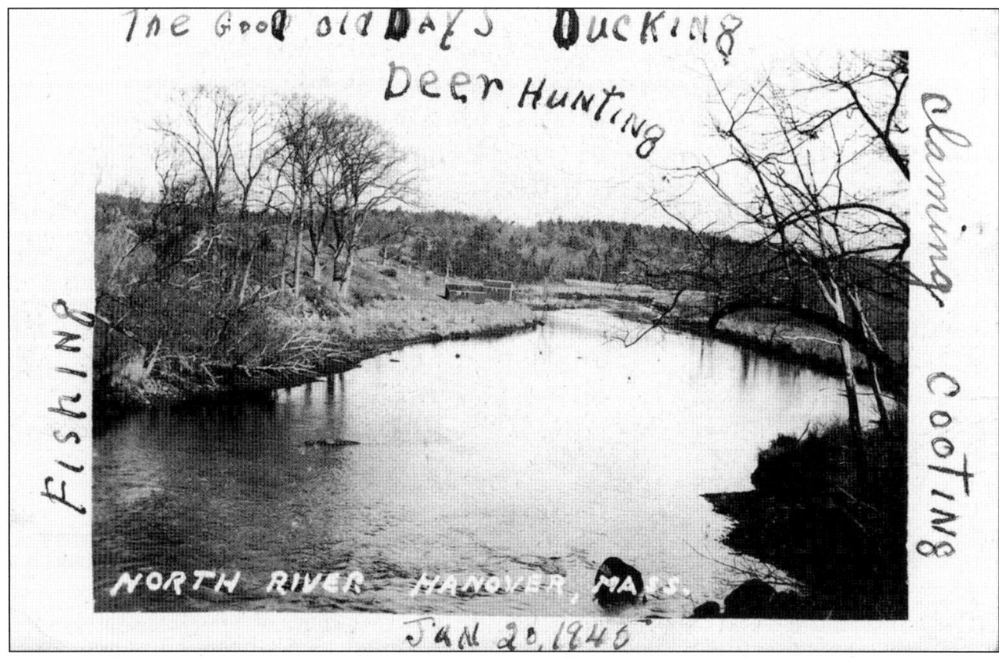

The reverse of this photograph of the North River has a written caption, "This reminds you of the good old days." The North River has always provided many recreational opportunities.

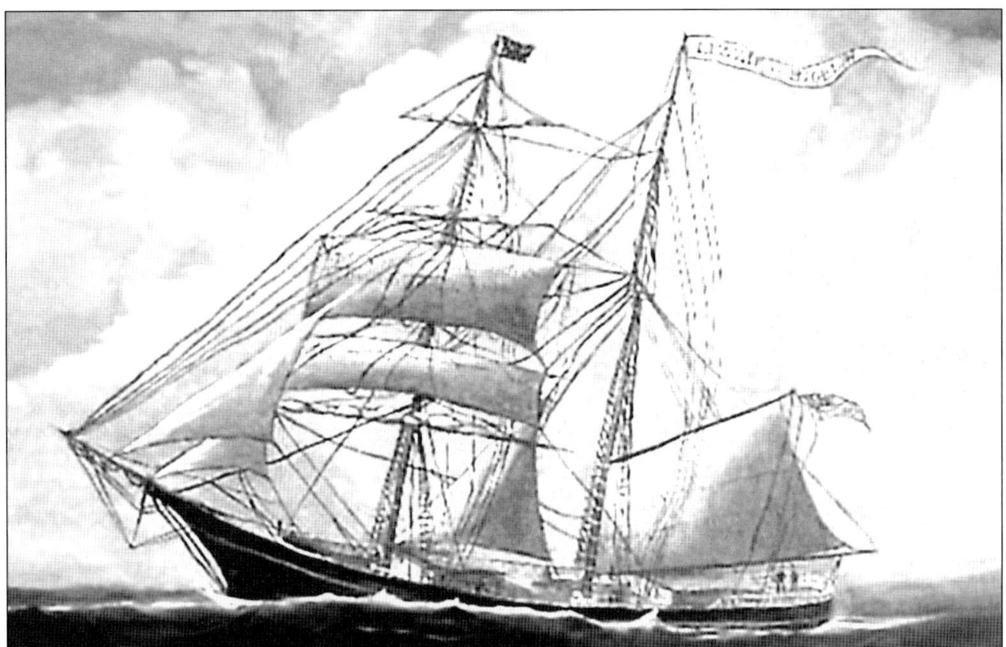

There are no known photographs of ships built in Hanover, but Webster Street artist Weston Bean was noted for painting ships on the lids of old sea chests for local antique dealers. This photograph shows Weston's oil painting of the hermaphrodite brig *Lizzie J. Bigelow*, built by Barstow and Waterman in 1866. The ship, once used in whaling, was lost at sea in 1885. Bean's painting was based on an engraving in L. Vernon Briggs's *Shipbuilding on the North River*.

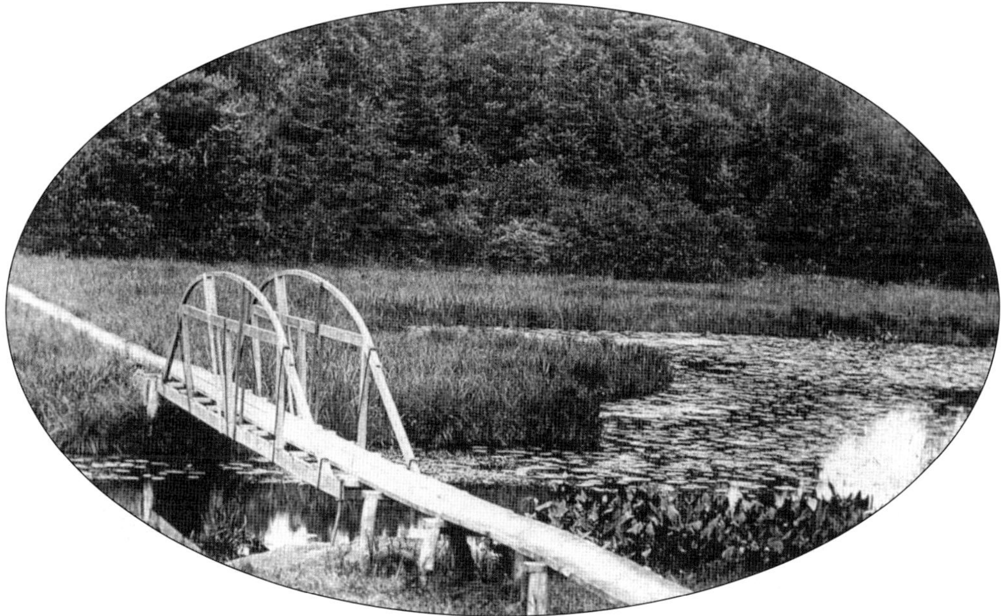

The Rainbow Bridge was a picturesque footbridge that spanned Third Herring Brook. It provided a crossing for the many South Scituate ship carpenters who labored in the North River shipyards in the early 1800s and later. A wooden-planked walkway above the level of the marsh is visible here. The so-called "Portland Gale" of 1898 brought about the demise of this local landmark.

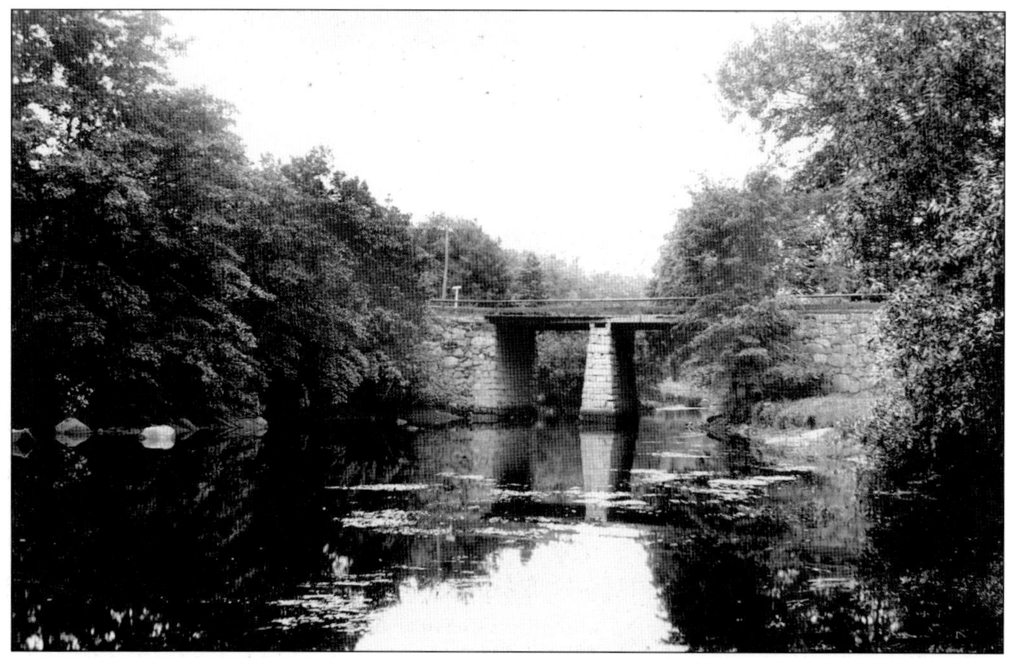

H. L. Sturtevant copyrighted this image of the Washington Street Bridge in 1903. In 1829, the stone bridge (pictured) was erected. This, the third bridge to span the North River at this spot, was replaced one year later with the current bridge.

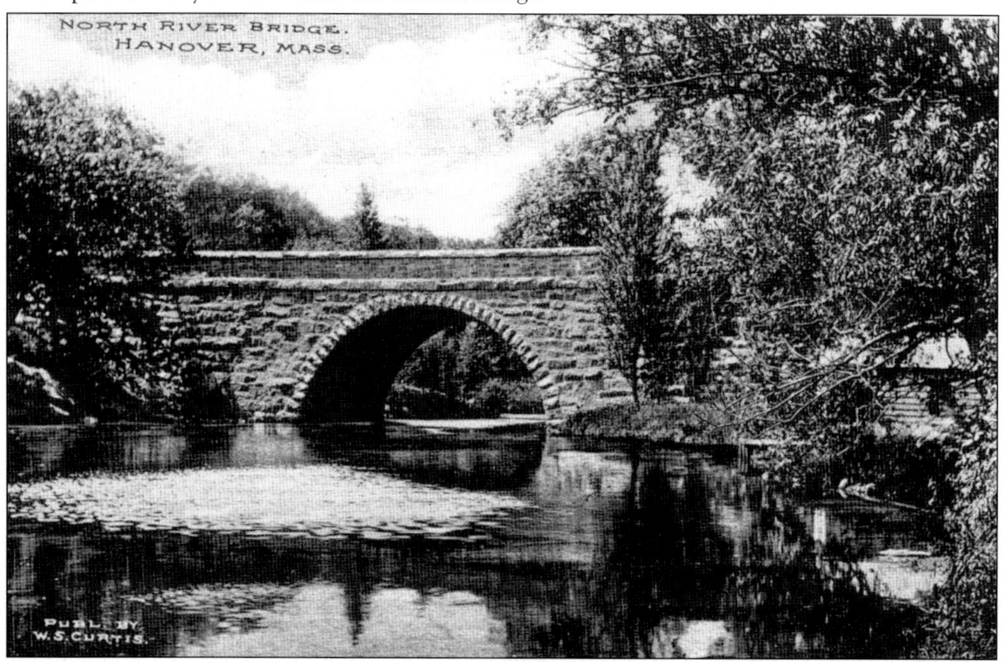

W. S. Curtis, druggist at the Four Corners, published this postcard of the North River's Washington Street Bridge *c.* 1910. Bronze tablets on the parapet of the bridge detail the history of the bridges and shipyards. The first bridge to join Hanover and Pembroke was built by William Barstow in 1656. It was replaced in 1682 by a cart bridge. In 1904, the bridge pictured here was built and it remains in use today.

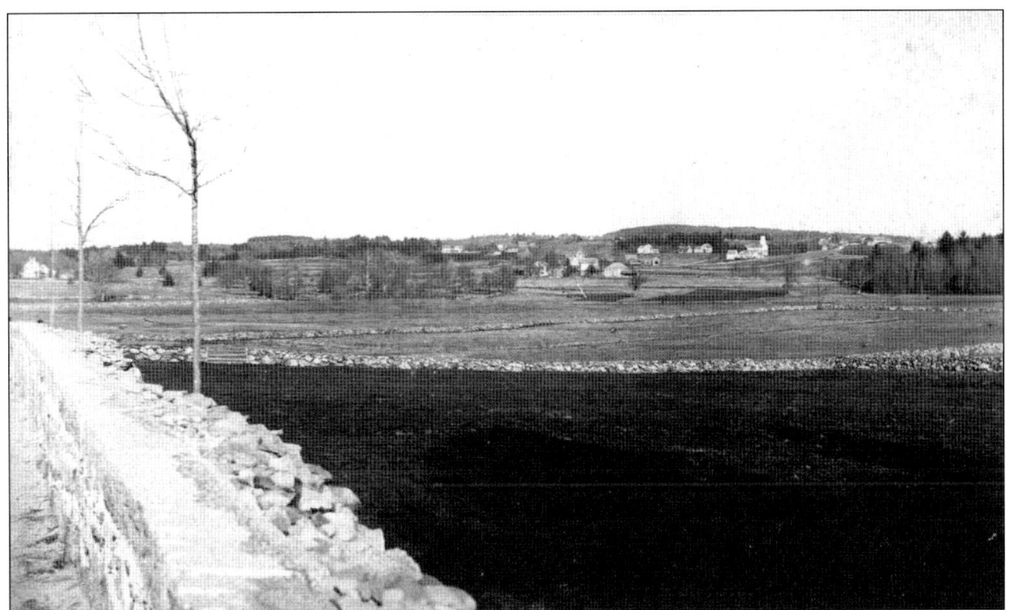

Church Hill in Norwell can be seen across E. Q. Sylvester's field in this 1887 view. The stone wall along Washington Street is in the foreground, while the spire of Church Hill Methodist Church rises on the horizon. Third Herring Brook, the boundary between Hanover and Norwell, flows unseen between the tree line and the stone walls in the background on the right.

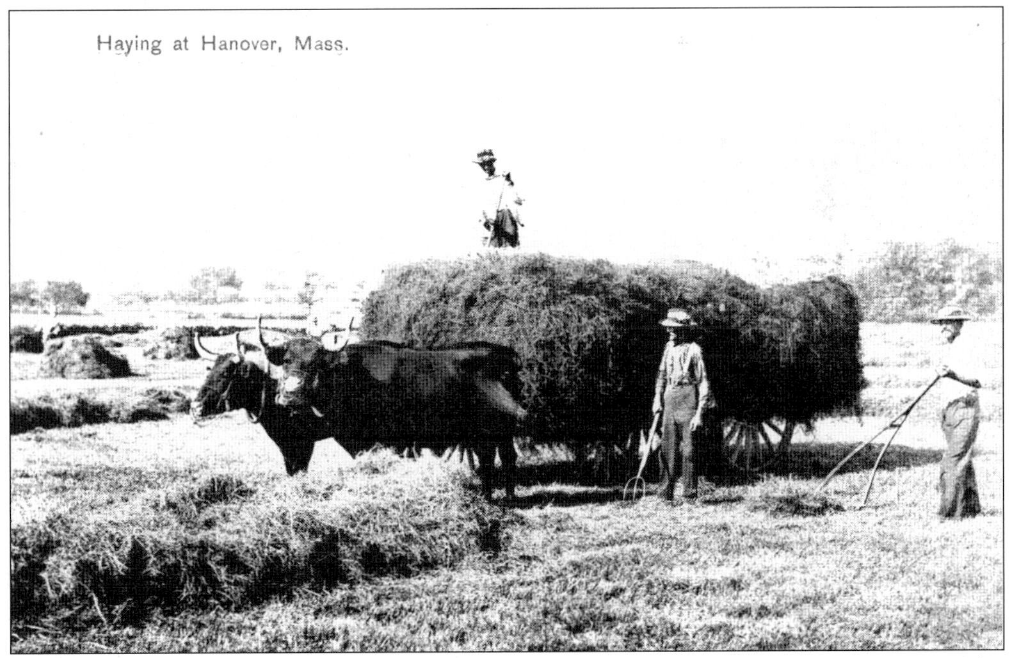

These fields have been owned for many years by the Sylvester family, and they form one of the more scenic vistas in modern Hanover. Sam Sylvester was the last of the Sylvester family to actively farm the land, which extends to Third Herring Brook and the North River. This H. A. Dickerman postcard was printed in Germany for George Lewis of Bryantville.

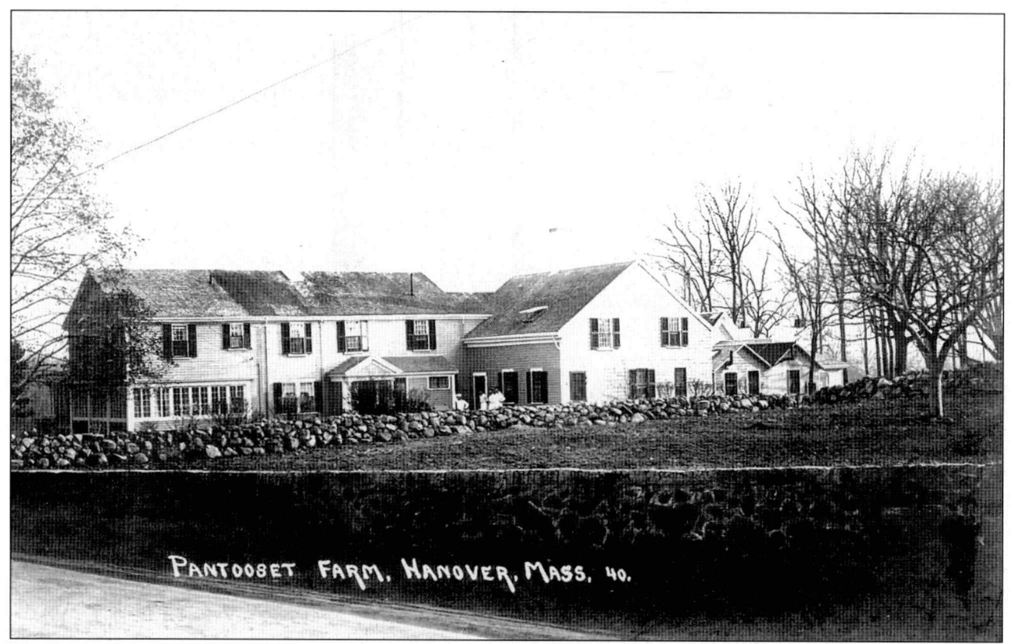

The original Pantooset estate was built in 1799 by Benjamin Whitman overlooking the North River on the west side of Washington Street. This house burned in 1901, and the Kendall family, then residents, moved across the field to the tenant farmer's house at 40 Washington Street. Theodore Guth renovated this house in 1904, and it became a restaurant known as Pantooset.

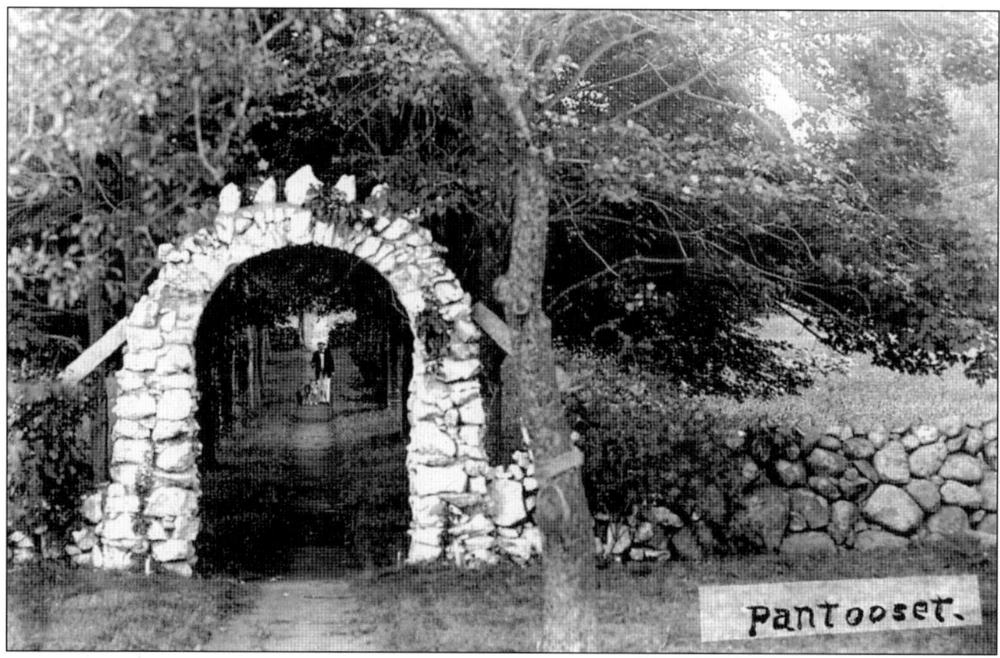

This elaborate stone gate opened to the original Pantooset estate. In Dwelley and Simmons's 1910 *History of Hanover*, it was said of the site, "The lawn was so thickly set with trees that the house could scarcely be seen from the road."

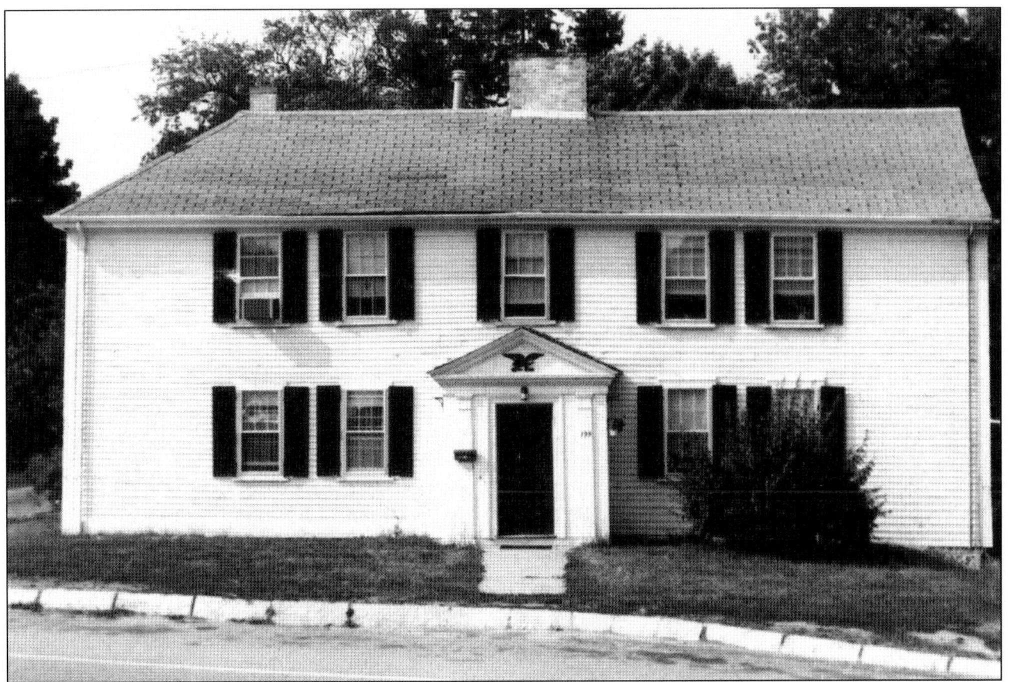

This Colonial house at 199 Washington Street, formerly the Wales Tavern, played host to many a tired traveler, perhaps none more illustrious than Paul Revere. Revere enjoyed the warmth of a blazing fire and a bit of refreshment during his overnight stay in 1794. He was in town to install the officers of the Old Colony Masonic Lodge and to dedicate the new rooms in the lodge hall on the opposite corner.

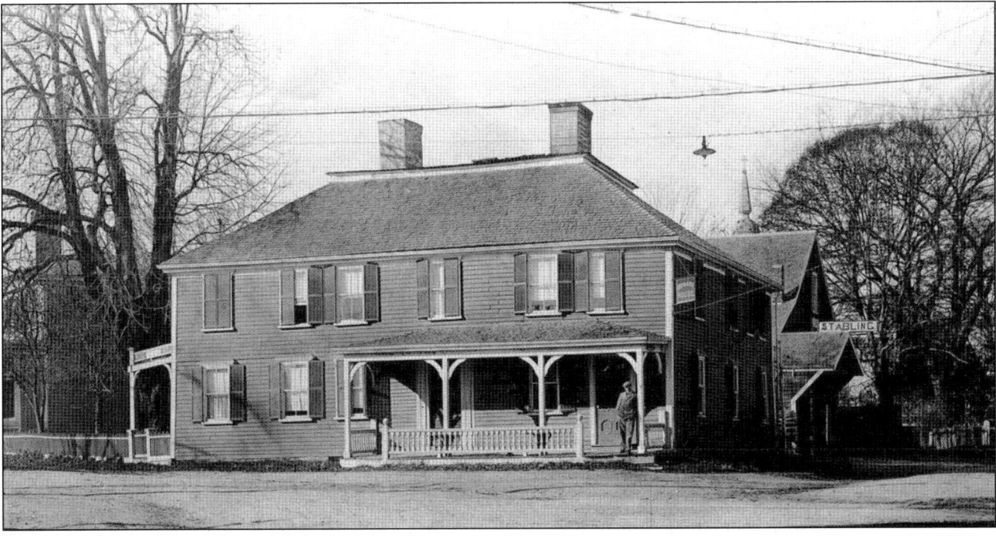

Beginning *c.* 1750, this was David Kingman's home; but from the late 1700s until demolition more than 75 years ago, it served as a hotel. Daniel Webster considered this a favorite stopping place. Generally known as the Howard House Hotel, its last operator was Joe Tripp, who married Franklin Howard's daughter. Tripp ran several businesses from this location. He is listed in directories as a barber, hairdresser, photographer, and telephone operator. He also sold stocks and bonds.

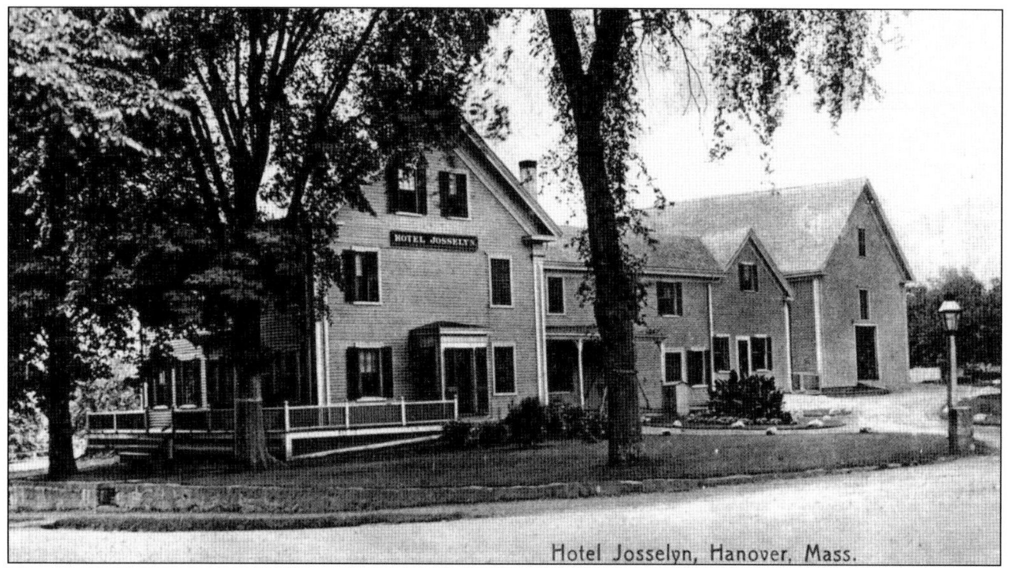

Hotel Josselyn was one of three hotels in the busy village of Four Corners, where the railroad terminated. Robert E. Dwelley built this as a private home in 1856 and raised his family here. For a time, he rented rooms to students attending Hanover Academy. In 1899 Alonzo Josselyn opened a hotel at the site and it was a popular gathering place for several years. The structure was later turned into apartments and eventually was torn down.

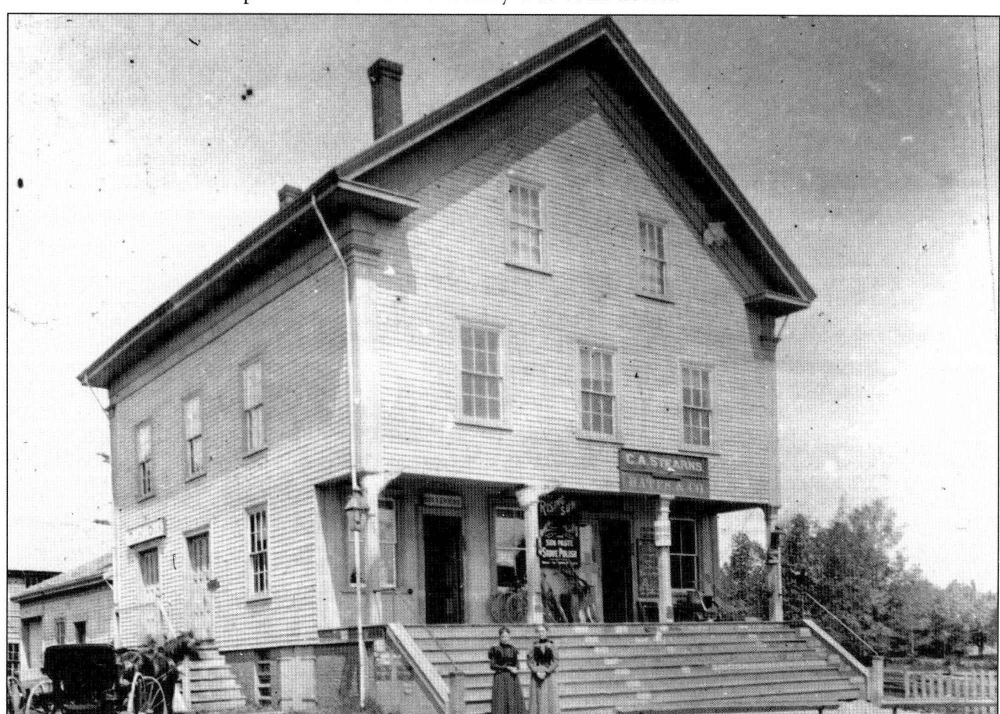

This photograph of the Bates Store in Four Corners was taken *c.* 1898. Henry and John Bates erected this store *c.* 1848 and continued in business for almost 50 years. The Masons and the Odd Fellows began meeting upstairs here in 1874. The Bates were followed in business at this location by Austin Stearns in 1896. Tragically, a fire destroyed the store 1898 and four men were killed.

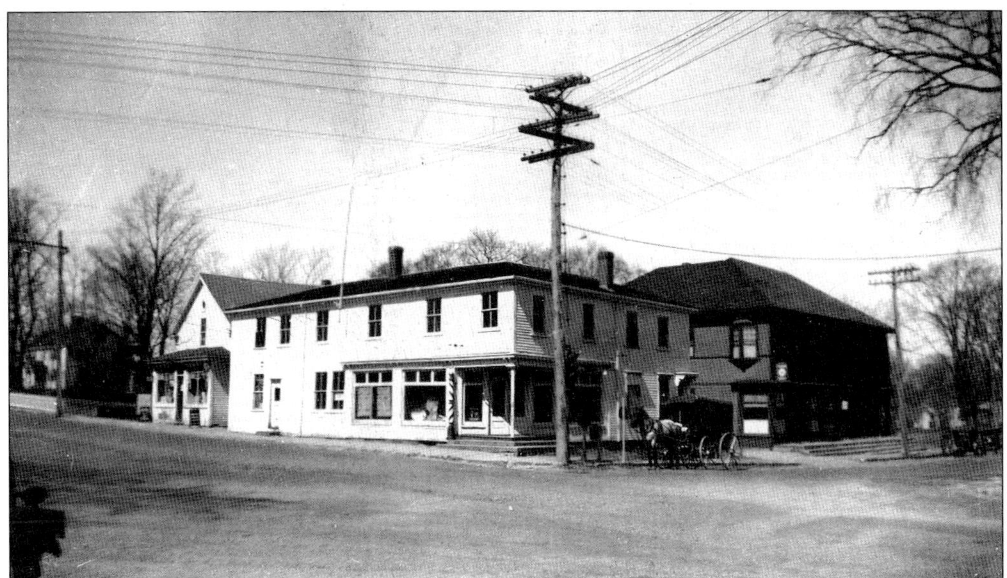

Morton's Store (center) was established on the northwest corner of Broadway and Washington Street early in the 1700s. This *c.* 1908 Charles Gleason photograph shows the Masonic building (right), Flavell's Store (center), and what was originally John Flavell's barn (left). Flavell's Store has been removed, and the barn is now Mary Lou's News. Gleason's wagon stands at the corner in this scene.

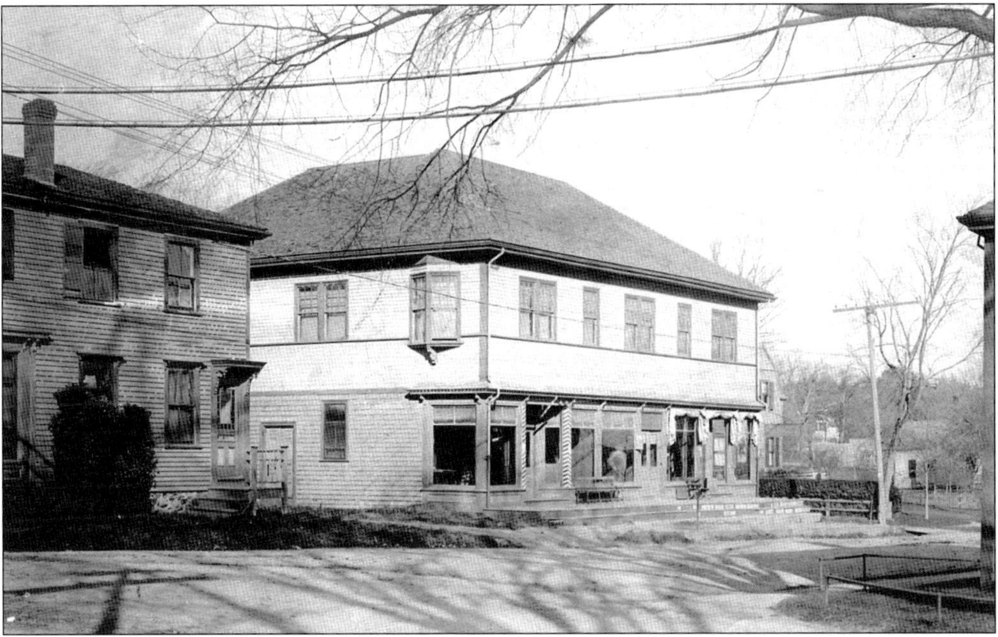

In 1899 the Masonic block was constructed on Broadway in Four Corners. The lodge met upstairs, and the establishments that occupied the lower floor were, from left to right, Duke Perry's barbershop, a Chinese laundry, and Sprague Brothers Meat and Provisions Shop. In 1904, after the murder of the laundry operator, the telephone office moved into the store in the center, and the post office later occupied the store on the right. Currently, Phoenix Lodge occupies the entire building.

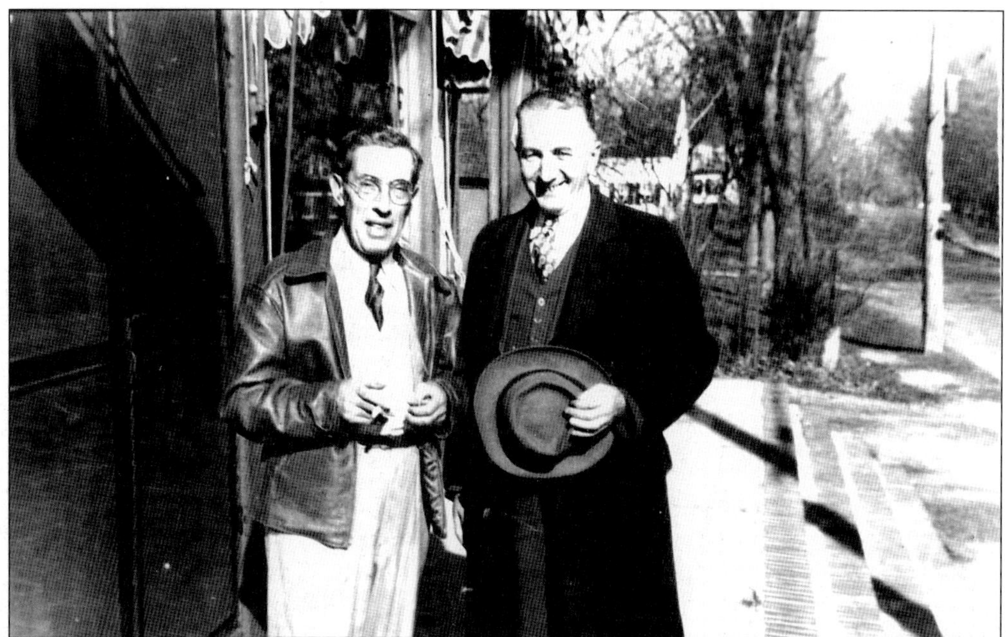

Domingo "Duke" Perry (left) was born in the Azores and came to Hanover in 1903. He was a friendly barber at the Four Corners, where he first worked for Joseph Tripp. Later, Perry operated his own shop in the Masonic Block for more than 40 years. Here, he chats with Bart Downing (right), Hanover native and postmaster at the Four Corners from 1935 to 1964.

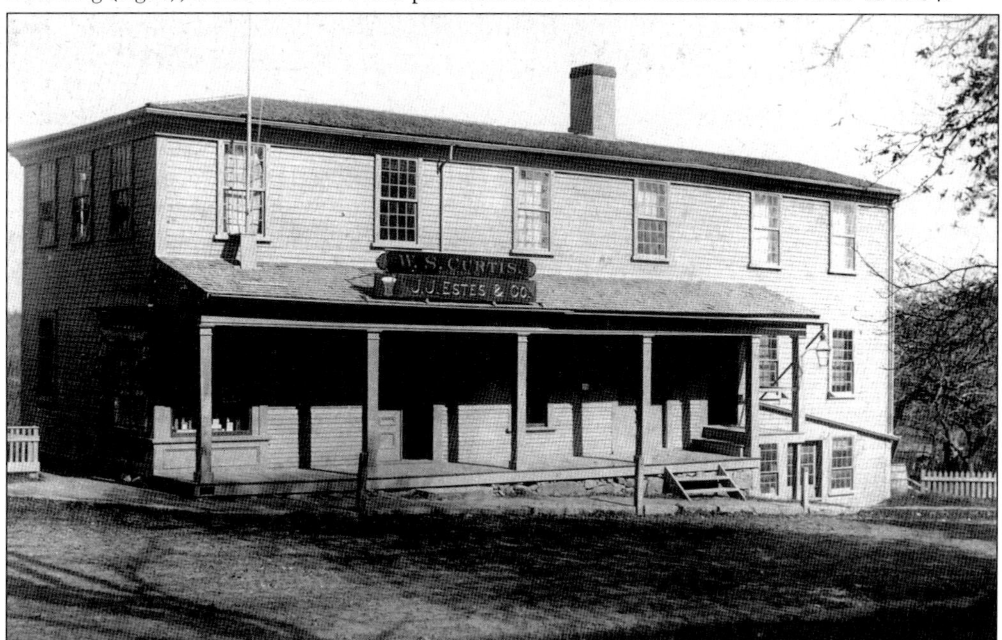

W. S. Curtis operated a drugstore and worked as postmaster in the first Hanover Academy building in 1887, when this photograph was taken. Rev. Calvin Chaddock, minister of the First Congregational Church, in 1808 built this structure in Hanover Center to house a private high school. The school closed in 1822, and the building was moved to its present location on Washington Street in the Four Corners.

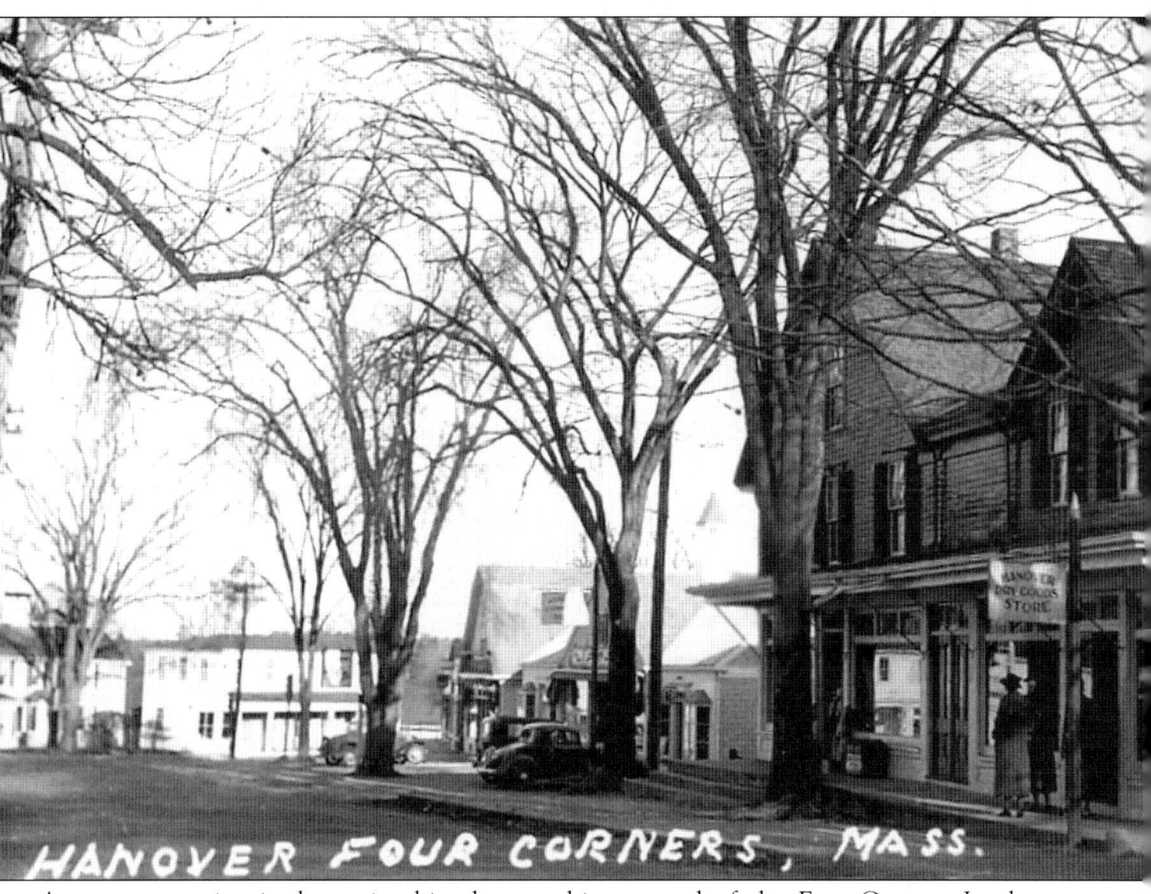

A rare perspective is shown in this photographic postcard of the Four Corners. In the foreground, ladies leave Belle Tucker's Hanover Dry Goods Store and head toward Fred Bowker's Grocery. This building, which had two apartments above, was moved here *c.* 1890 and was torn down in 1941. The other buildings in the picture look much the same today, including Wales Tavern and Hanover Academy, seen in the background.

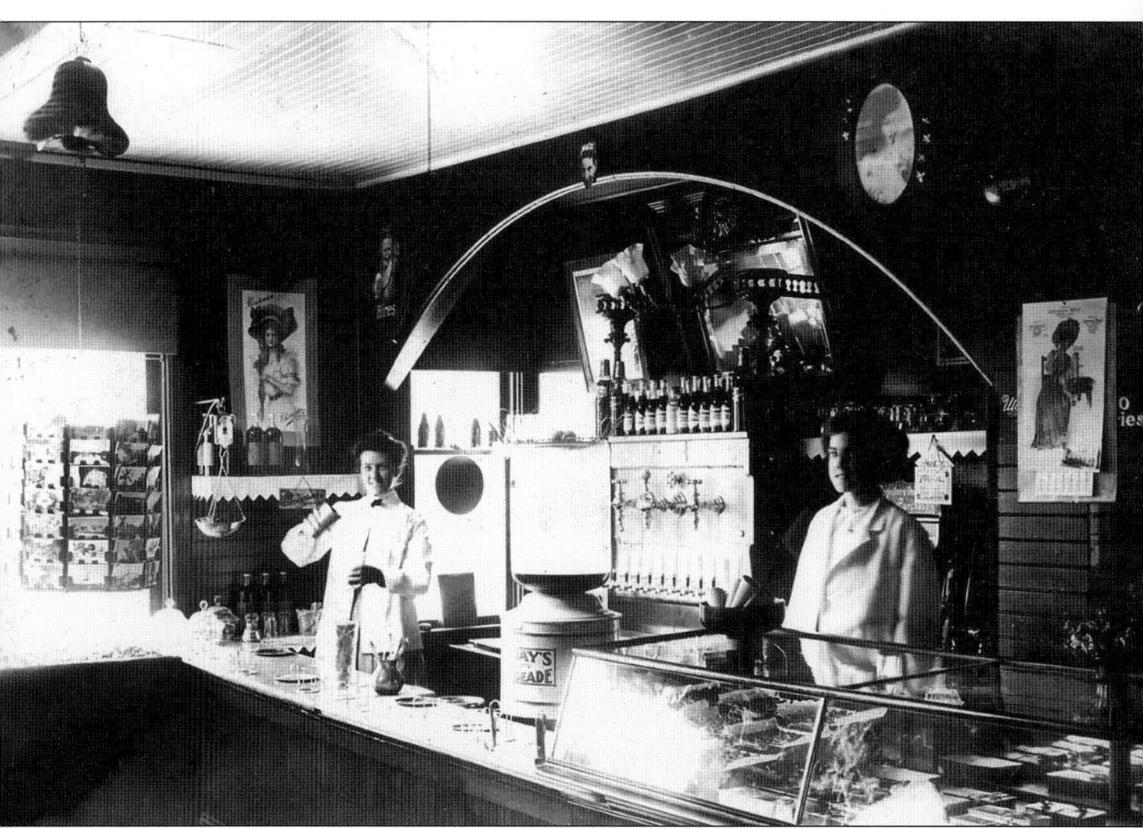

Grace Beal, in her recollections of the Four Corners in 1915, states that Gus Bryant and his wife operated a restaurant that served railroad people on Broadway, across from the house of John Williams Beal. They also served homemade ice cream from the ice-cream parlor and soda fountain shown here.

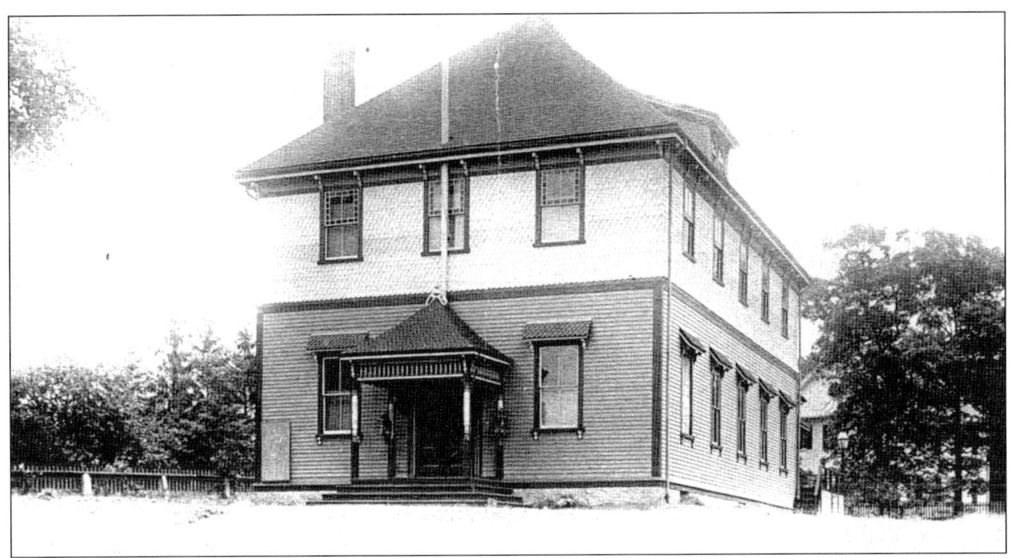

Odd Fellows Hall was constructed in front of the third Hanover Academy building, on Broadway west of the Four Corners, in 1888. The two-story lodge had a stage, which made it a site of many social events. The structure was razed in 1960, after years of disuse. The Hanover Academy can be seen at the rear in this photographic postcard, postmarked in 1907.

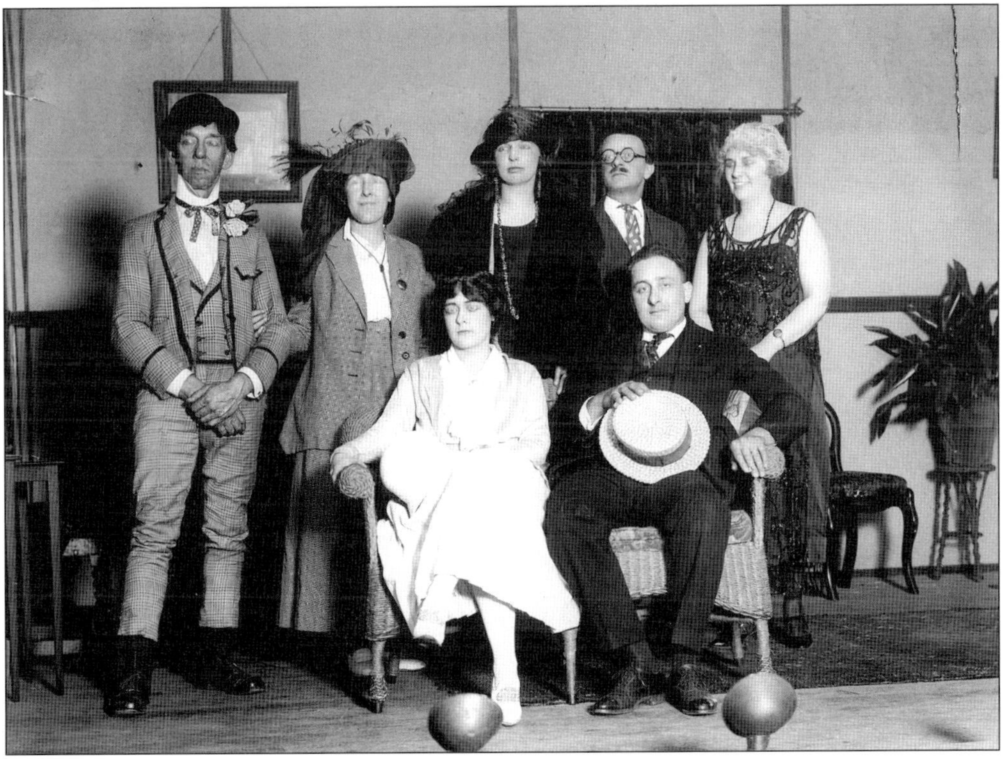

"Amateur Players at Hanover Please Crowd" read the 1920 newspaper headline about a play presented at the Odd Fellows Hall. In the show, Jared Gardner played the foppish son, and Irving Sylvester was the country idiot. Other stars of the production included Alice Church Merritt, Theodore Dyer, Gracia Peck Soule, Lois Clapp Turner, and Grace Sproul.

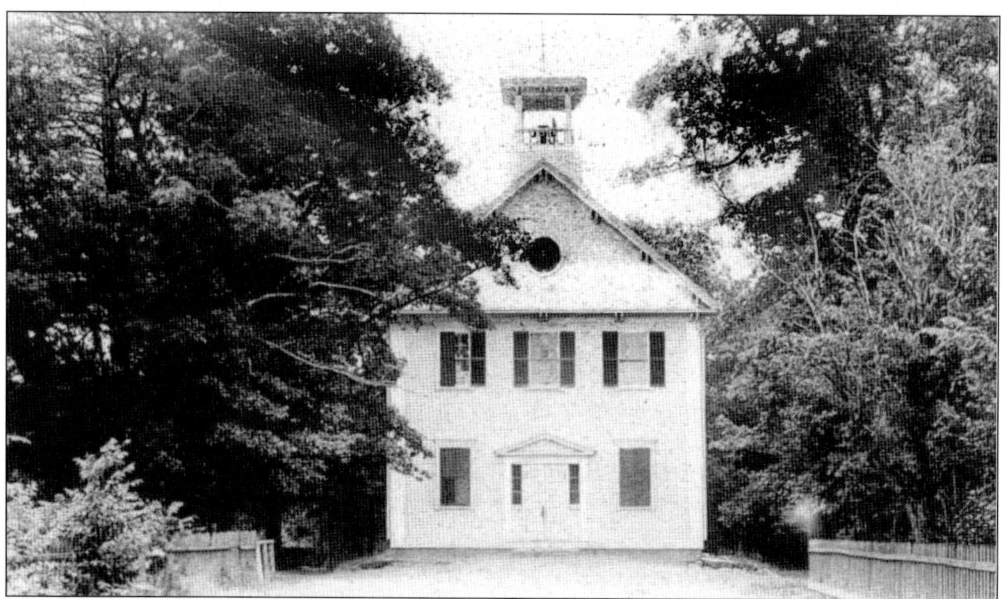

This photographic postcard shows the third Hanover Academy building, built in 1854. It was located 15 rods back from Broadway at the site of the current Salmond School, which replaced it in 1931. Capt. Nathan Dwelley and his wife donated the land for the academy. Samuel Salmond bought the most shares. His eldest daughter, Mary, donated the bell, which was saved and installed in the present Salmond School.

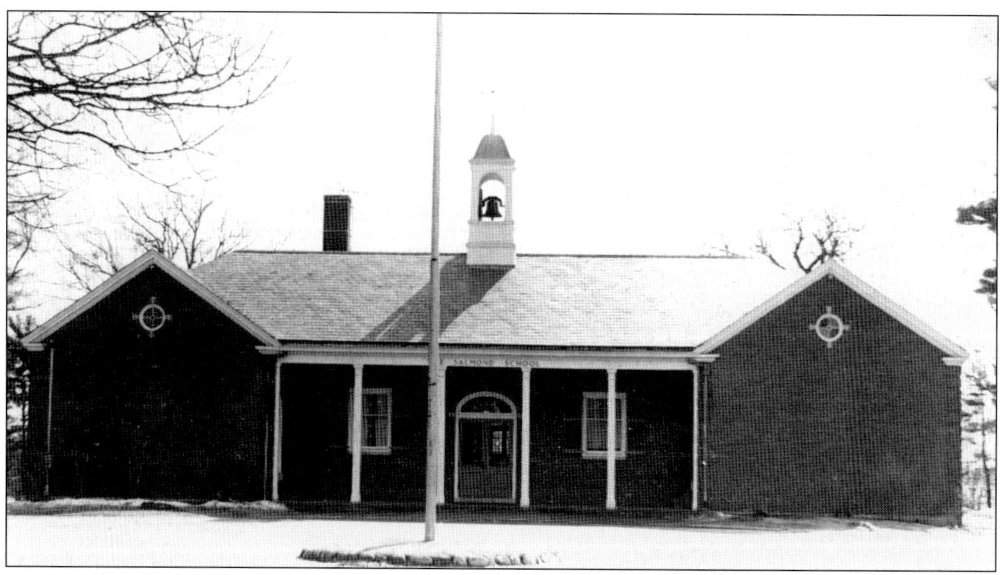

In 1931, Salmond School replaced the third Hanover Academy building on this site, set back from Broadway. The academy closed in 1901, and the old building was sold to the town to be used as a new location for the District Two (or Broad Oak) School. Salmond School, designed by John Williams Beal, remained a school building until 1978 and currently houses school department offices.

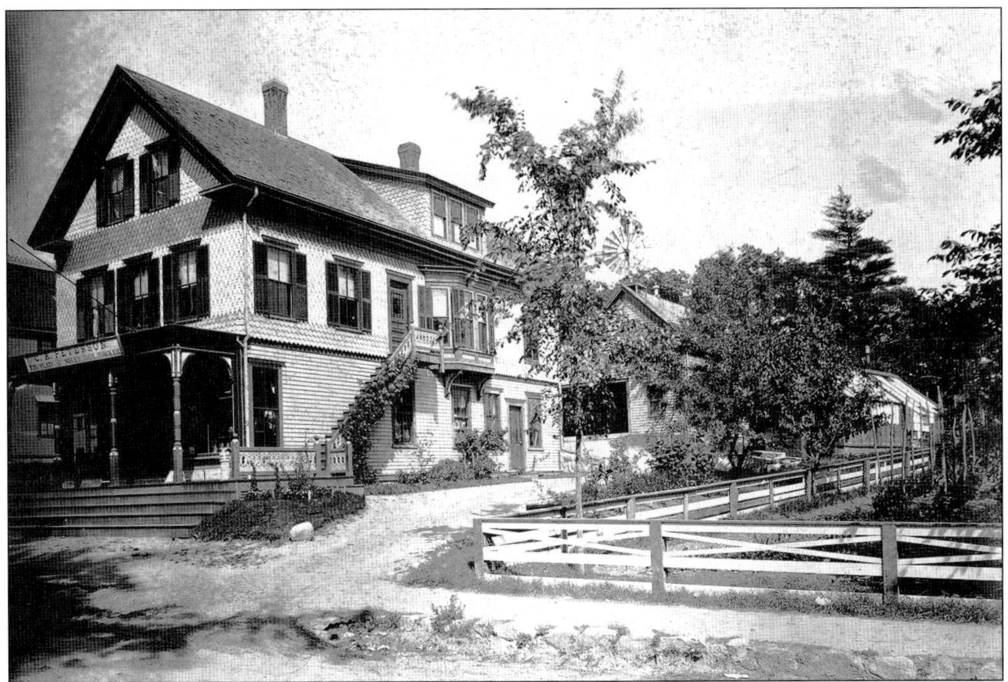

Charles Petersons built this tall Victorian building *c.* 1890 at 208 Broadway, from which he operated a successful stove and hardware business. He, like a few residents, had a windmill constructed for pumping water. Peterson was killed in the disastrous 1898 fire at the Four Corners, but his wife and daughter, Lottie, remained here. They lived upstairs and rented out the lower floor to various businesses. Today, the structure is used for offices and has retained many of its period features.

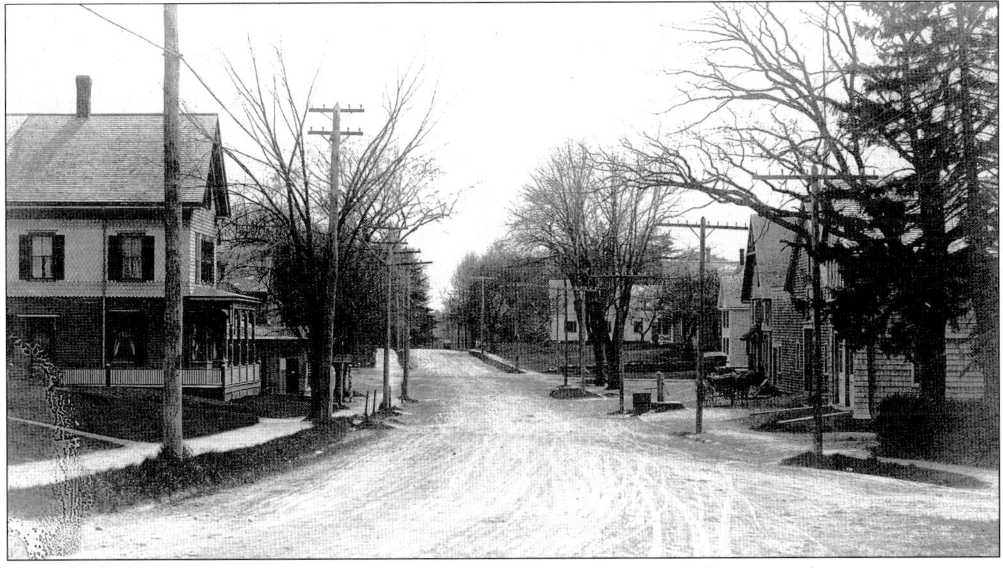

In this view looking west on Broadway in 1910, Lottie Peterson's house and store are seen on the left. The nicely restored shingle-style structure is now used for medical offices. On the right are the blacksmith shop and the Four Corners Fire Station. Route 53 (Columbia Road) now crosses from left to right just beyond Peterson's house.

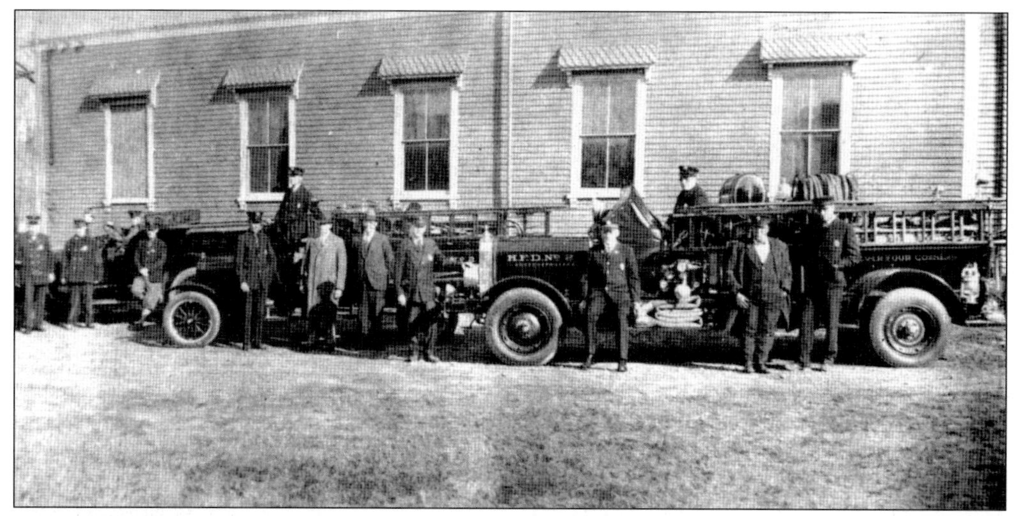

Members of the Four Corners Fire Department and their equipment are shown in this *c.* 1930 photograph. Shown from left to right are Will Gardner, ? Joyce, Percy Bonney, Ed Bailey, Ernest Hunt, Walter Beech, Albert L. Sylvester, John Beal, ? Stockbridge, Bob Henderson, Burt Gardner, Charles Waite, and Joseph Sylvester Jr.

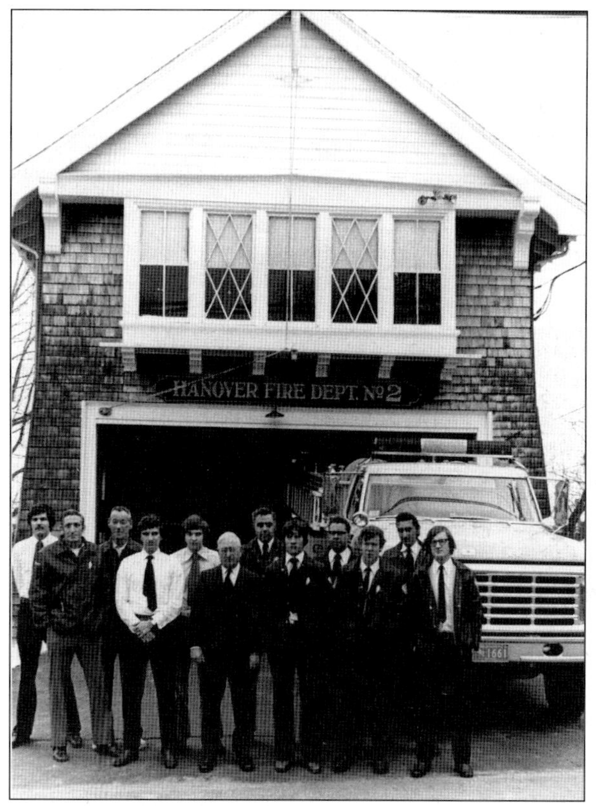

The Four Corners Fire Company No. 2 station, designed in 1908 by noted architect John Williams Beal, still serves the community. This 1977 photograph by Anthony Acampora features, from left to right, Steve Richardson, David Grady, Richard Brown, Thomas Salvucci, unidentified, Edgar Packard, Donald Winn, Brian Boates, Peter Muncey, John Stewart, Dan Salvucci, and John Tolman.

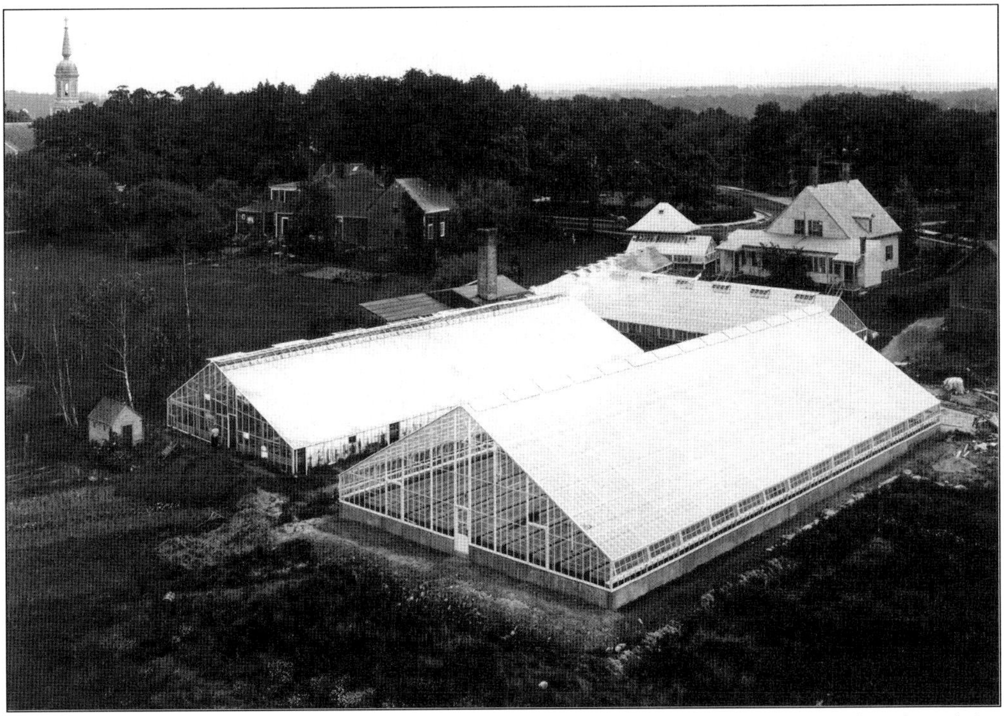

The J. W. Beal Flower Shop and Greenhouse was located between St. Andrew's Church and the Beal house, on the corner of Church and Rockland Streets. The shop specialized in carnations. Beal's growing fields and greenhouses were located behind both the shop and the house. Most of the flowers were sold wholesale and shipped to the market in Boston via the railroad.

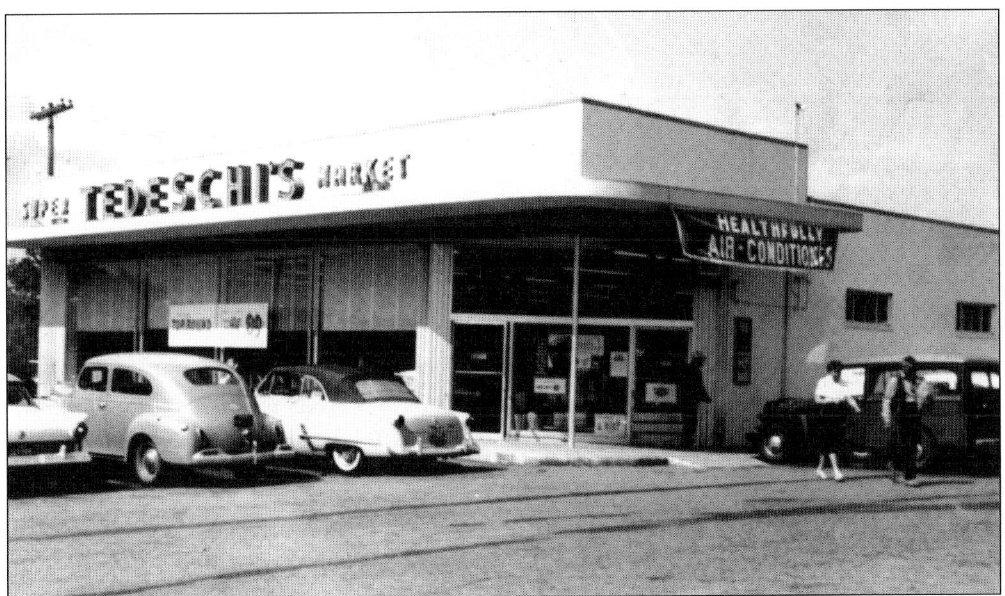

Soon after the railroad left the Four Corners in 1938, the Beal greenhouses were taken down, and the fields were later sold. Some years later, the property became the site for construction of the first supermarket in town. Ralph Tedeschi, from Rockland, built this market *c.* 1954.

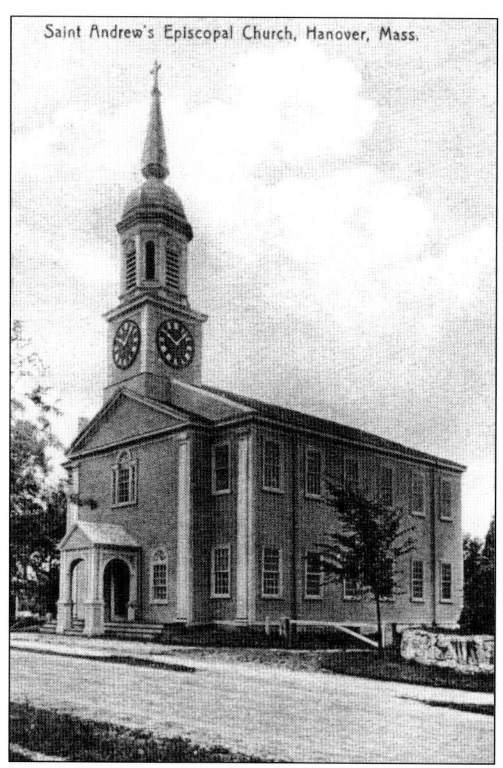

This William S. Curtis postcard shows St. Andrew's Episcopal Church, which was erected on Church Street in 1810 on land belonging to Capt. John Cushing. Prior to 1810, the church (founded in 1725) was located atop Church Hill in Norwell. The Sylvester family provided funds to remodel the church c. 1930, adding Sunday school rooms within and pillars in front.

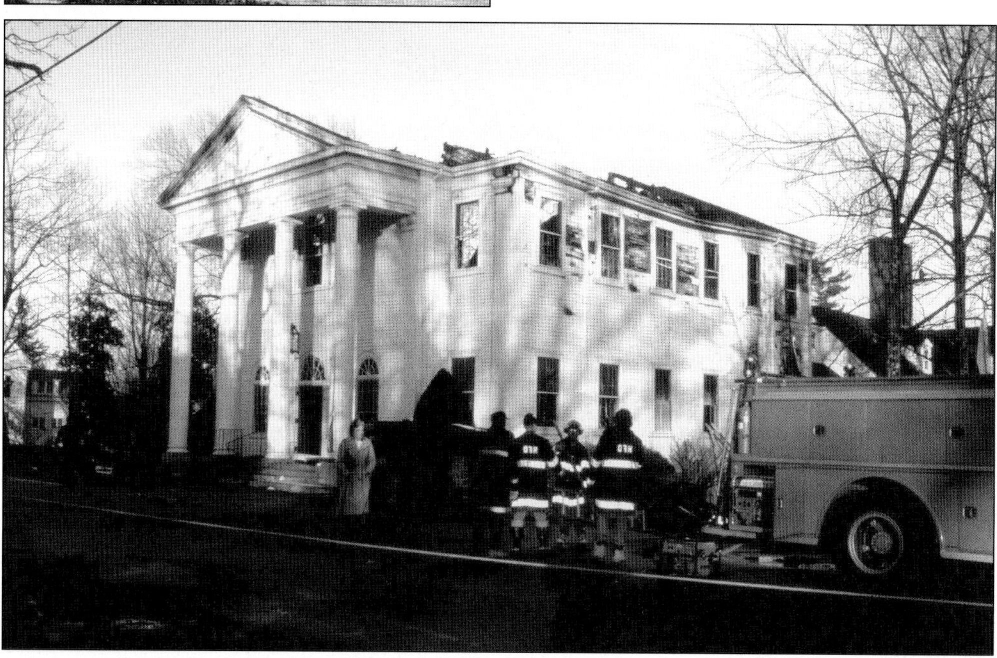

On the night of December 25, 1983, St. Andrew's Church was consumed by fire, causing the roof to fall in and leaving only the walls standing. Jean Migre was on the scene while the fire was active, taking many photographs of firemen vainly trying to save the historic structure. This picture, taken the next morning, shows the extent of the damage. The church has been rebuilt in the same architectural style as the original.

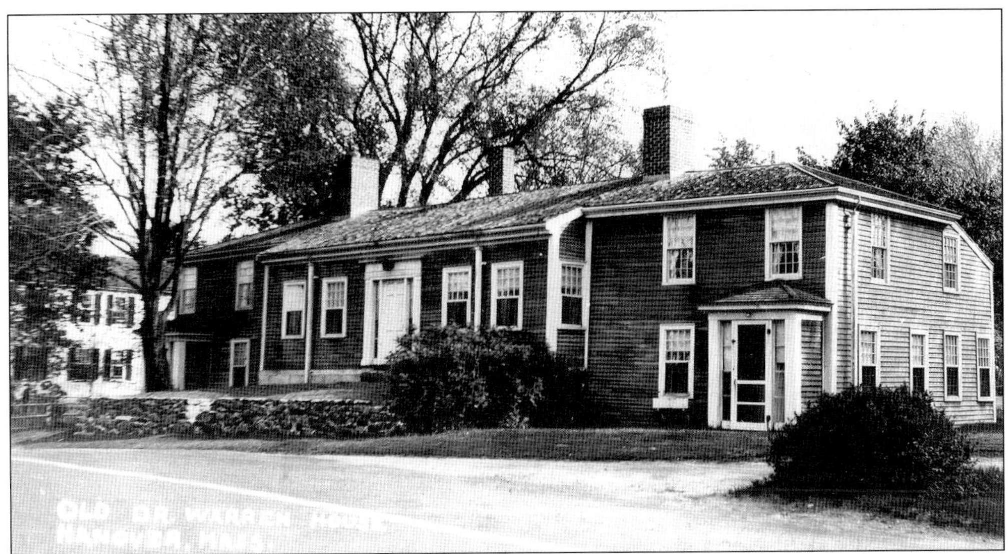

Antique expert Wallace Nutting called this home at 240 Washington Street, in the Four Corners, the first split-level house in America. The house began as a small Cape in 1810; lower wings were added later. There are fireplaces on four levels. On this photographic postcard, it is called the Dr. Warren House, named for Dr. Ira Warren. Dr. Warren lived in the house in the 1830s and is best known for his book *The Household Physician*.

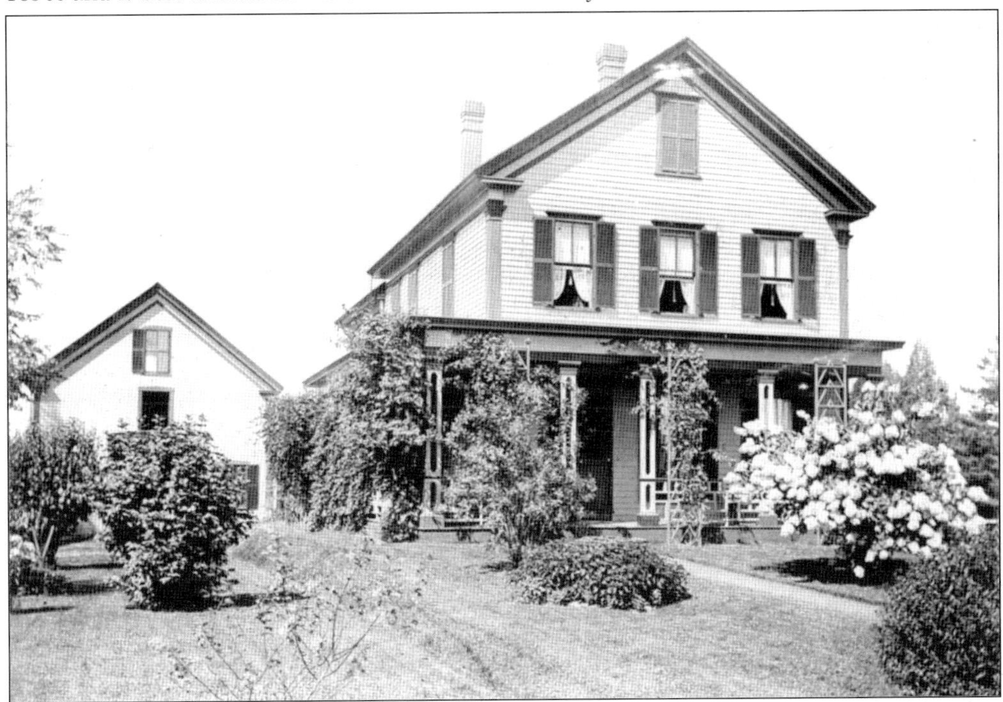

When Dr. Charles Hammond came to Hanover in 1906, he lived in this house at 262 Washington Street, built by R. C. Waterman c. 1866. Dr. Hammond was a family physician and school doctor for more than 50 years in Hanover. Although he had no children of his own, he left a large endowment for scholarships to benefit Hanover High School graduates each year. His legacy lives on.

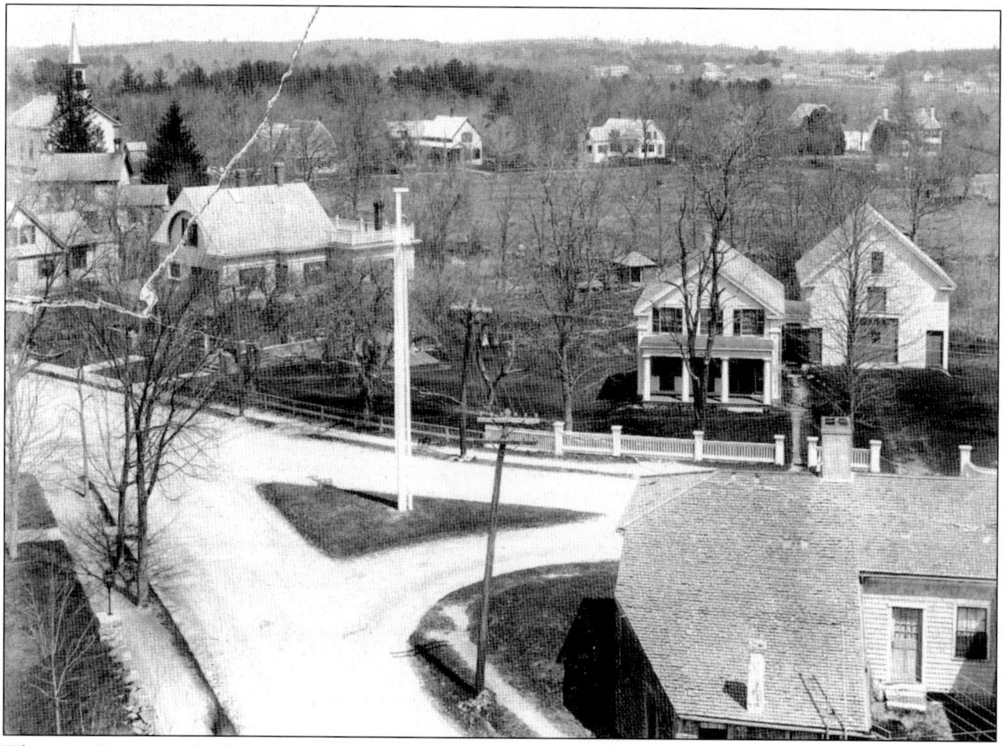

Thomas Drew took this picture from the steeple of St. Andrew's Church. It shows the Liberty Pole, which stood on a triangle formed by the intersection of Church and Washington Streets. In 1874, a bandstand was built around the flagpole, and the Hanover Brass Band gave open-air concerts there. The pole was removed in 1956, due to traffic problems, despite the objections of some townspeople. The Second Congregational Church and homes on Oakland Avenue can be seen in the background of this photograph.

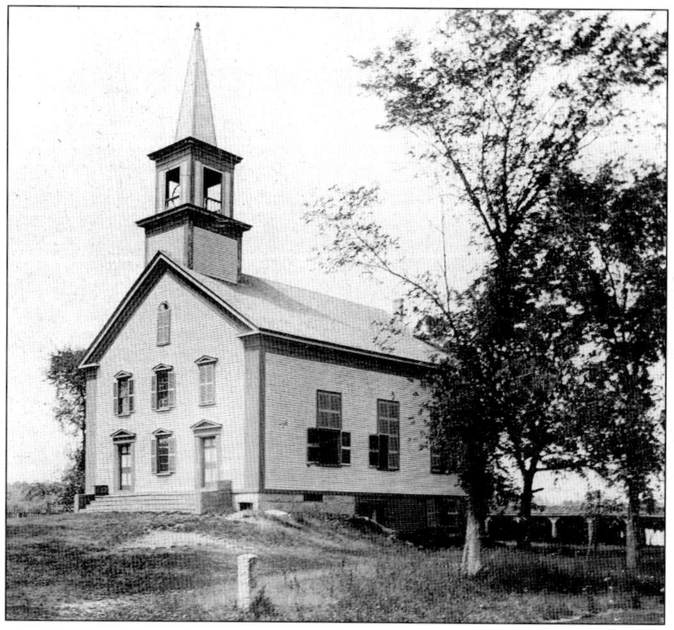

The Second Congregational Church, sometimes called the Orthodox Church or the Trinitarian Church, was founded *c.* 1854 by discontented members of St. Andrew's Episcopal Church and the First Congregational Church. The building was moved to 48 Oakland Avenue from Abington, and services were held until 1936. The structure was dismantled and moved to a farm in Pembroke, where it was rebuilt and used as a pigsty.

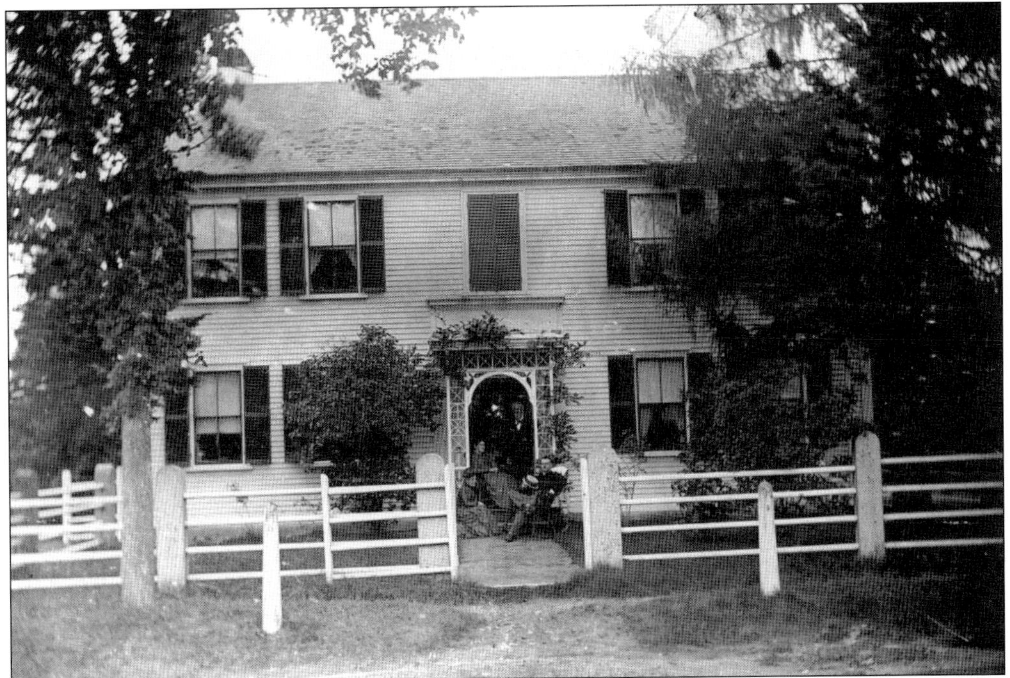

Rev. Joab Cooper constructed the first rectory of St. Andrew's Church in 1811 at 94 Oakland Avenue. Timbers from the first Episcopal Church, located on Church Hill, were used in the construction. Several doctors later resided here, before E. Perry bought the house and traded it with the Tolman family from Norwell. Morgianna Tolman, a schoolteacher for 50 years, spent her life in this house. She is one of the family members shown at the center of this *c.* 1900 photograph.

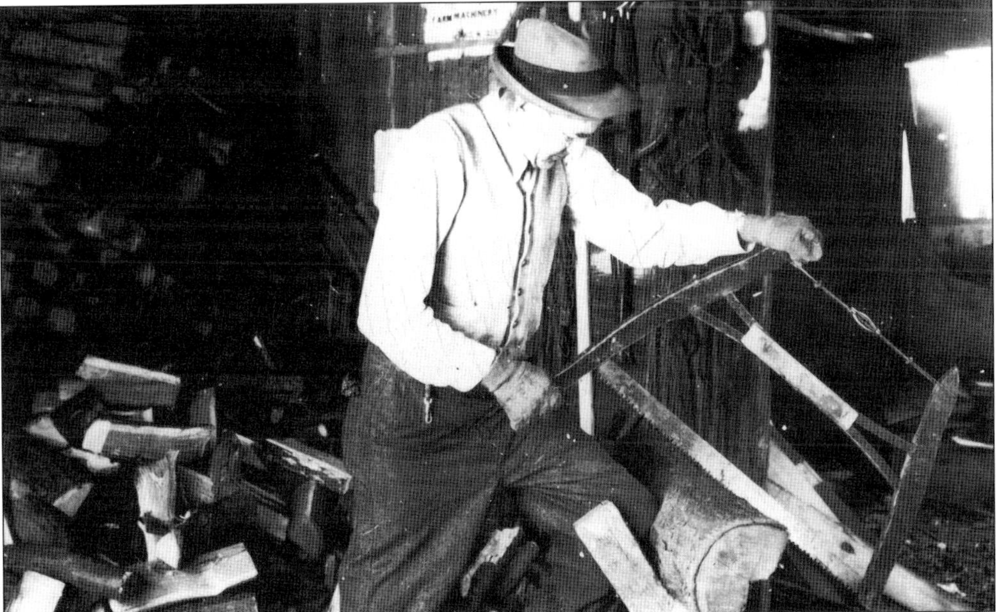

Charles Gleason, a hardworking man, saws his winter wood supply. In addition to peddling his goods, he served the town as assessor, overseer of the poor, and selectman for 13 years. His many photograph albums made him one of Hanover's best historians of the first half of the 20th century.

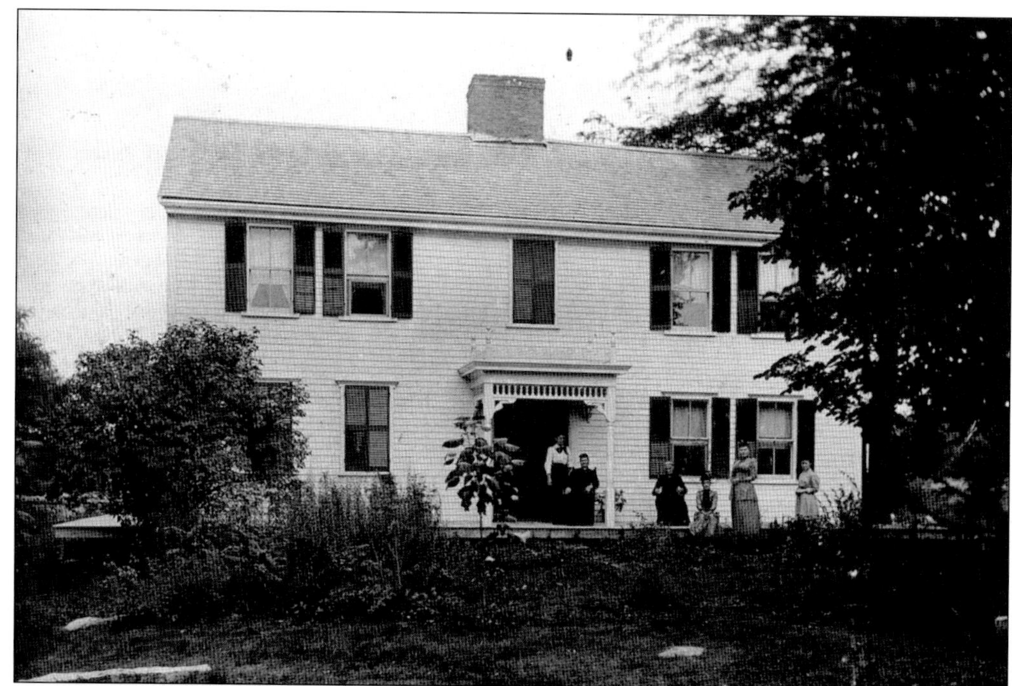

On the corner of Oakland Avenue and Washington Street is an old house built by the son or grandson of the first settler of Hanover, William Barstow. John Bailey, a Quaker clockmaker, lived here, at 323 Washington Street, for a short time. Among those pictured is Georgie Barstow, daughter of Edward Barstow, a sea captain who died in 1898. Georgie passed away in 1960, and was the last of her line to live in the house.

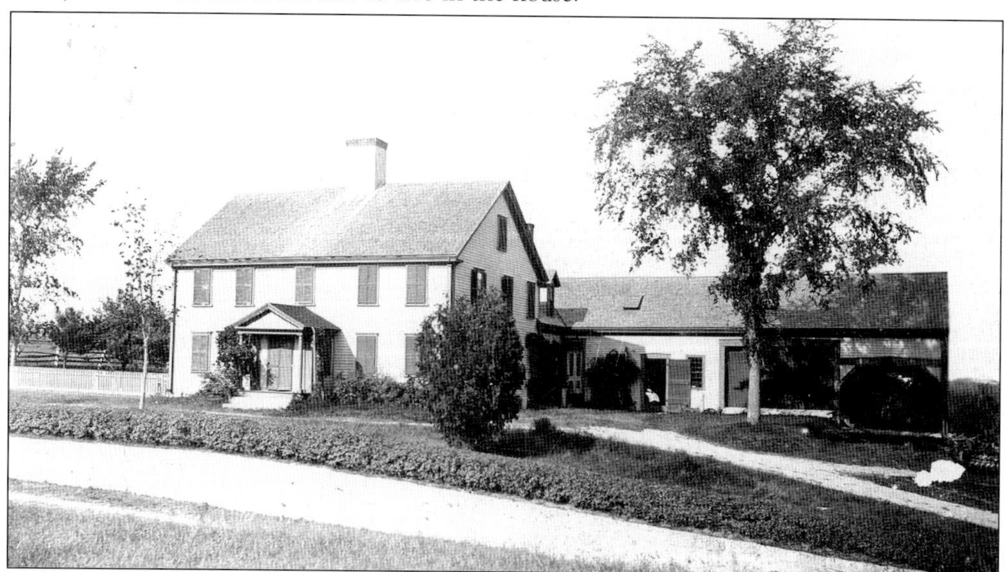

The Robert Sylvester house, at 417 Washington Street, was home to seven generations of the Sylvester family. The property was sold *c.* 1905, and the house next door became the Iron Kettle Inn. The Mitton family later used the estate as a gentleman's farm and sold high-quality milk to the Boston market. In 1947, the property was given to Archbishop Cushing and the Sisters of St. Francis to be operated as a school for children with special needs.

Descendants of William Palmer probably built this small Cape-style house, located on a little-used path back from County Road. The home came into farmer Amos Sylvester's family in 1724 and was used for many years as a tenant's house. The "lone house at Cricket Hole," pictured in this H. L. Sturtevant photograph, at one time was used to shelter French Acadians who had been driven out of Nova Scotia by the British in the mid-1700s. Many of the Acadian exiles continued moving southward to settle in the bayous of Louisiana.

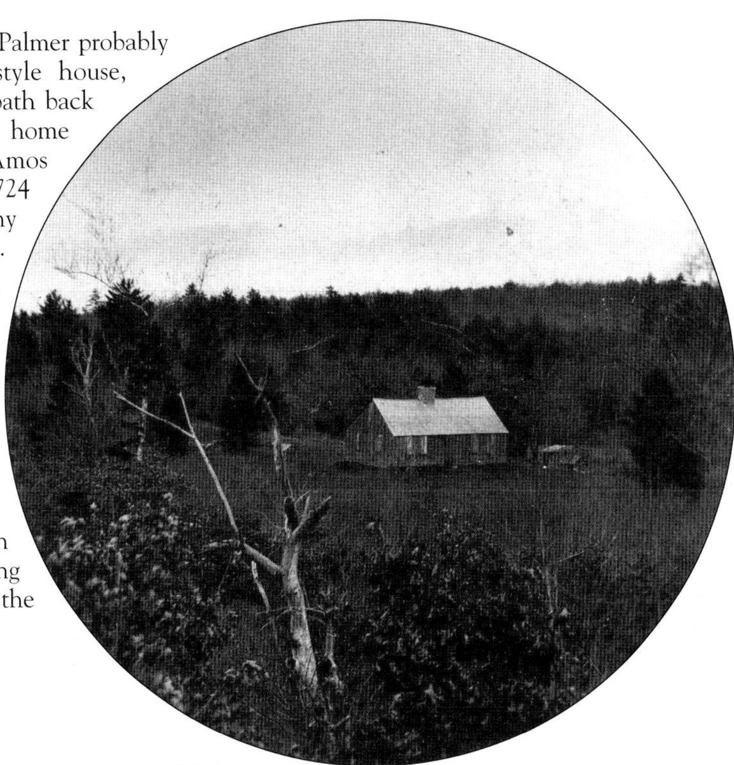

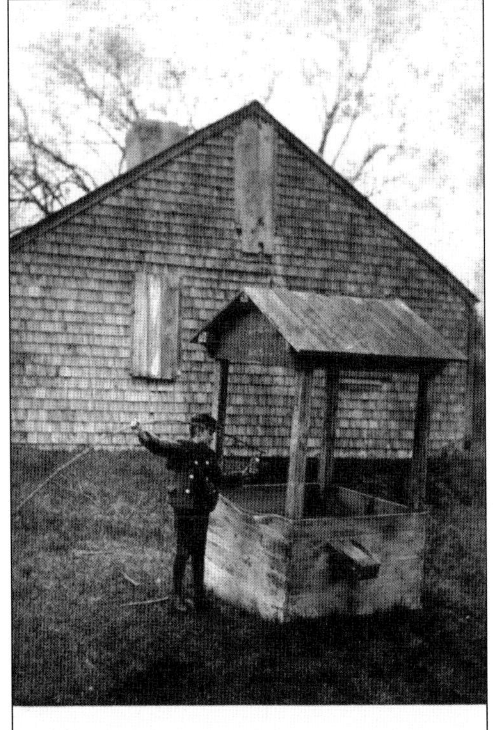

This H. L. Sturtevant cabinet card is titled on the reverse "Moss covered bucket that hung in the well." The young man prepares to lower a tin can so he can quench his thirst at the well near the old house in Cricket Hole, which was abandoned *c.* 1900. The foundation and well site are still visible in the woods far behind Cardinal Cushing School.

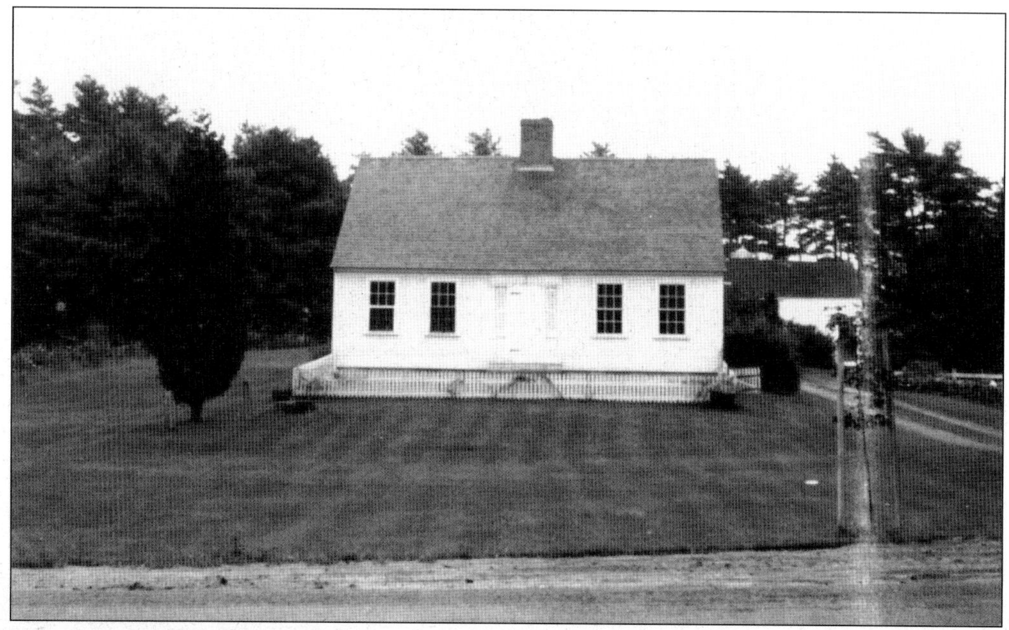

Isaac Perry, a shipbuilder and farmer, built this Cape-style farmhouse on Washington Street, near the path to Cricket Hole. Several families farmed this land over a span of more than 150 years. The Sullivan Funeral Home has operated from this location for the past 30 years. The proprietors have preserved the open fields at the edge of the woodland, as well as many of the features of the old house.

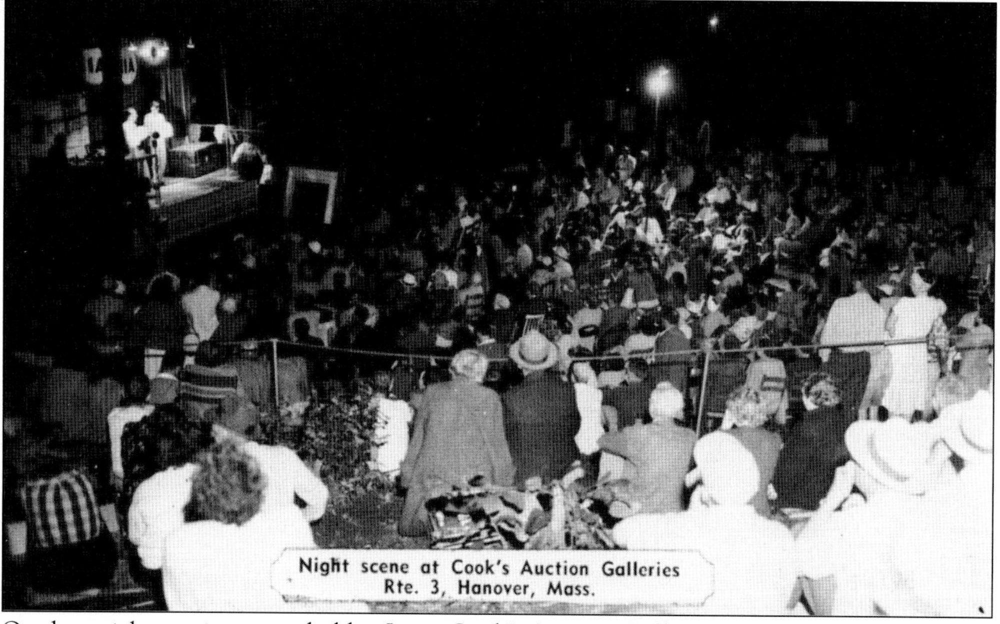

Outdoor night auctions were held at Louis Cook's Auction Gallery, just off Washington Street on Old Hanover Street. In the 1950s and 1960s, the events provided an evening's entertainment and a chance to purchase some treasures. In the auction's 20th year in Hanover, more than 2,000 people attended an anniversary auction held outside, surrounded by the pine trees on the ridge.

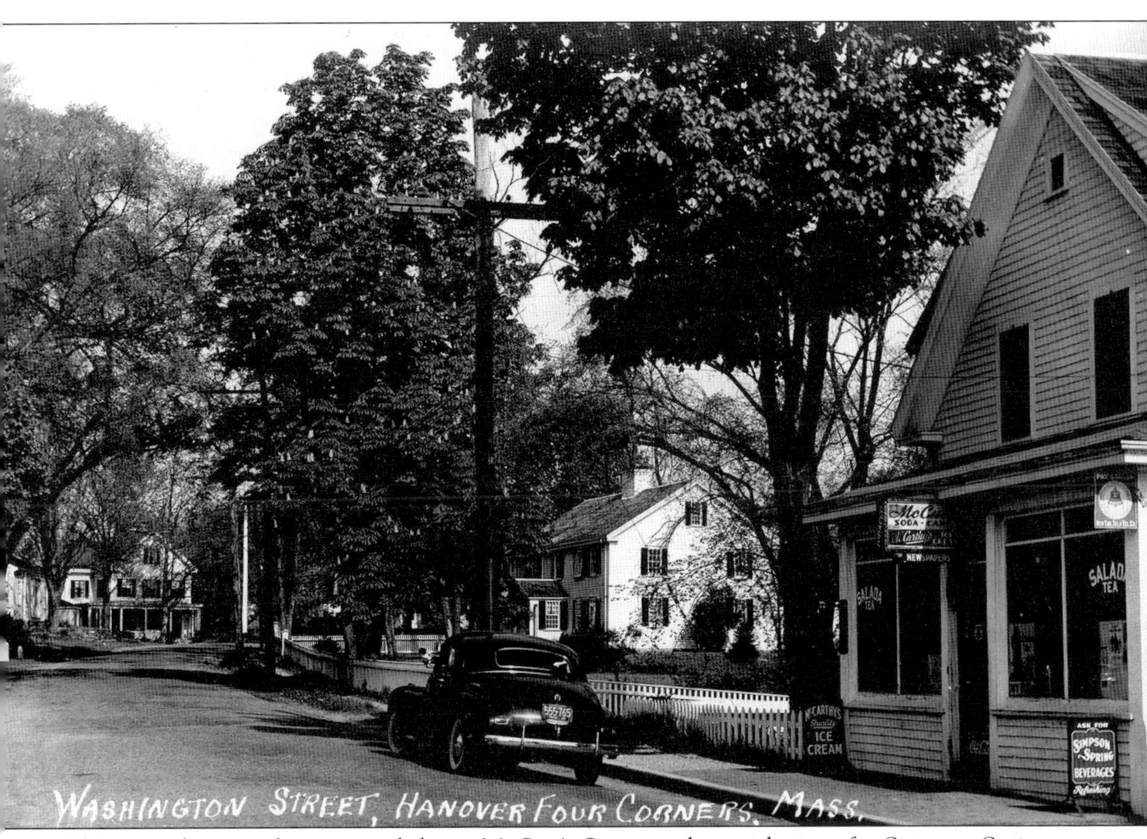

This rare photographic postcard shows McCue's Store, replete with signs for Simpson Springs Soda and McCarthy's Ice Cream. Salada Tea is advertised in the window, and a telephone pay station and newspapers are offered. This store began operating in what was originally John Flavell's barn. Later proprietors have included Mr. Jones, the Scotts, and Jack Murphy, among others. It has gained quite a reputation as Mary Lou's News, thanks to her famous coffee.

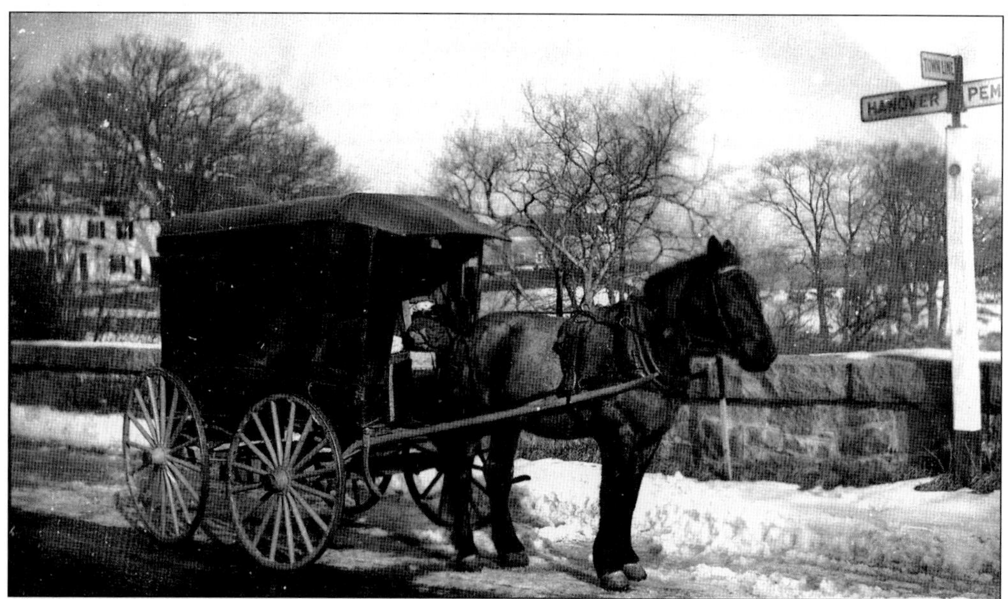

Charles Gleason crosses the Washington Street Bridge on his way to Pembroke aboard his peddlers wagon. Gleason sold his wares in Hanover, Pembroke, and Marshfield.

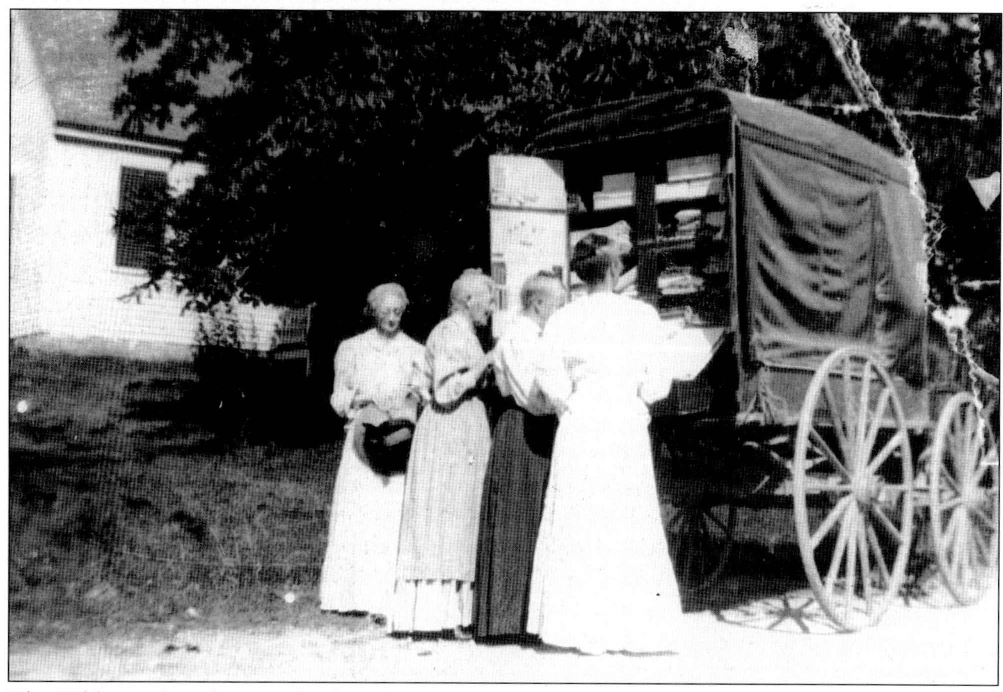

The Tilden girls gather at Charles Gleason's wagon to purchase dry goods c. 1910. In Gleason's scrapbook, he noted: "My peddlar cart was very attractive to the ladies. They came out and stood at the back of the wagon and picked out dress goods, spool cotton, and things to wear. Yes, I even had to fit corsets on them. Them were the good old days." The wagon was retired in 1939 and is now owned by the Hanover Historical Society.

Augustus "Gus" Tolman, born in Norwell in 1861, built a blacksmith shop on Broadway, near the site of the present Four Corners Fire Station. He resided on Church Street. After his death in the 1898 fire, Tolman's wife carried on the business, before selling it to L. J. Haywood.

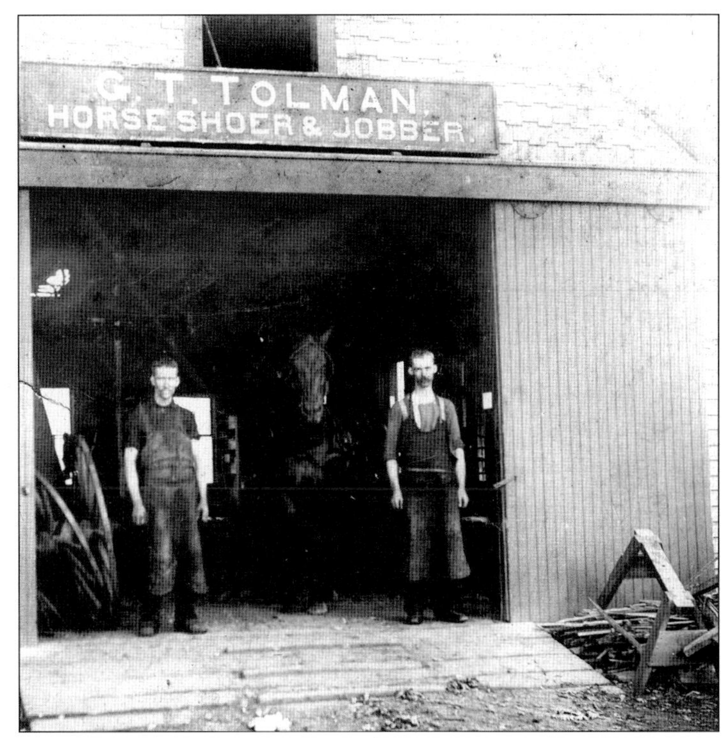

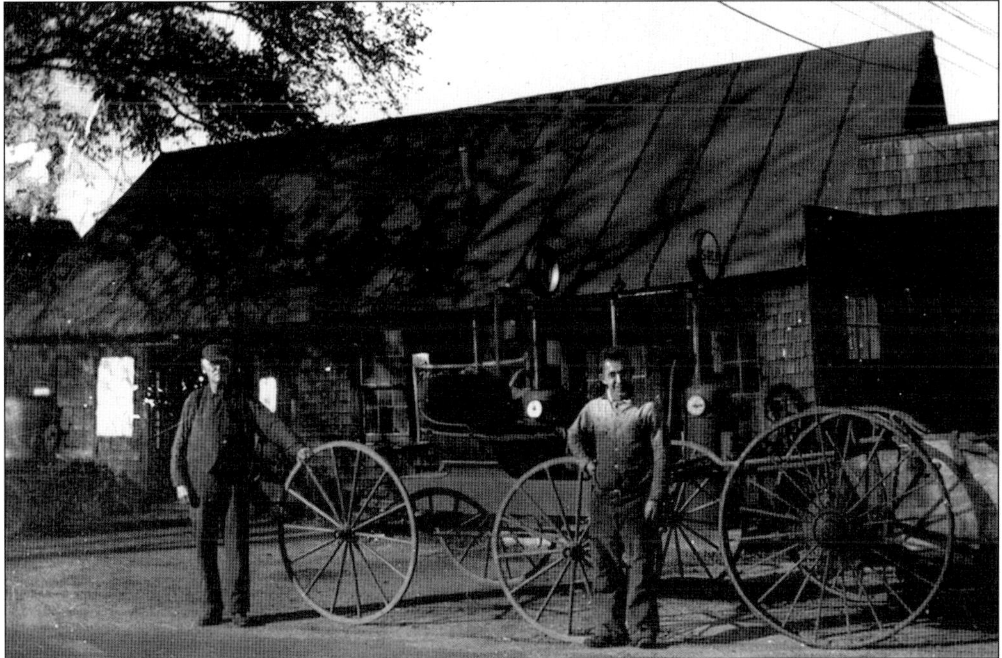

Each village had at least one blacksmith shop to shoe horses, fix wagon wheels, and such. A note written on this photograph, from the collection of Charles Gleason, reads, "Frank Merritt of Hanover came here in the 1850s after learning the trade from Warren Wright. Merritt passed it on to Harry Winslow 50 years ago." Notice the electric and telephone lines and gas pumps in this view, an indication that the photograph was probably taken in the early 1900s.

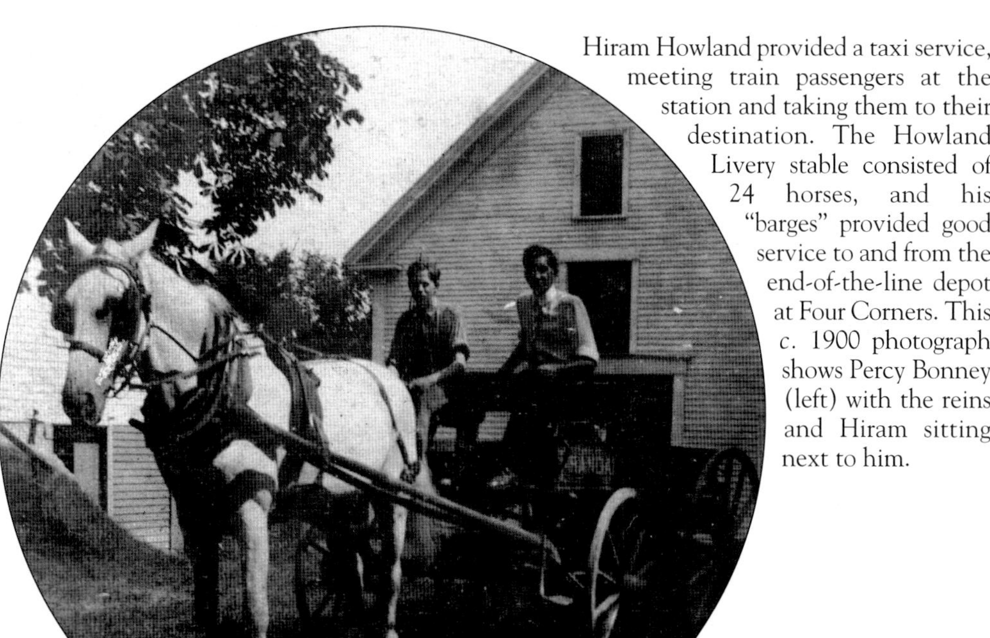

Hiram Howland provided a taxi service, meeting train passengers at the station and taking them to their destination. The Howland Livery stable consisted of 24 horses, and his "barges" provided good service to and from the end-of-the-line depot at Four Corners. This c. 1900 photograph shows Percy Bonney (left) with the reins and Hiram sitting next to him.

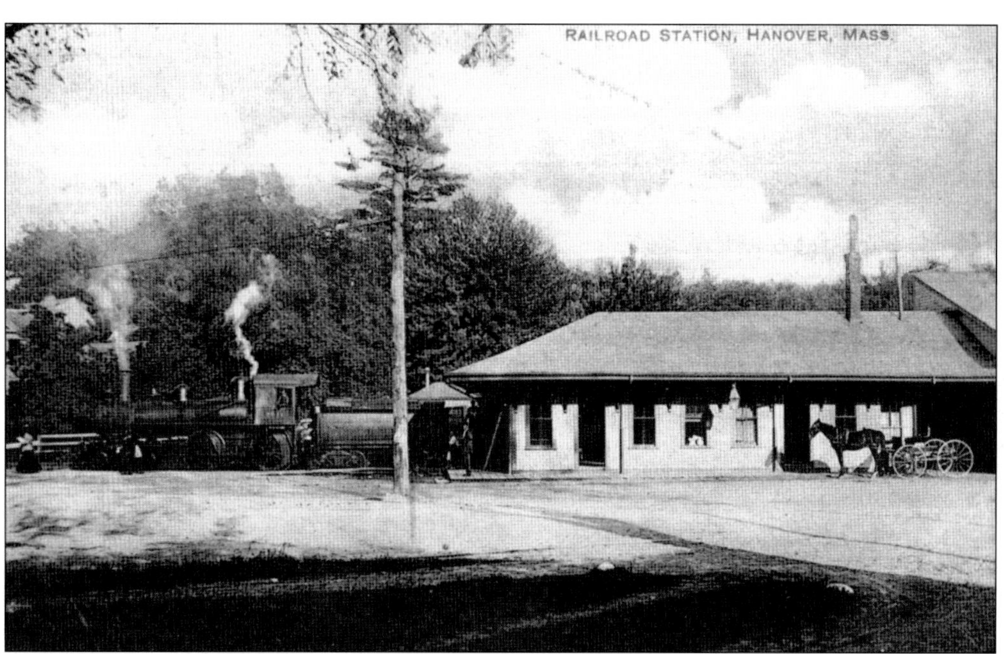

The end-of-the-line Hanover station was off Broadway, opposite Phillips, Bates & Company (now Sylvester Hardware Company). A turntable was located next to the station so that the locomotive could be turned around for the return trip to Boston.

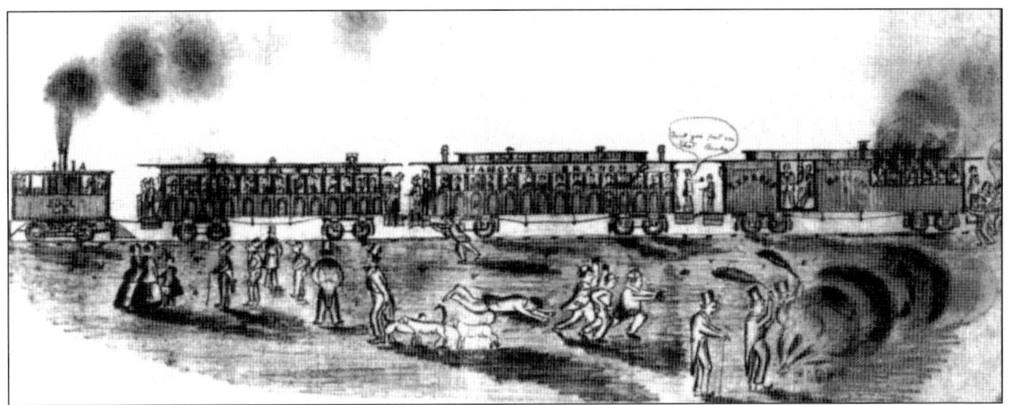

Harry McLaughlin, one of the first engineers on the Hanover Branch Railroad, was a musician, mechanic, and artist. His pencil sketch here depicts the so-called "dummy engine," which was used when the Hanover Branch Railroad began service in 1868. The smoke seen rising from the car on the right is due to passengers smoking, and onlookers at the right are attempting to extinguish fires started by sparks from the train.

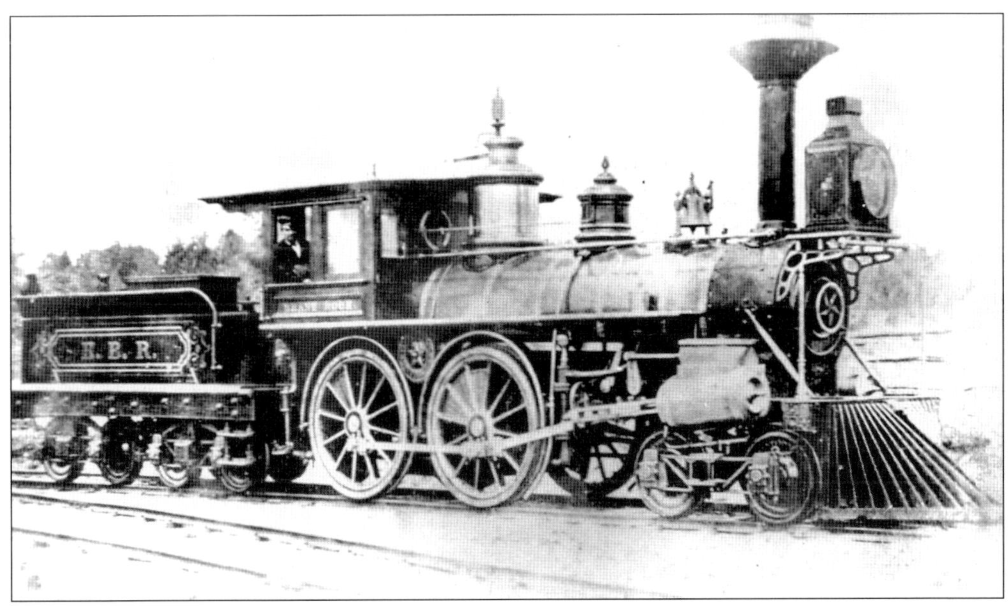

The Portland Locomotive Works built the Hanover Branch Railroad locomotive No. 1, the Brant Rock, in 1869. State of the art for its day, it had brass bands around the boiler and brass cylinder jackets. It became engine No. 13 when the Old Colony Railroad took over the eight-mile line in 1887. The Old Colony was, in turn, absorbed into the New Haven railroad system in 1893. (Collection of Mark Jacobson.)

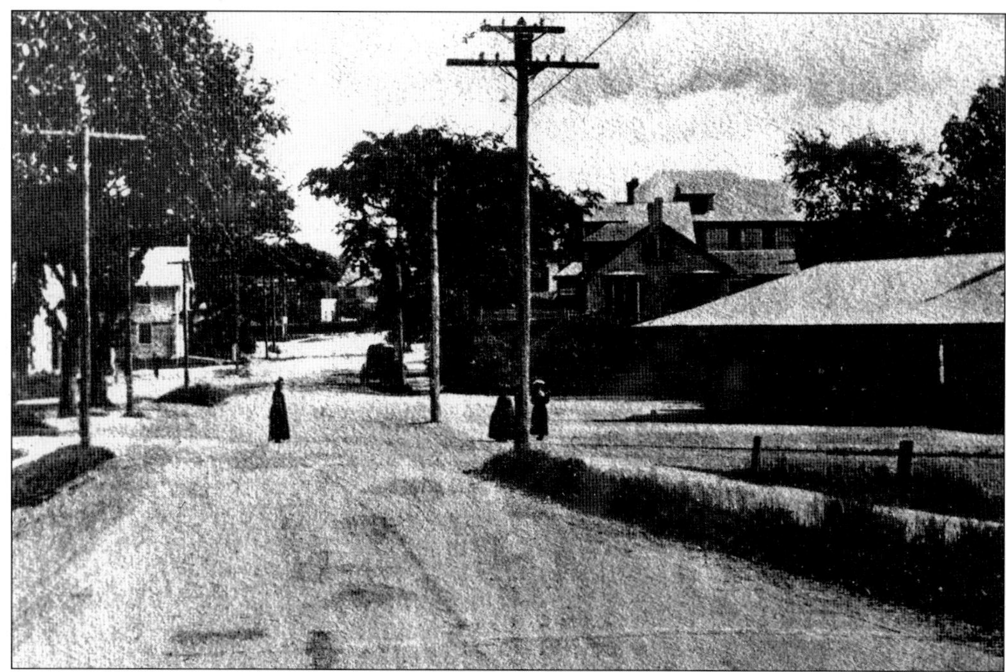

This lantern slide was titled "Hanover Depot Before the Big Hanover Fire of August 22, 1913." This postcard view looks up Broadway toward the Four Corners. The railroad station is on the right.

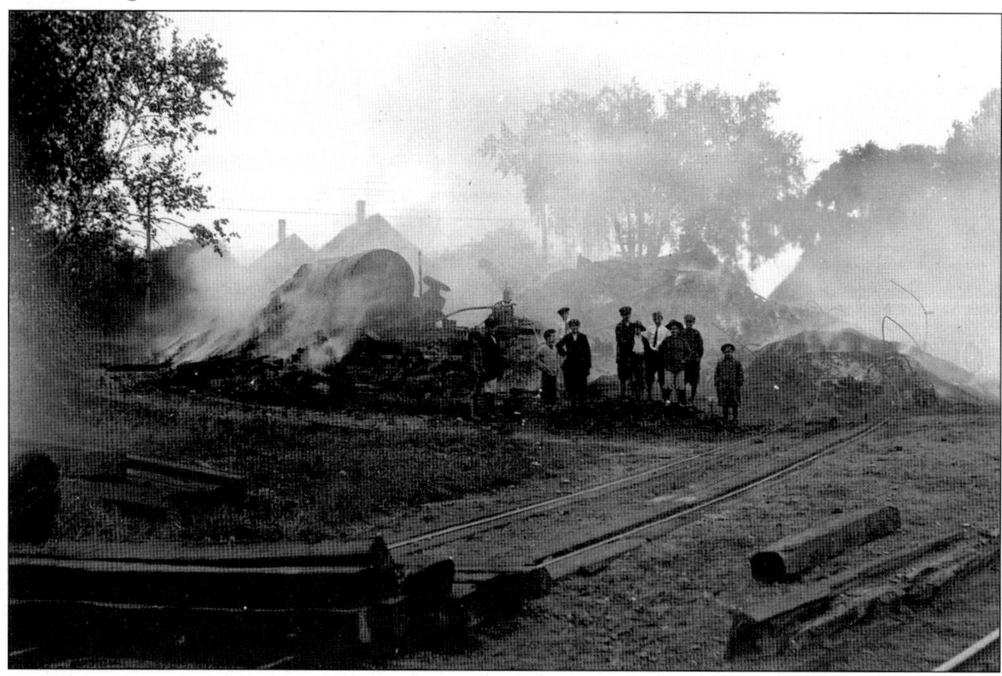

Smoke is still rising from the remains of the Four Corners railroad station, train cars, and the Phillips, Bates & Company grain elevator that were consumed by fire on August 22, 1913. Homes on Broadway can be seen in the background of this lantern slide, titled "200 Tons of Grain Burning."

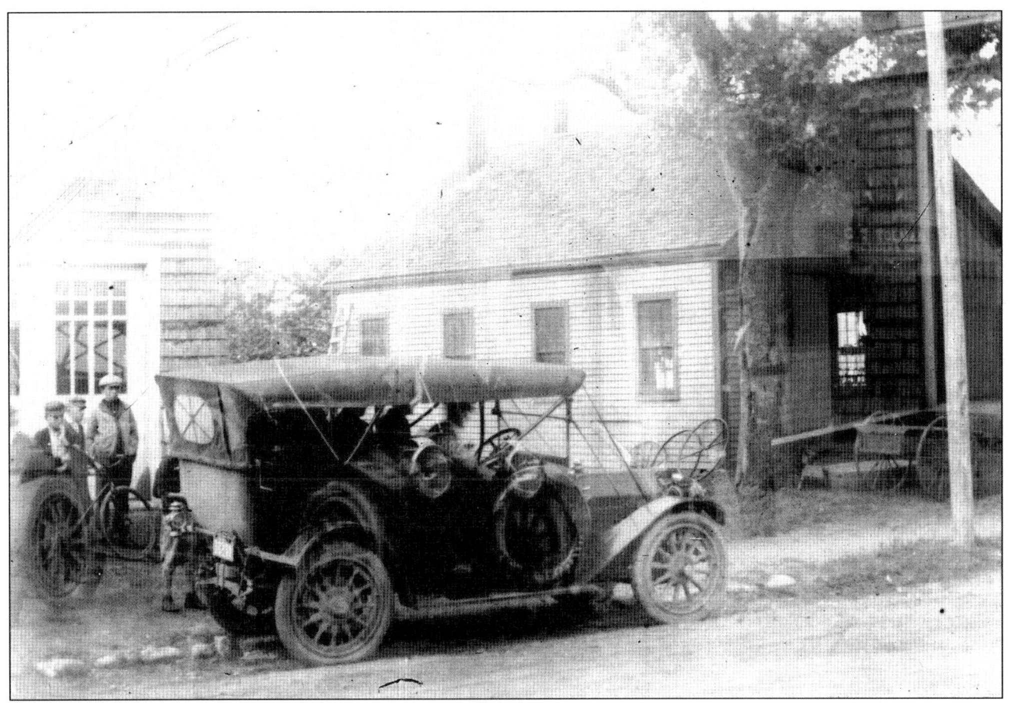

This rare lantern slide is titled "Police and Detectives Automobile." It is one of a series of images showing the results of the August 22, 1913 fire at the Four Corners. The auto is seen in front of the fire station on Broadway.

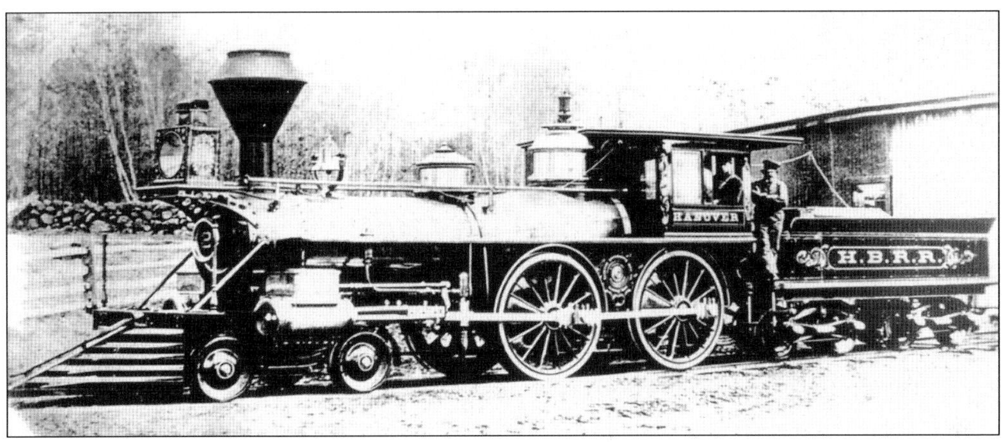

The Hanover Branch Railroad tracks entered Hanover at the Rockland town line, near the end of Circuit Street. The tracks wound their way through West Hanover into South Hanover and ended at the Hanover station, behind the current Citizens Bank. An engine house, turntable, repair shop, and coal shed were built at the end of the line. Engine No. 2, the Hanover (pictured), of the Hanover Branch Railroad, later became Old Colony Railroad engine No. 49.

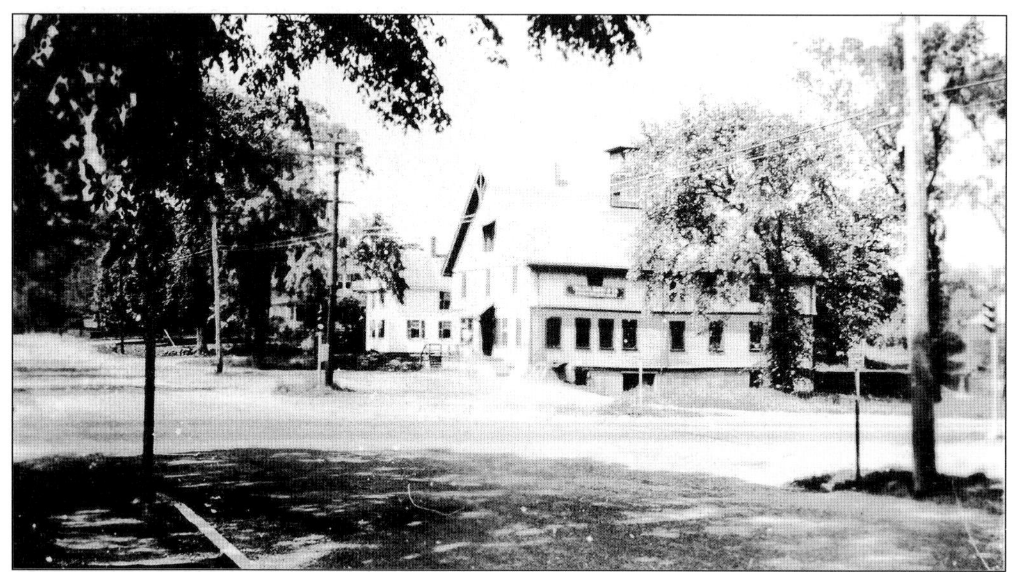

Phillips, Bates & Company, business successors to Samuel Church and Robert Sylvester, occupied the building that is now home to the Sylvester Hardware Company. A spur track crossed the road to the railroad station, and, according to Charles Gleason's scrapbook, "It was a common sight to see Mose Young come rushing out of the office with a red flag to warn the public of an approaching engine." Gleason took this photograph after 1931, as Columbia Road (constructed in that year) is visible in the foreground.

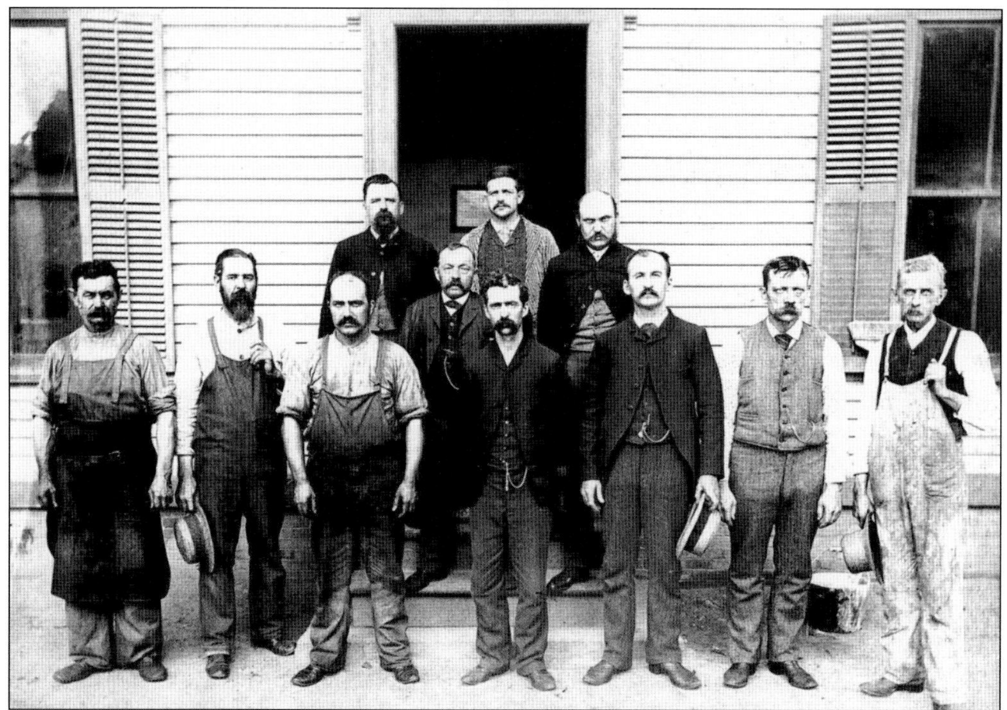

Mose Young is one of the Phillips, Bates & Company workers in this c. 1900 image. The company, established in 1868, advertised in 1907 as a store that sold grain, flour, cereal, coal, hardware, hay, and straw.

James Waterman and his dog are the subject of this H. L. Sturtevant cabinet card. James and his wife, Sarah (Bates), lived at 1 Church Street, on the corner of Rockland Street. The house was on the site of Captain Cushing's "Folly Hill" house.

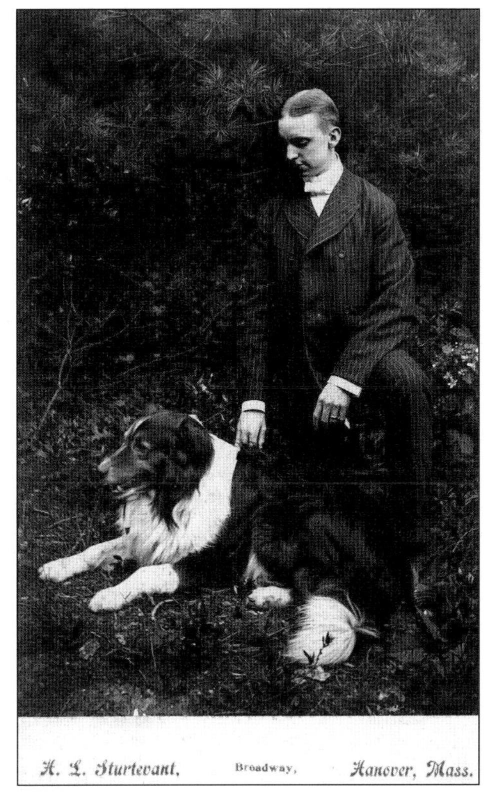

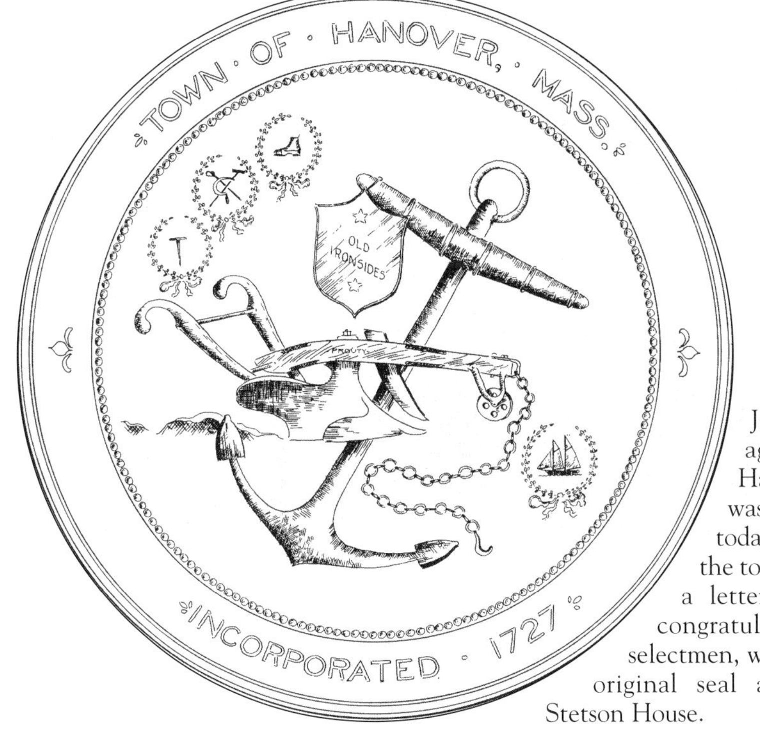

James C. Waterman, at age 20, designed this Hanover town seal, which was simplified and is used today as the official seal of the town. Waterman received a letter of appreciation and congratulations from the selectmen, which is framed with the original seal and displayed at the Stetson House.

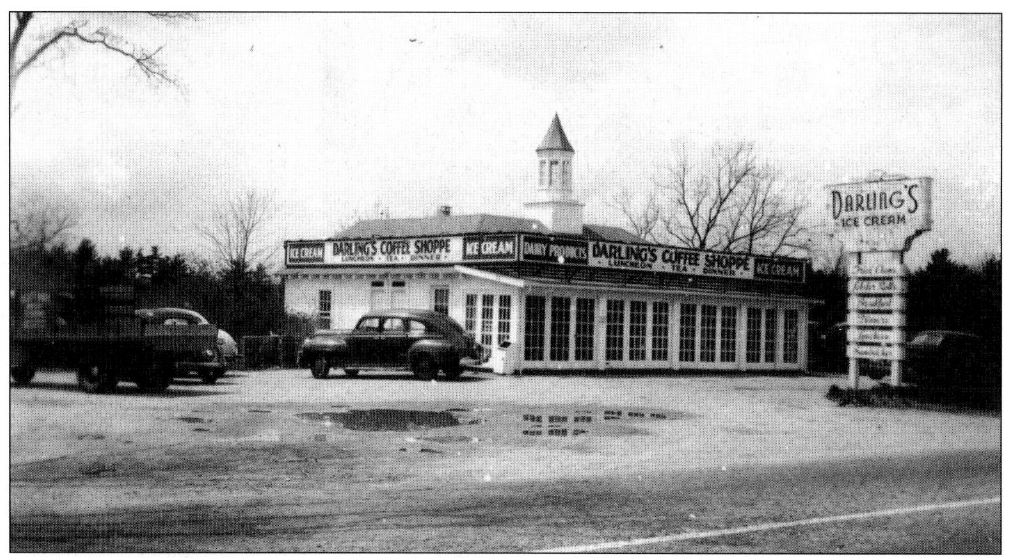

Charles Gleason's description for this 1940s photograph says, "Darling's eating place at the corner of Columbia Road and the Folly Road [Rockland Street] do a good business." Judging from the signage, it appears the eatery offered quite a selection. Since then, the restaurant has operated under several names, including Doran's and Ridders, and is now known as Crossroads. The cupola has disappeared.

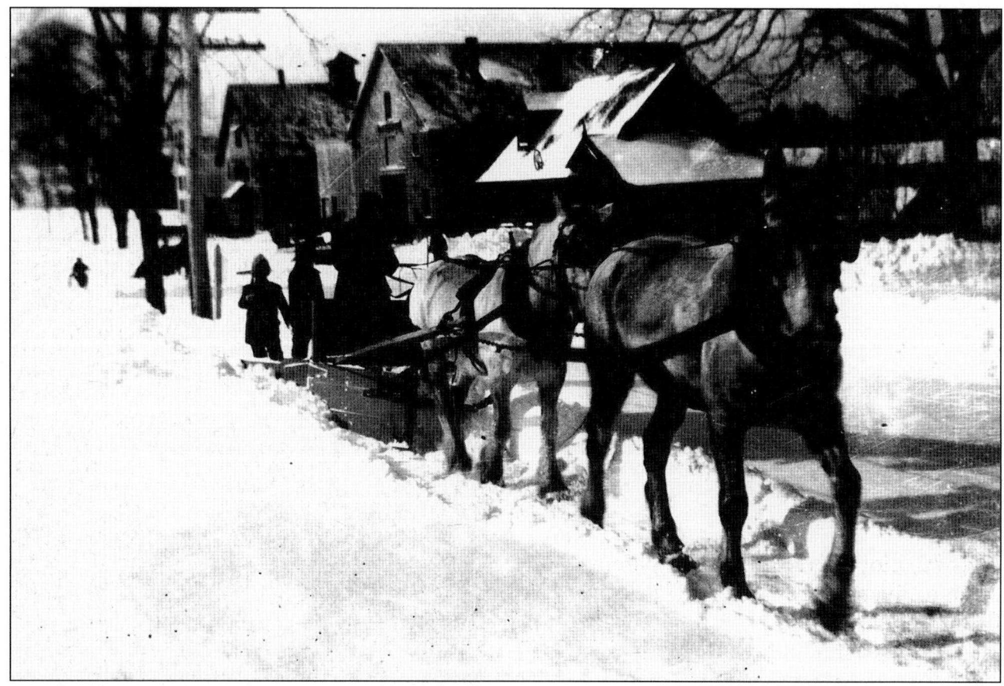

Stanley Briggs is shown here plowing the sidewalk at the Four Corners with his two-horse team. Sylvester Lumber Company is the building with the cupola in the background. The large building in front of it was Hiram Randall's Stable, a structure removed in 1930 when Columbia Road was constructed. Percy Bonney's shop, the next-door building (with a snow-covered roof), remains at the corner of Broadway and Route 53.

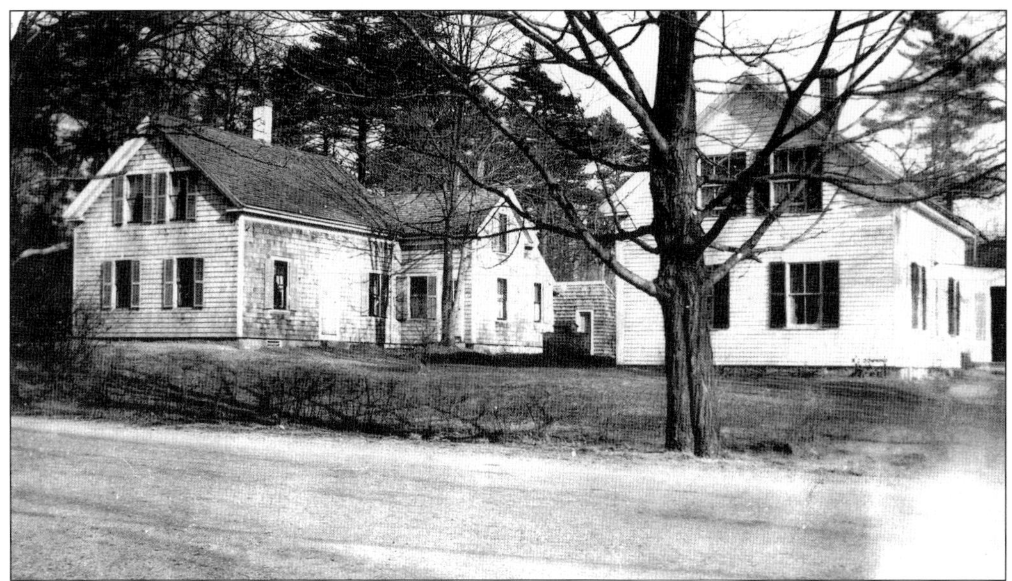

These homes at 304 and 312 Broadway were built *c.* 1870 by E. Y. Perry, founder and president of the Hanover Branch Railroad. Fred Tower (engineer), Frank Tower (conductor), and their families occupied these houses for many years. Fred and Frank did not have to travel far to get to work; the railroad tracks ran behind the houses, and the station was about 500 yards up the street.

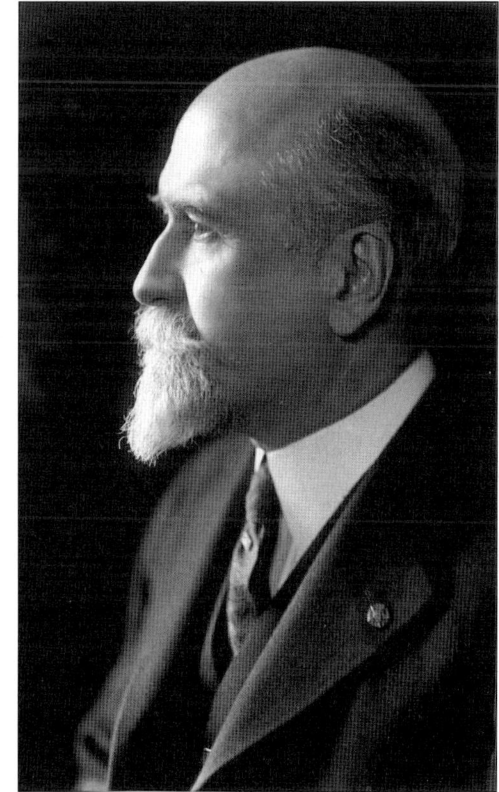

In 1870, Lloyd Vernon Briggs's parents came to live at 8 Elm Street in Hanover. Briggs (pictured) was born in Boston and received his early education in the public schools and at Hanover Academy. He attended lectures at Harvard Medical School by the age of 15, and later received his doctorate in medicine from the Medical College of Virginia. Briggs was a crusader for better treatment of the mentally ill.

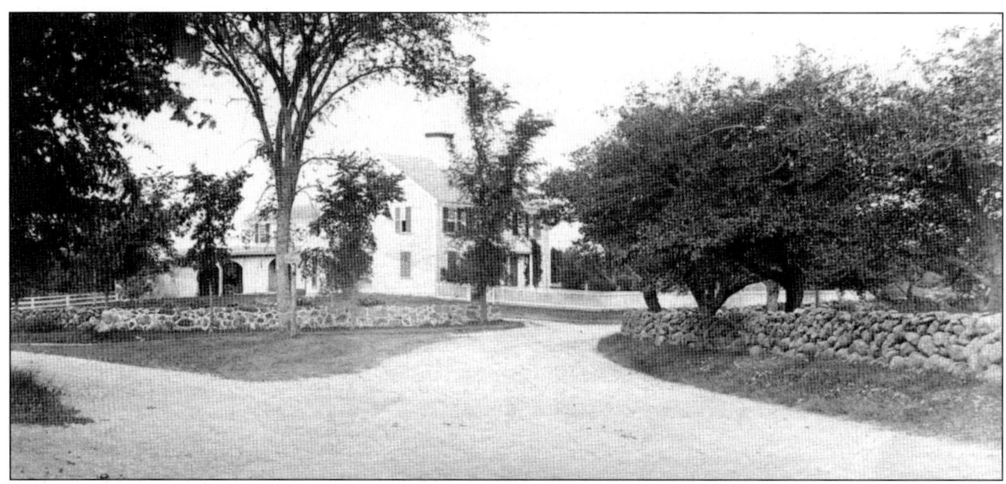

This *c.* 1890 H. L. Sturtevant photograph shows Broad Oak Farm before the road was moved farther away from the front of the house. Located on the corner of Broadway and Elm Street, the house was built in 1799 and was the home of Col. John Barstow, a shipbuilder. It later became the residence of Dr. L. Vernon Briggs, a prominent Boston psychiatrist and author of *Shipbuilding on the North River*, genealogy books about the Briggs and Cabot families, and numerous history and medical volumes.

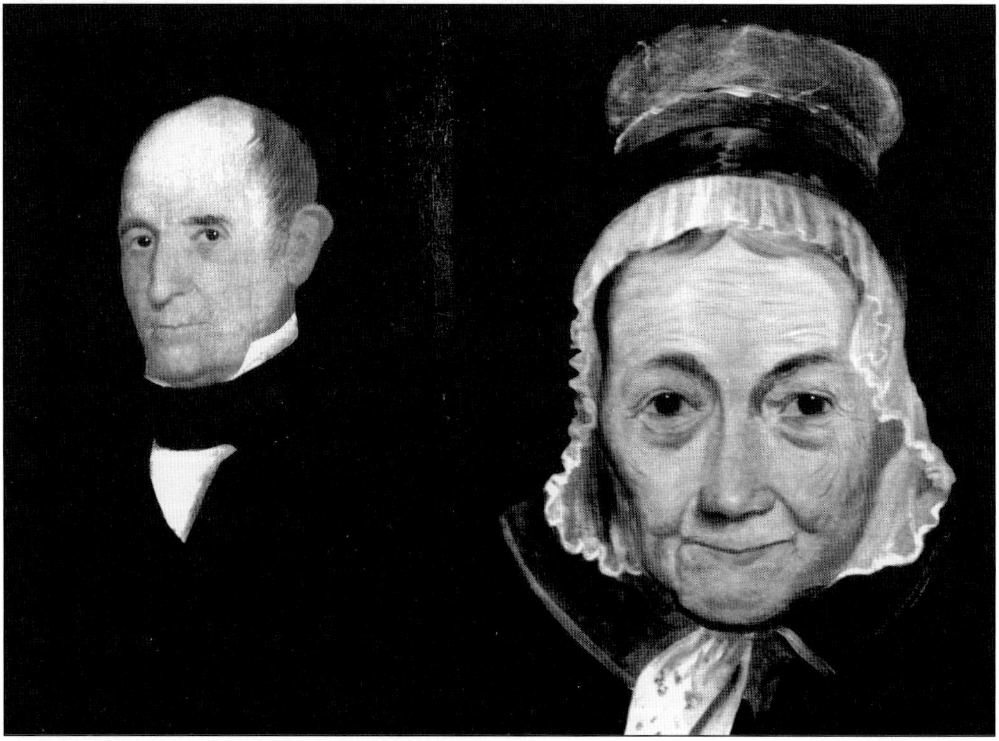

Col. and Mrs. John B. Barstow were both from old Hanover shipbuilding families. Many North River ships were built in the Barstow yards, including the whale ship *Oeno*, which sailed the South Pacific from Nantucket. In 1825, the ship struck a reef in the Fiji Islands, and natives killed 21 of the 22-man crew. Barstow and his wife, Betsy, lived at Broad Oak Farm. Their portraits hang in the Stetson House.

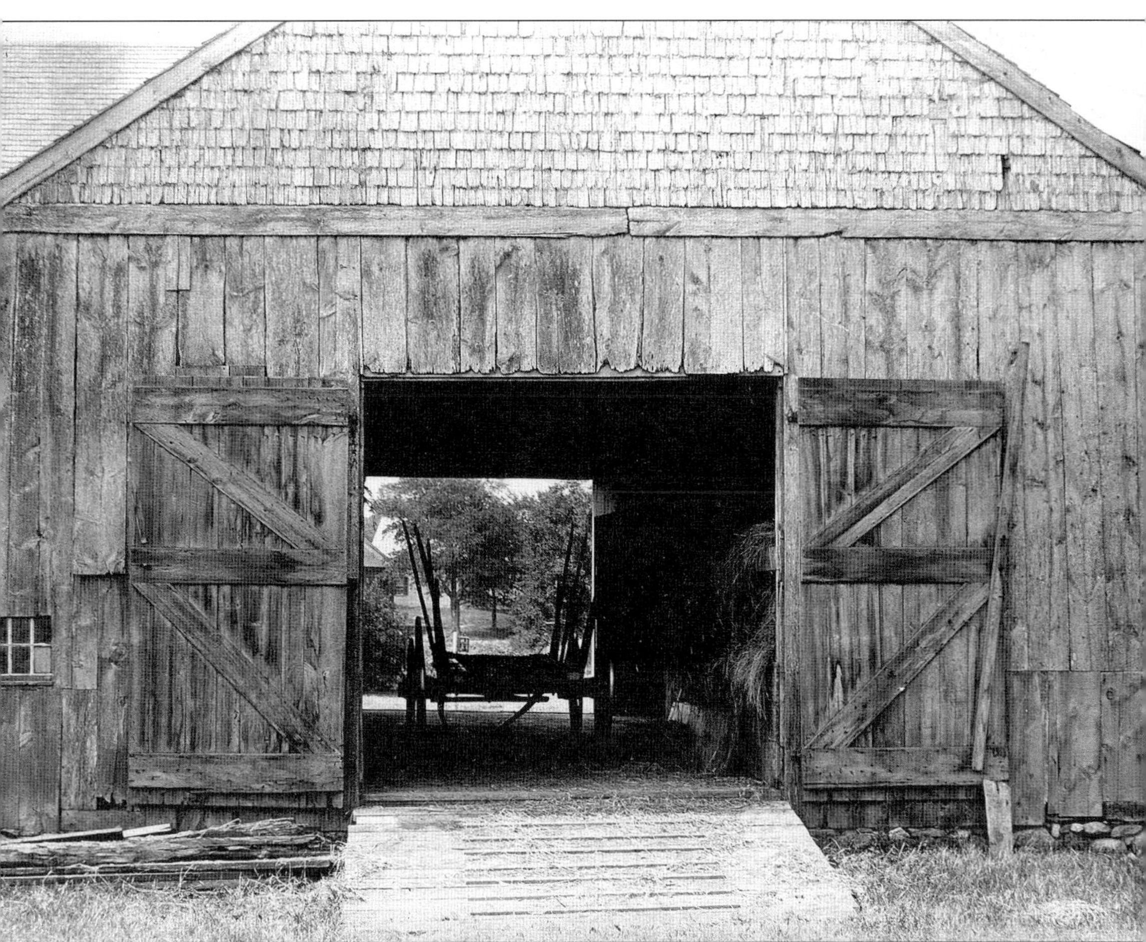

H. L. Sturtevant recorded this scene for posterity on July 3, 1896, at Reuben Donnell's barn at 80 Elm Street, near Water Street. Donnell ran a dairy farm and was one of several milkmen in Hanover. He had no milk bottles at that time. Instead, Donnell filled pitchers from an eight-quart milk can. By 1909, Charles Gleason reported that milk was 8¢ a quart.

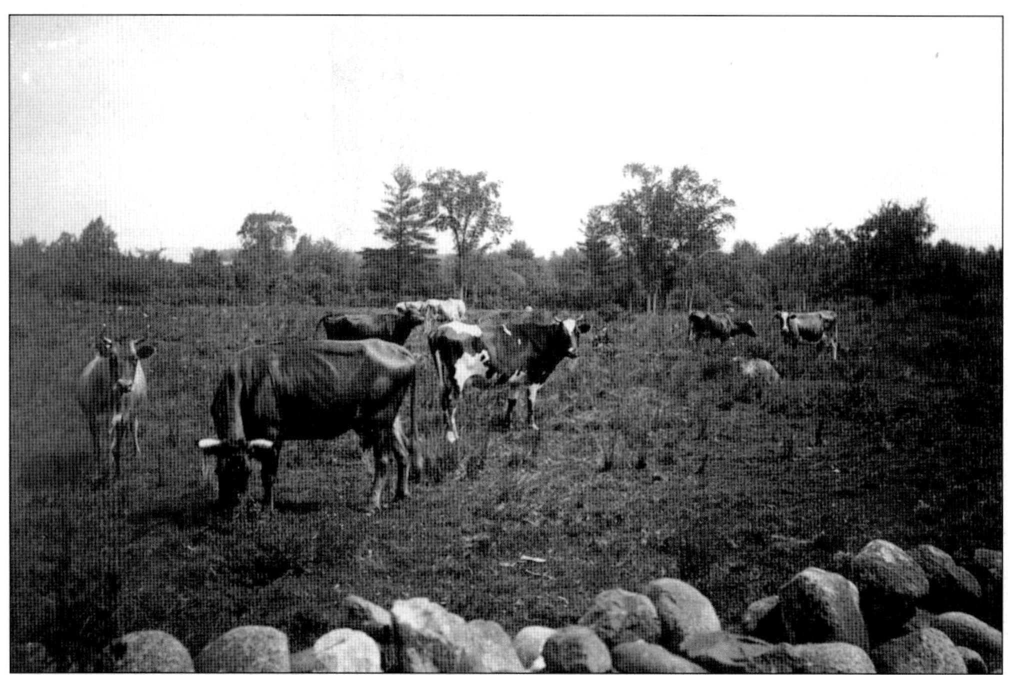

Two of Reuben Donnell's dairy cows watched as H. L. Sturtevant captured their image on July 3, 1896.

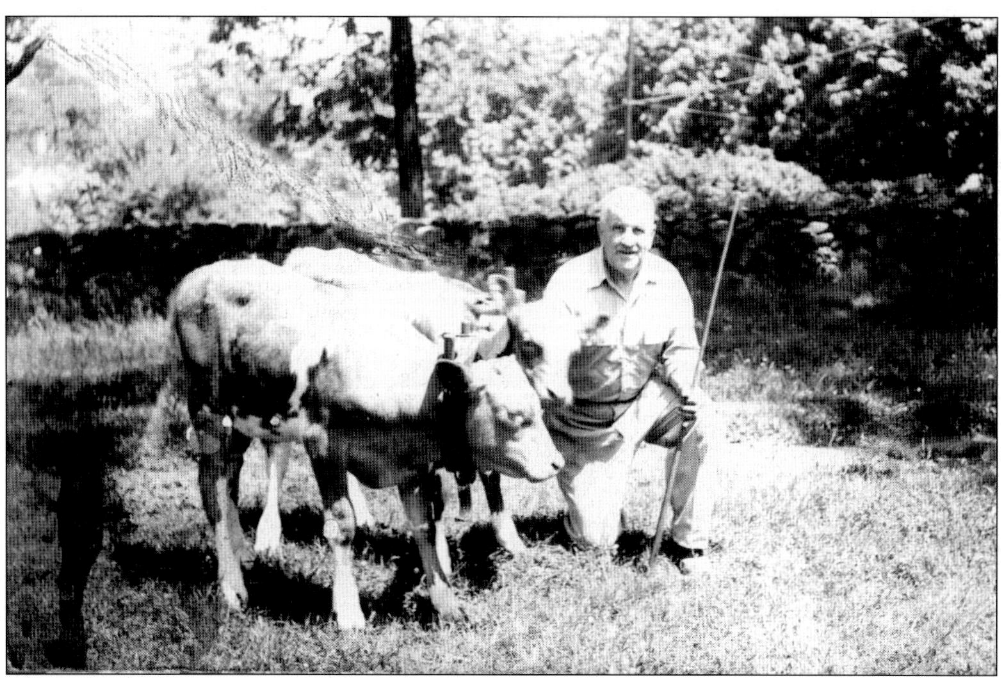

Oxen were a familiar sight on the Sylvester farm for many years. Fred Sanders worked for Sam Sylvester and was in charge of the farm animals. Here, Fred poses with his twin steers, Pete and Repeat, for a Charles Gleason photograph.

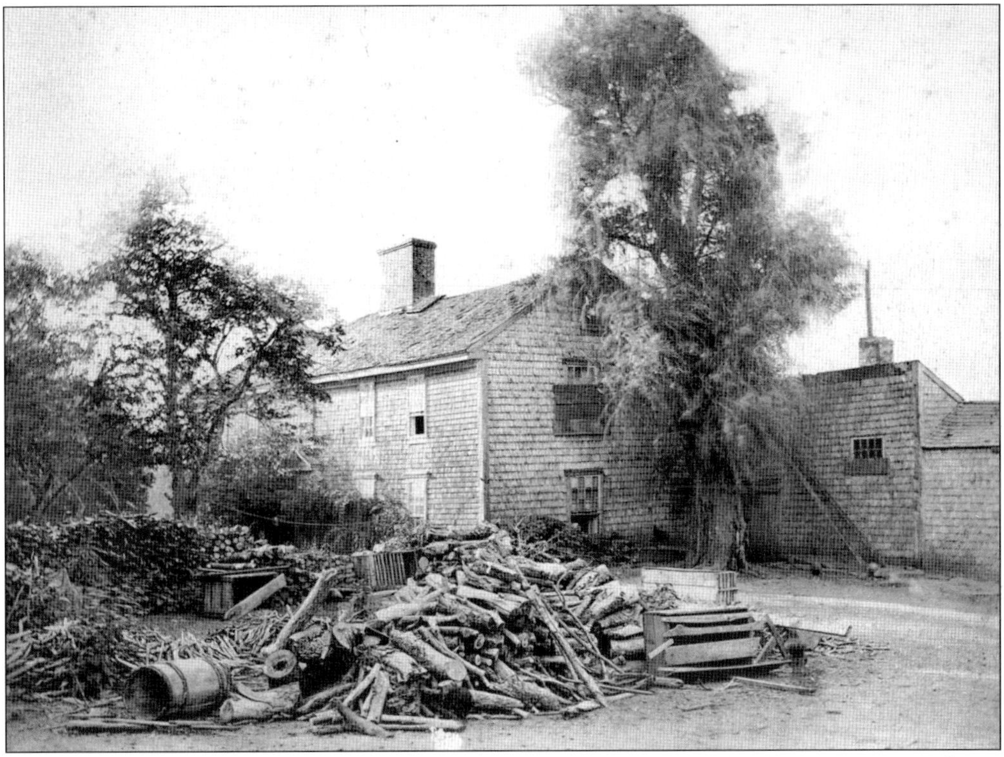

The Benjamin Pratt home, at 167 Elm Street, was built *c.* 1820. The house appears to be in need of repair here, but there is a good supply of wood for winter. In the early 1900s, the barn and part of the house burned, but the house was later renovated and is still standing today.

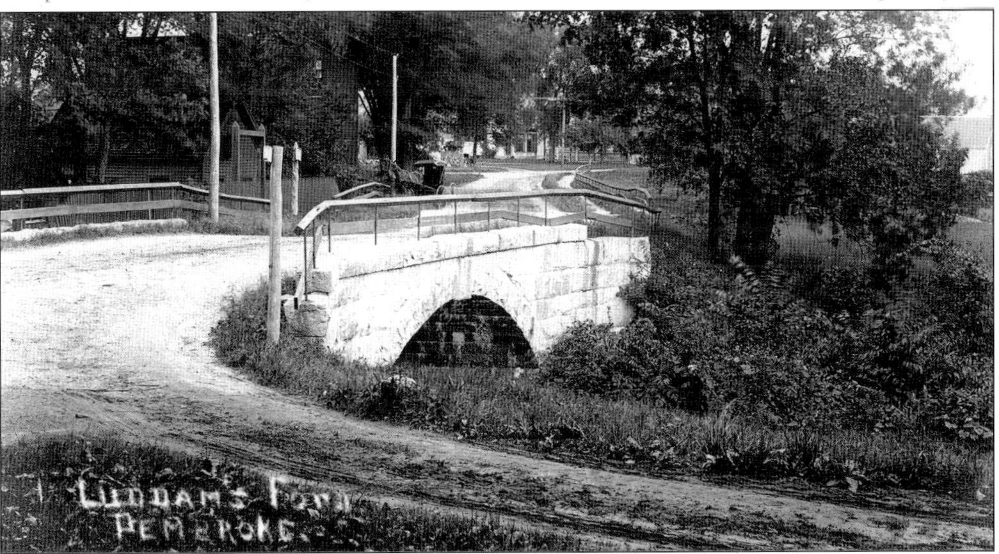

In 1632, James Luddam guided Mass Bay Colony governor John Winthrop on a visit to Plymouth Colony. The men followed the Plymouth and Bay Path. When they reached the Indian Head River at this site, it is said that Luddam carried his guest through the river. In 1704, the first bridge was built over the Indian Head River. The current stone arched bridge was constructed in 1894, at a cost of $900.

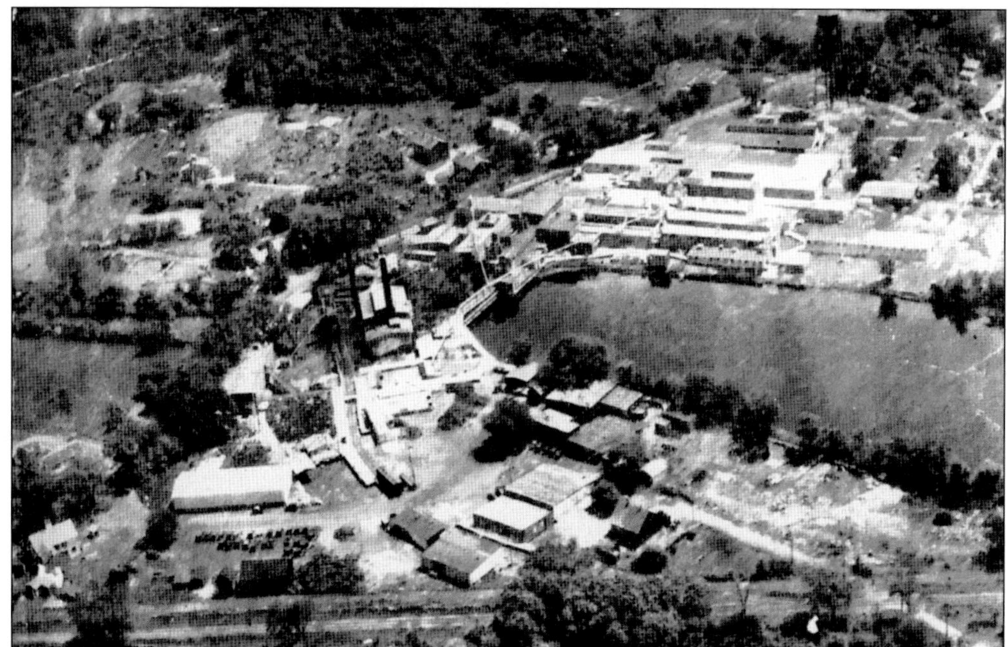

The E. H. Clapp Rubber Mill, shown in this 1920s aerial photograph, began on this site at Luddam's Ford, on Elm Street in South Hanover, in 1870. Eugene H. Clapp's company recycled rubber products and operated from 1892 to the late 1930s. The former mill site, which spans the Indian Head River, now is preserved as conservation land by the towns of Hanover and Pembroke.

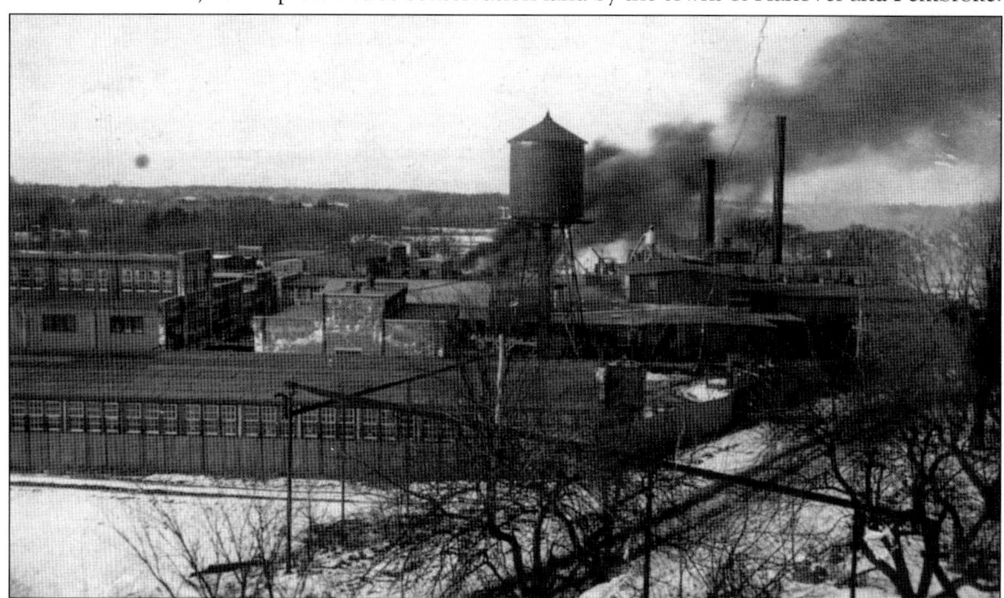

Who could have guessed that this gritty industrial scene of Clapp Rubber Mill in 1924 would be replaced by the pastoral beauty today of Luddam's Ford? The harnessing of waterpower for industry led to 200 years of pollution and abuse of the river. Today, organizations such as the North and South Rivers Watershed Association (www.nsrwa.org) monitor river conditions and conduct periodic cleanups. The river is probably cleaner today than at any time since the Native Americans lived here.

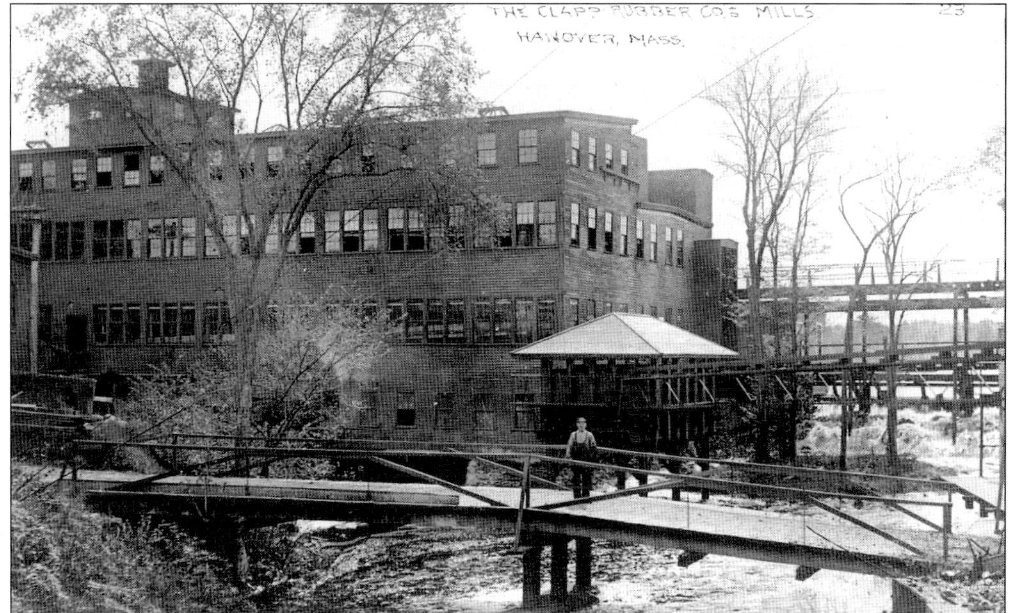

Few residents realize the immense size of the Clapp rubber mill facility that once spanned the Indian Head River at Luddam's Ford. This photograph, taken from the Elm Street bridge, is a view looking west toward the dam, seen in the background.

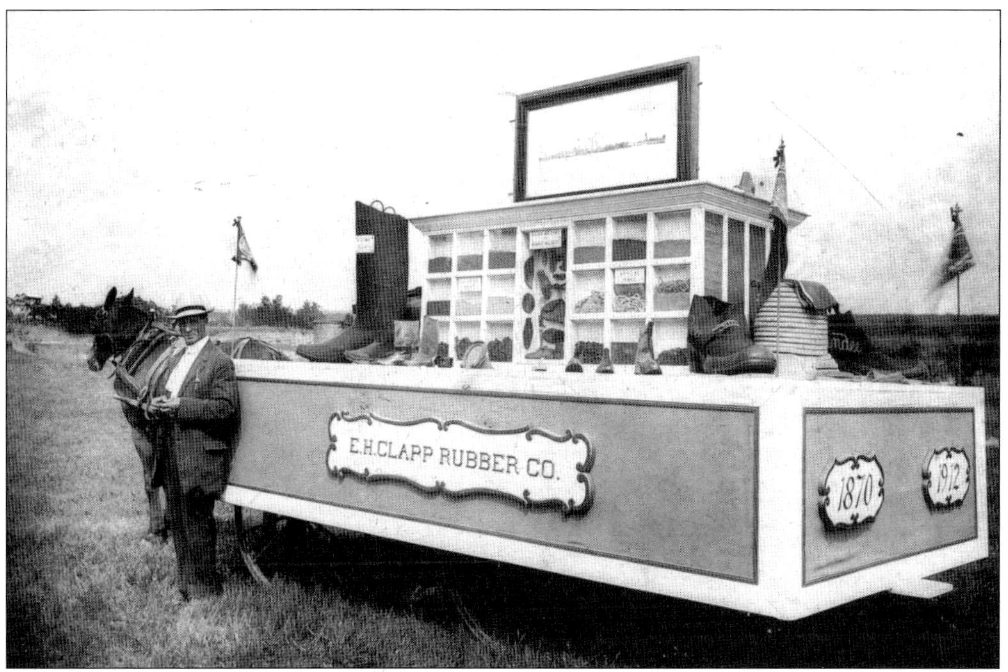

The E. H. Clapp Rubber Company float participated in a 1912 parade and showcased the firm's business. A large photograph of the plant sits on top of the float. The cubicles in the box beneath the photograph show what the company recycled. A sign on the large worn-out boot reads, "What we buy." A sign in a middle compartment says, "What we find in what we buy," while another reads, "What we make."

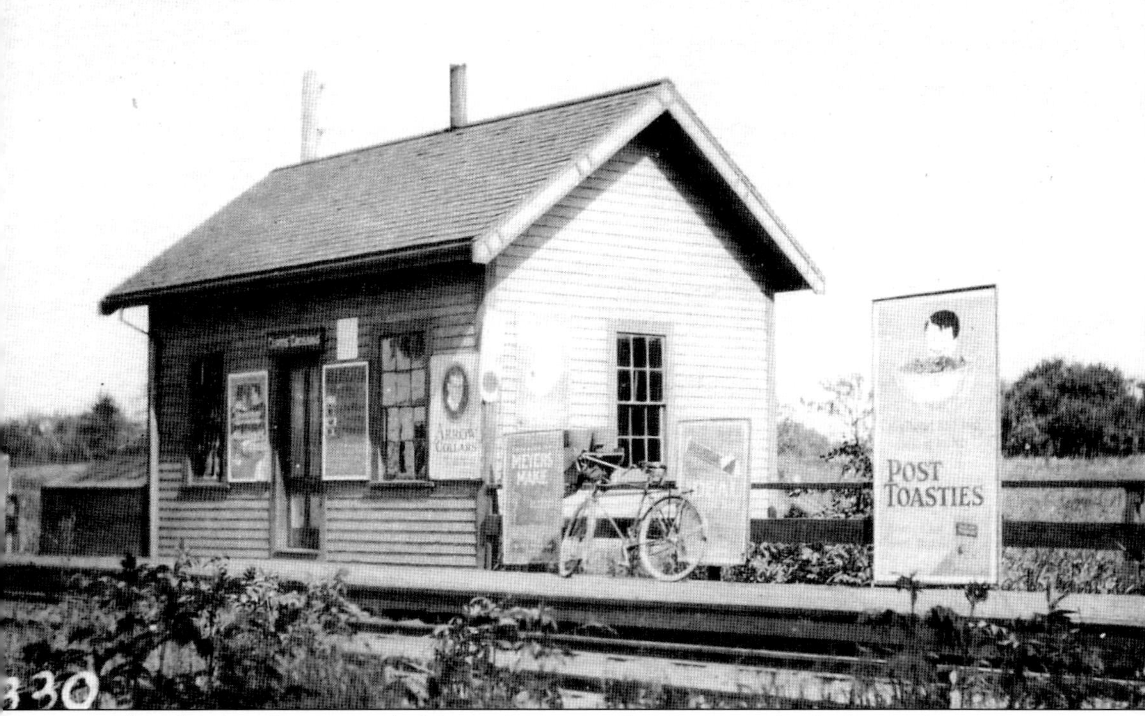

This photographic postcard of Curtis Crossing railroad station clearly shows advertising posters. Signs promoting Arrow Collars, Meyers Make, and Post Toasties are three of the advertisements posted at the station where Clapp Rubber Mill employees disembarked trains on their way to to work. (Collection of Mark Jacobson.)

Three
South Hanover

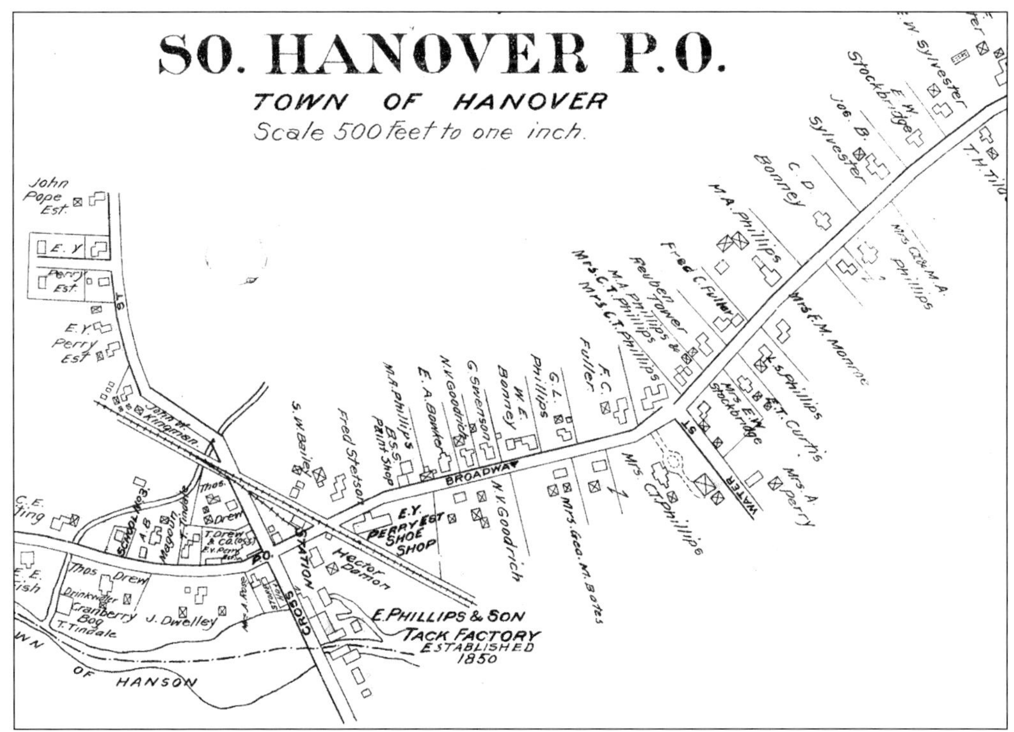

Detail from Plate 14, *Atlas of Plymouth County*, 1903.

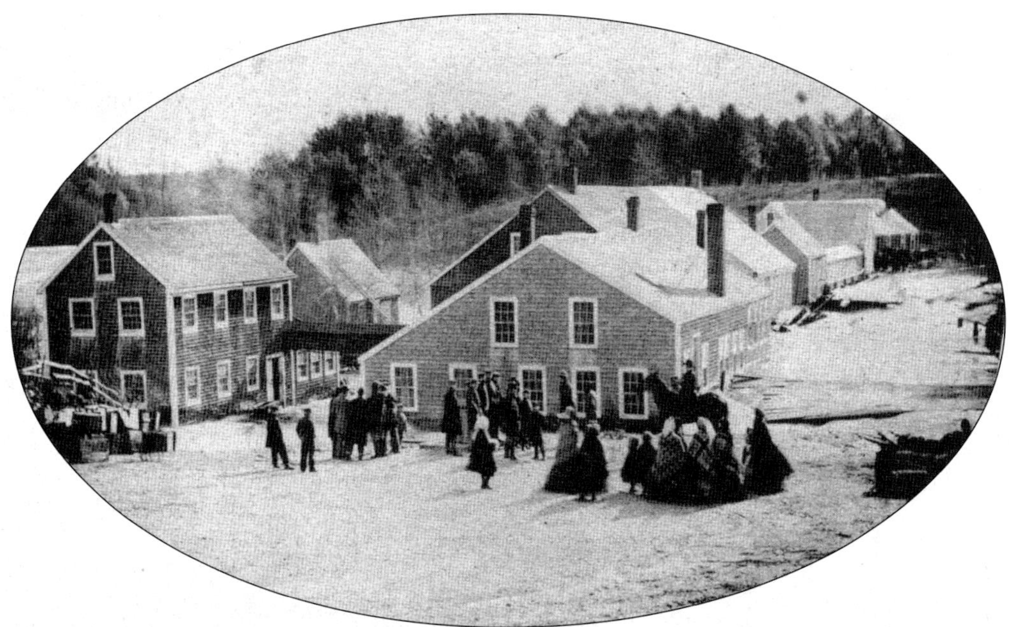

One of the earliest photographic images of Hanover, this *c.* 1865 winter scene shows a gathering at the E. Phillips and Sons tack factory in South Hanover. Rufus Bates is identified as the man on the horse. Eva Bonney, daughter of William E. "Ink" Bonney, is the little girl with the white bonnet and muff (near center). She was born in 1853, according to Dwelley and Simmons's *History of Hanover*. The two other small girls (seen below the horse's head) are identified as Ruthena Stockbridge (left) and Lizzie Robbins.

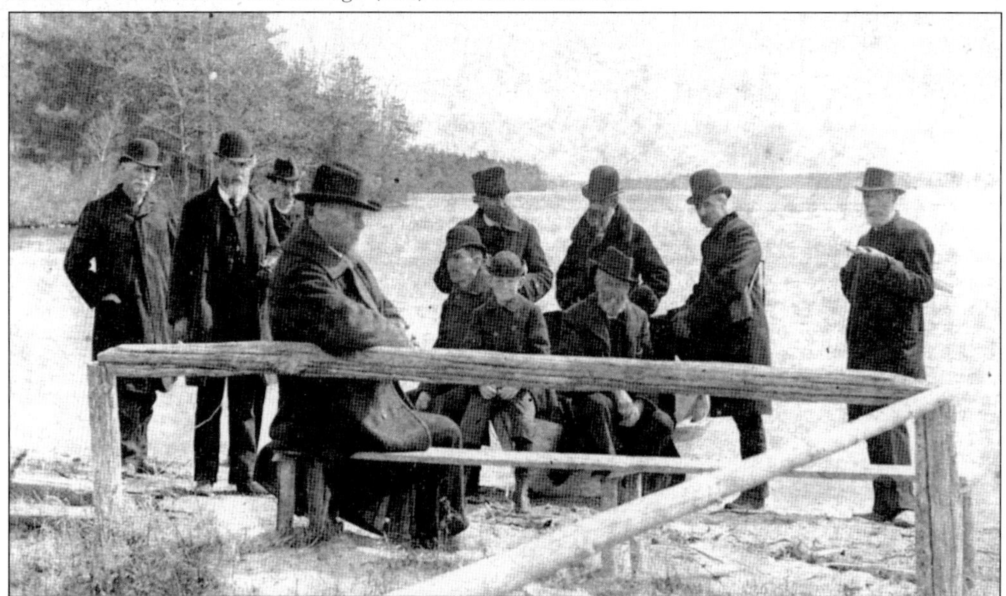

These gentlemen, dressed in their Sunday best, are members of the North River Historical Association, photographed at the river before 1890. From left to right are the following: (seated) Francis Arnold, Fred Phillips, and John Knight; (standing) Jedidiah Dwelley, Edward Sweeney, John Monroe, Lot Phillips, Calvin Phillips, Morrill Phillips, and John Tower. The boy seated at center is a grandson of Sweeney.

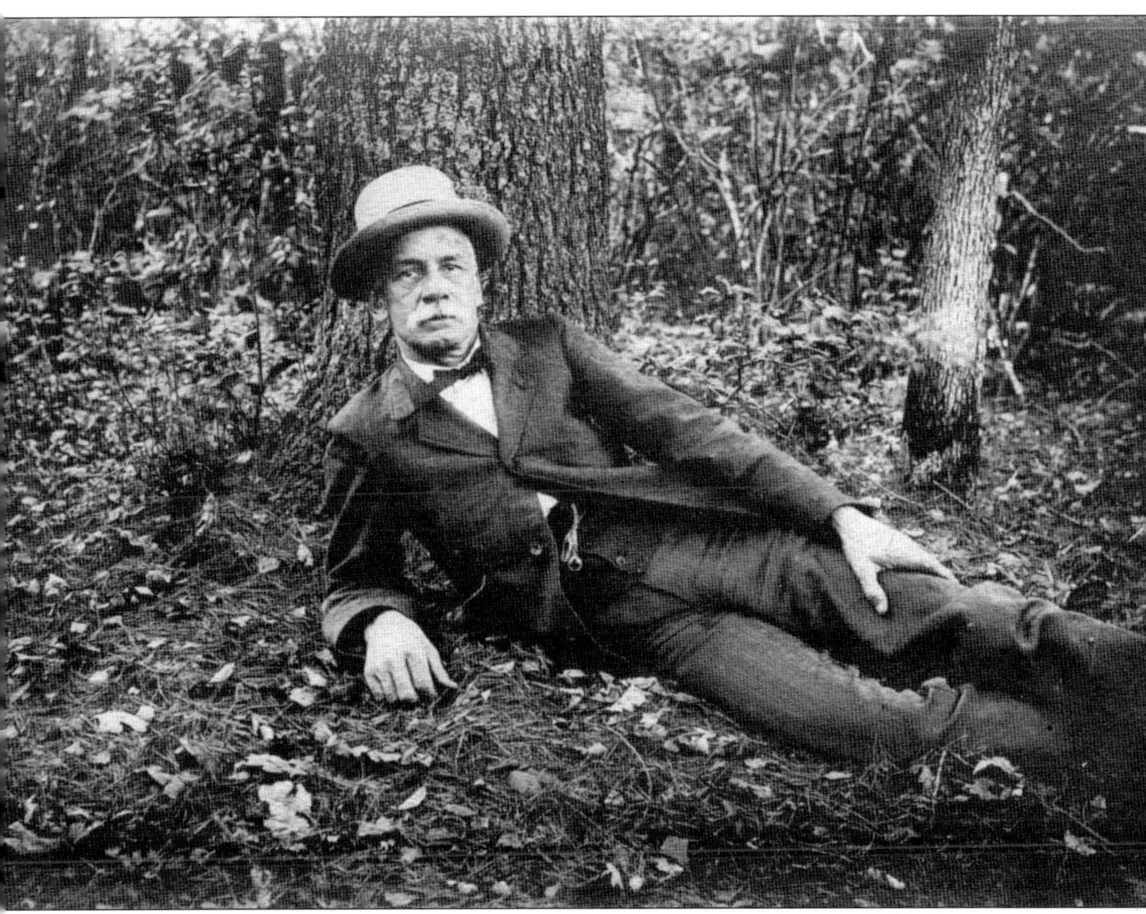

Thomas Drew, one of the more prolific Hanover photographers, was born in 1845. After service in the Civil War, he was a storekeeper and postmaster in South Hanover. Many of Drew's large-format, glass-plate negatives of his relatives, neighbors, and the structures in and around Hanover have survived. This self-portrait was taken *c.* 1900.

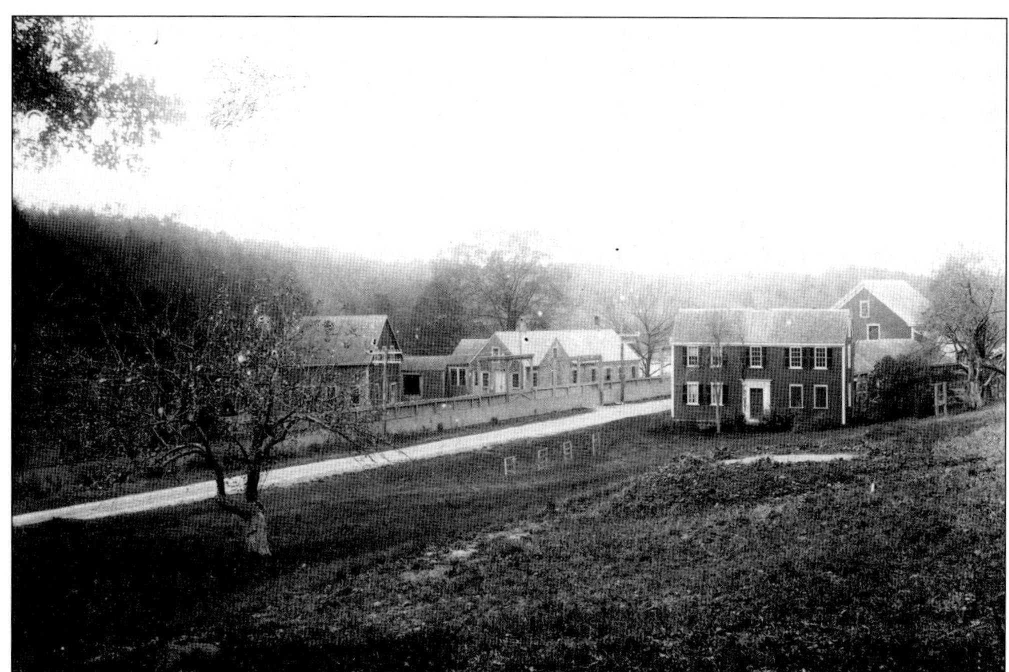

A dam was built c. 1726 on the Indian Head River opposite an early house at 361 Water Street. A fulling mill began early operation at this site, followed by a sawmill and a gristmill. Later, a tack factory was operated here by Elihu Hobart, E. Y. Perry, and Nathaniel Curtis, and, for many years, by the Watermans. It was a scenic spot along the river, and the area has been called "Project Dale" for as long as anyone can remember.

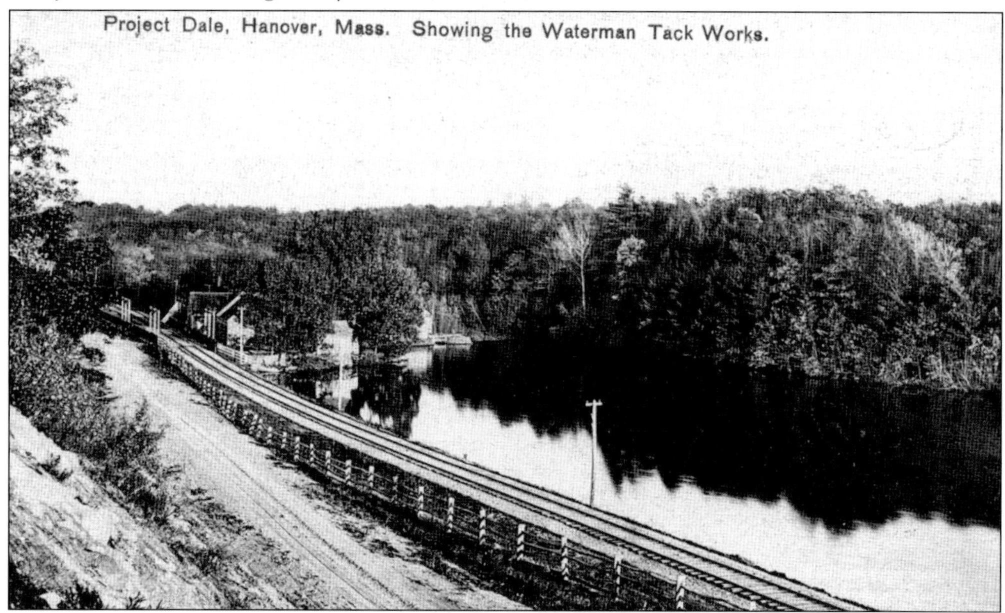

A Thomas Drew photograph led to the production of this H. A. Dickerman postcard of Project Dale in South Hanover.The building shown here, the Waterman Tack factory, remains today. The dam, which impounded water for the pond, was destroyed in the Hurricane of 1938, and the Indian Head River now winds its way many feet below the road.

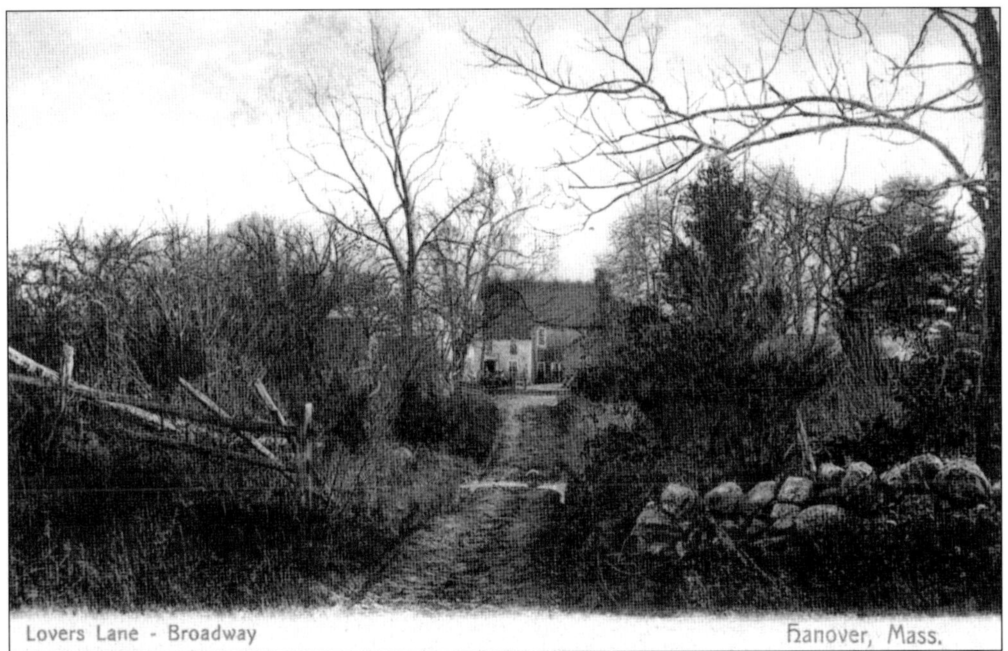

Thomas Drew had this postcard printed in Germany. Titled "Lovers Lane–Broadway," it shows the end of a path behind 607 Broadway. The 1850 map of Hanover shows this path leading from the top of Woodward Hill on Hanover Street through the woods, emerging just behind the Martin Stetson house.

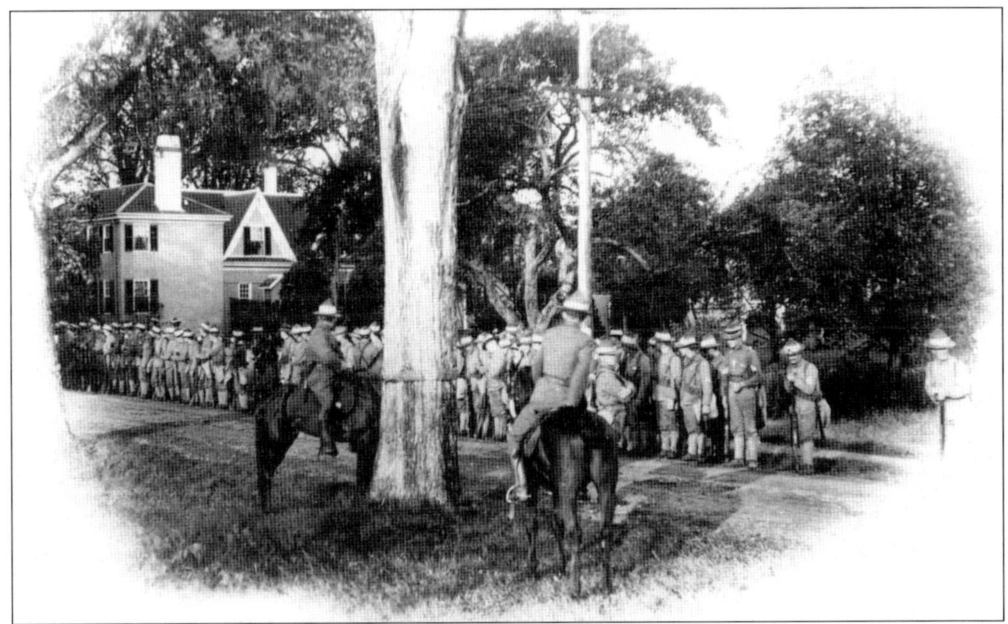

In August 1909, the Massachusetts State Militia, in conjunction with the U.S. government, carried out a mock military skirmish, which involved 10,000 to 12,000 participants. The so-called Blue and Red War was conducted through many South Shore towns, including Hanover. A large encampment was set up on the Sylvester Fields in the Four Corners. This photograph by Morrill Phillips shows a dress parade paused on Broadway, with the Phillips home in the background.

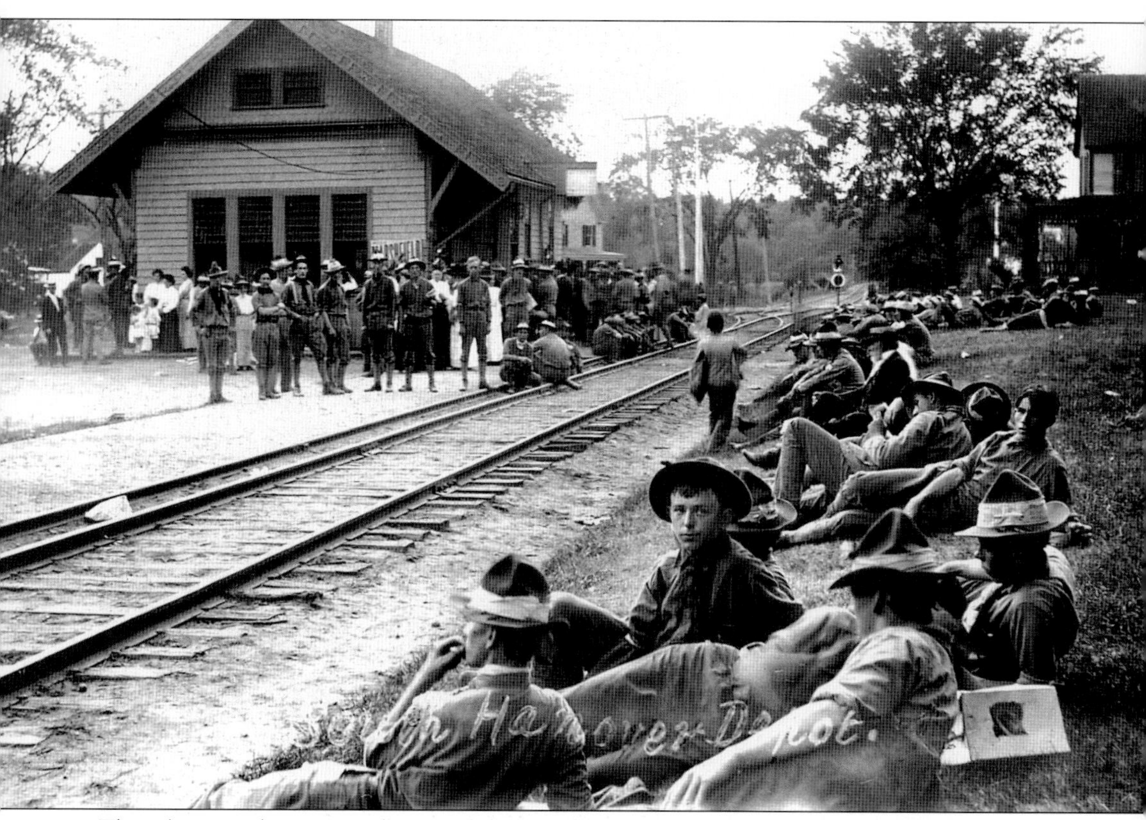

This photographic postcard view of the South Hanover depot and the troops of the Blue and Red War of 1909 looks westward down what is now Cross Street. The home on the right remains today at the corner of Broadway and Cross Street. The Blue and Red War was a military training exercise that involved thousands of troops and reserves engaging in mock skirmishes from Bridgewater to Hanover.

Fanny H. Phillips, affectionately known as Aunt Fan, was born in Hanover in 1888. The Phillips family was active in the tack business in South Hanover, and also participated in St. Andrew's Church activities and town affairs. After Aunt Fan graduated from Radcliffe College, she taught for 30 years at the Brearley School in New York. A past president of the Hanover Historical Society, she edited the updated *History of Hanover 1910–1977*. Aunt Fan was an important chronicler of Hanover history.

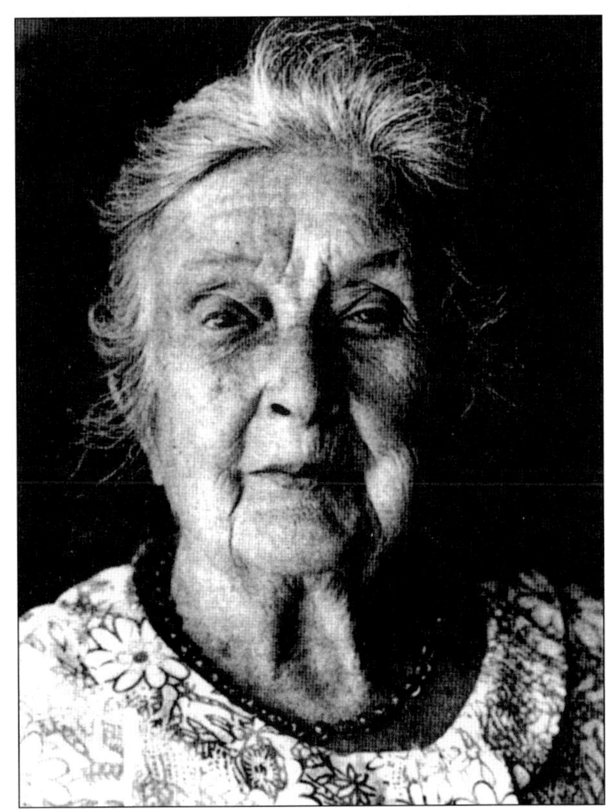

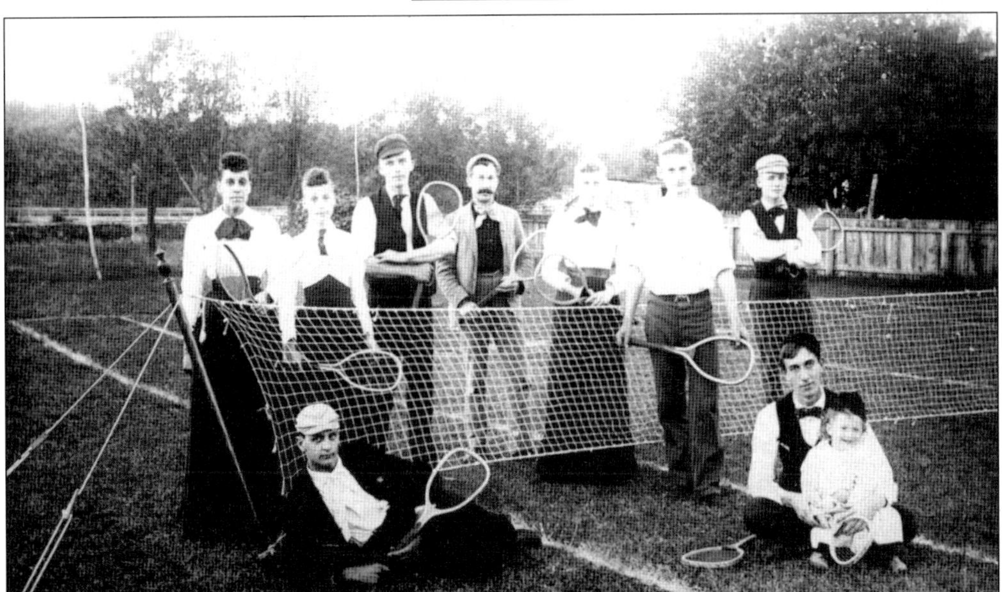

In the late 1890s, Morrill Phillips, Aunt Fan's father, had a grass tennis court constructed at his home at 947 Broadway, and it was a great hit with his family and neighbors. Pictured courtside are, from left to right, the following: (front) Sumner Chapman and Bert Luther, who is holding Howard Magoun; (back) Alice Smith, Jennie Drew, unidentified, Irving Kingman, Annie House, Calvin Tilden, and Walton Drew.

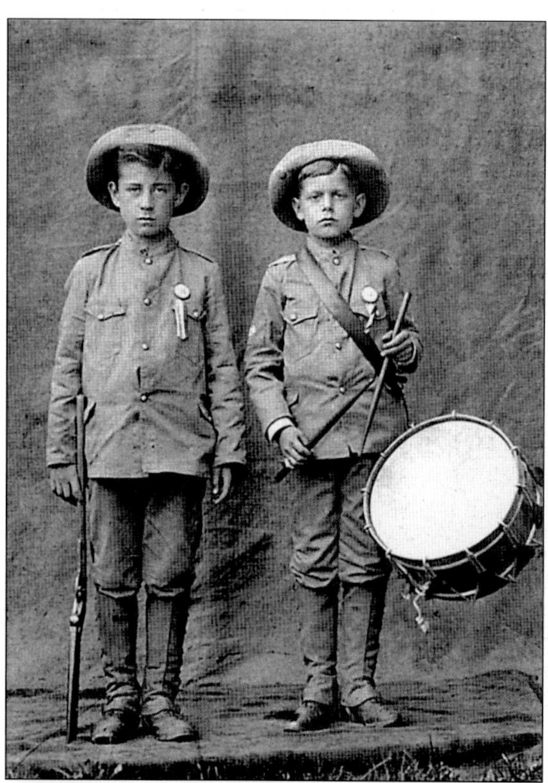

This photograph of two cadets was taken by Thomas Drew *c.* 1905. These Hanover boys have been identified as Raymond Oldham (left) and Stanley Curtis. Oldham was the grandson of Civil War Capt. George B. Oldham.

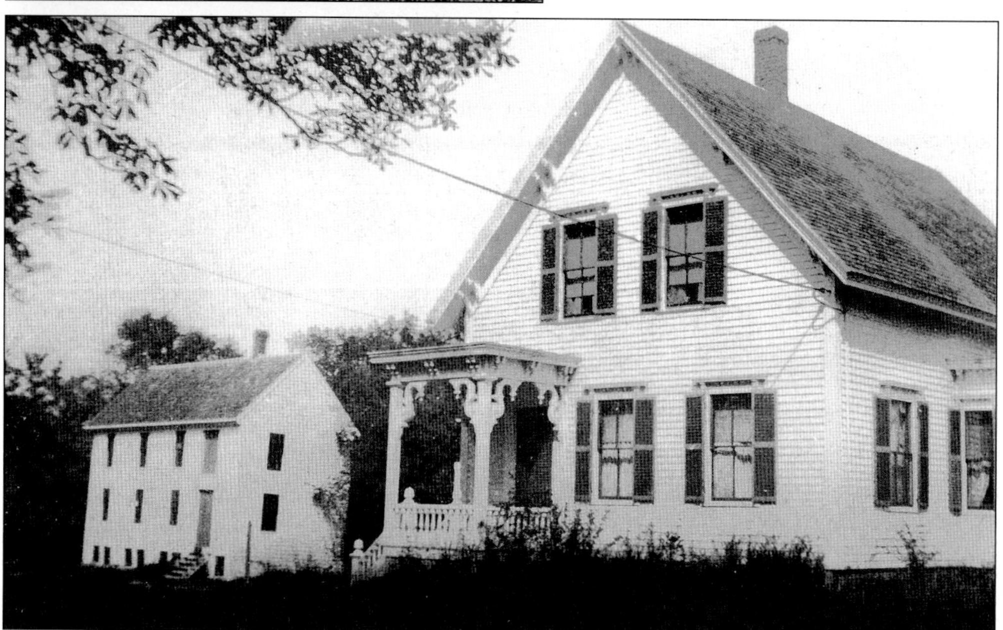

William E. "Ink" Bonney lived at 1049 Broadway (in what is now a private residence at 1057 Broadway) and operated an ink factory next door. This 1937 Charles Gleason photograph shows the factory on the left. Bonney manufactured his own secret-formula, high-quality ink for 40 years. His daughter Cora ran the business for a few years after his death, and later sold the dyes and formulas to the Carter Ink Company.

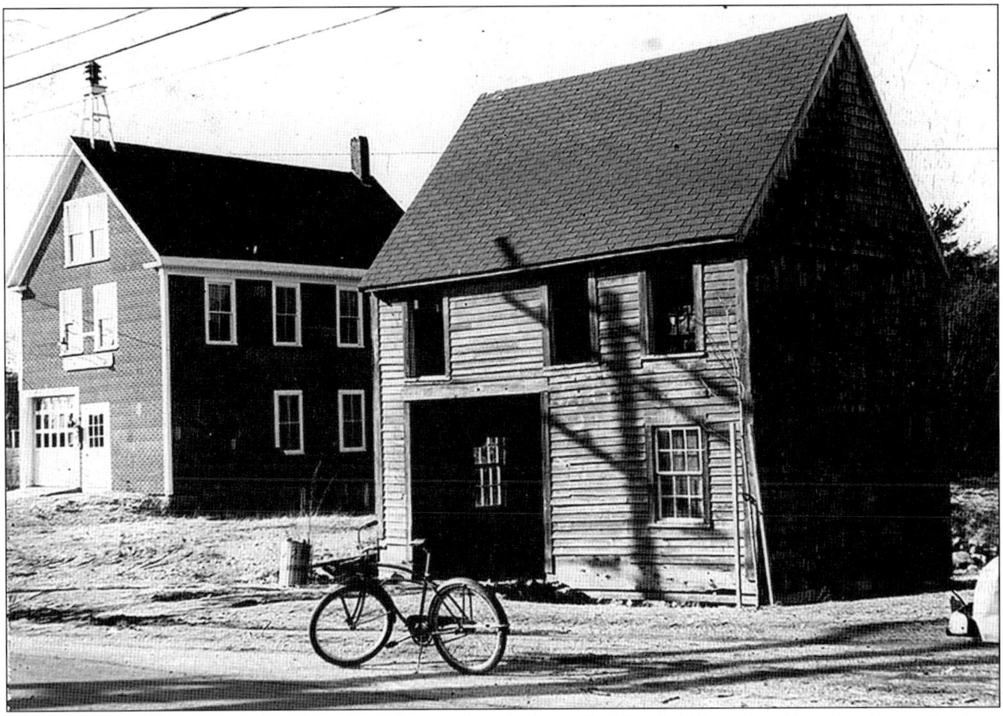

Charles Gleason wrote this caption in scrapbook No. 40: "Fred White had his blacksmith shop here and S. Bonney a paint shop, now the South Hanover Fire Station. There was a time when every village had its blacksmith shop to repair wagons, carriages and carts to be painted." Note Charles's bicycle in the foreground, in front of the paint shop.

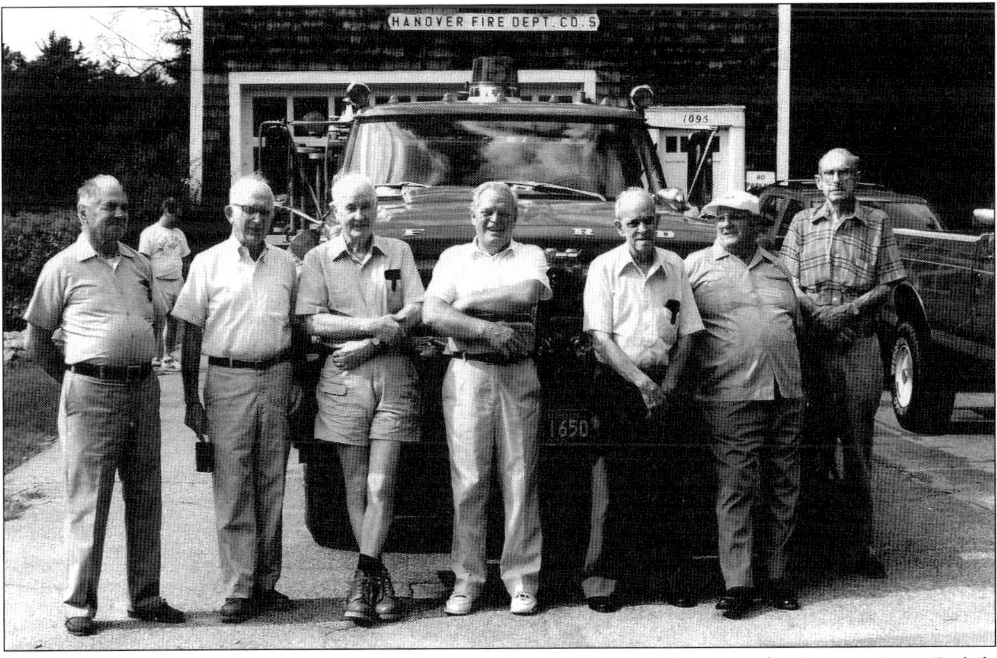

Hanover Fire veterans socializing at station No. 5 include, from left to right, Harry Nava, Ralph Josselyn, Stuart Oldham, Joe Hannigan, Lawrence Slaney, Harold Smith, and Bob Montgomery.

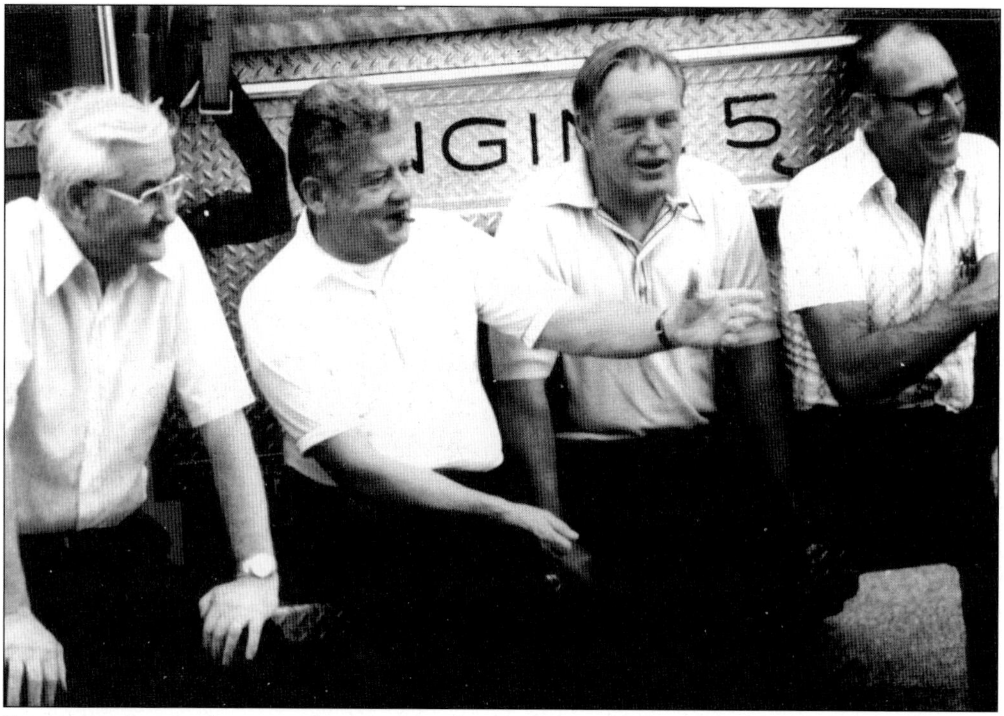

Sitting on the rear bumper of engine No. 5 and swapping tales of their service as members of the Hanover Fire Department are, from left to right, Stu Oldham, Bud Blanchard, Joe Hannigan, and Bob Montgomery.

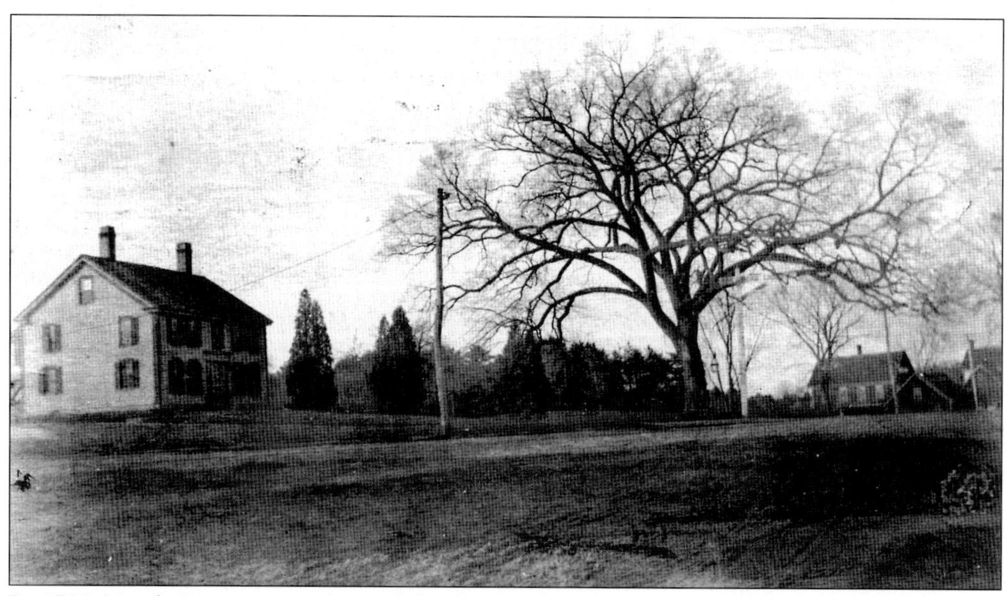

In 1720 Joseph Barstow, grandson of the first settler of Hanover, built this square, Colonial-style house at 1119 Broadway, within view of the Indian Head River. This branch of the Barstow family was involved with the forge nearby. I. G. Stetson later lived here and operated a grocery business across the street. The house burned in a tragic fire in 1982.

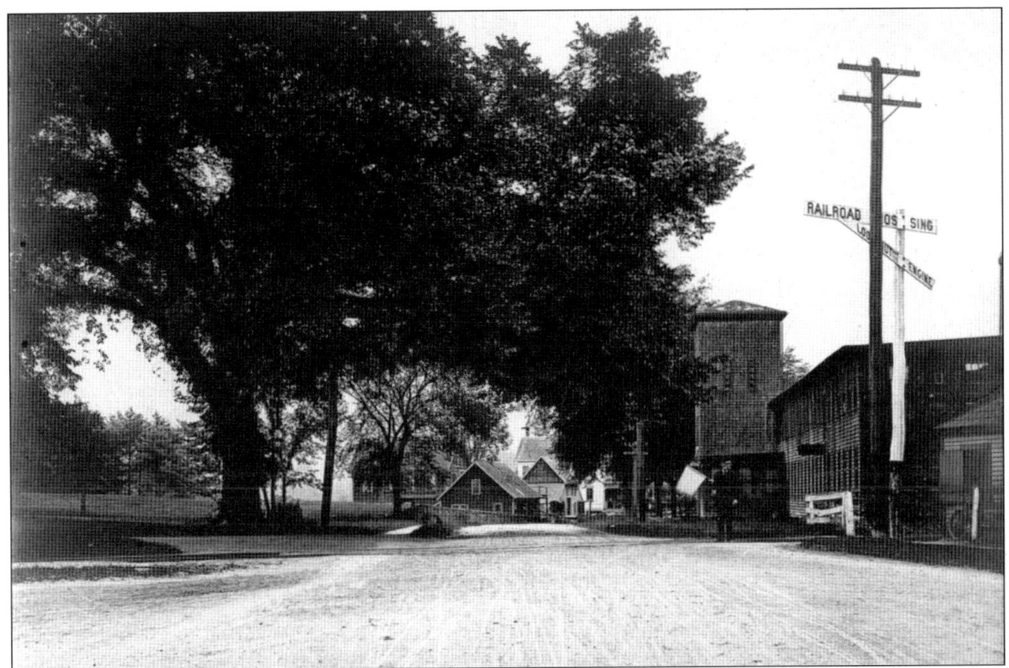

This crossing guard stands with his warning flag at the Broadway railroad crossing in South Hanover. The Hanover Branch Railroad was chartered in 1864 by E. Y. Perry, and businesses were encouraged to locate along the line. Nathan V. Goodrich's shoe factory is seen on the right in the foreground, while further down Broadway to the east, a paint shop, district No. 5 fire station, and residences can be seen.

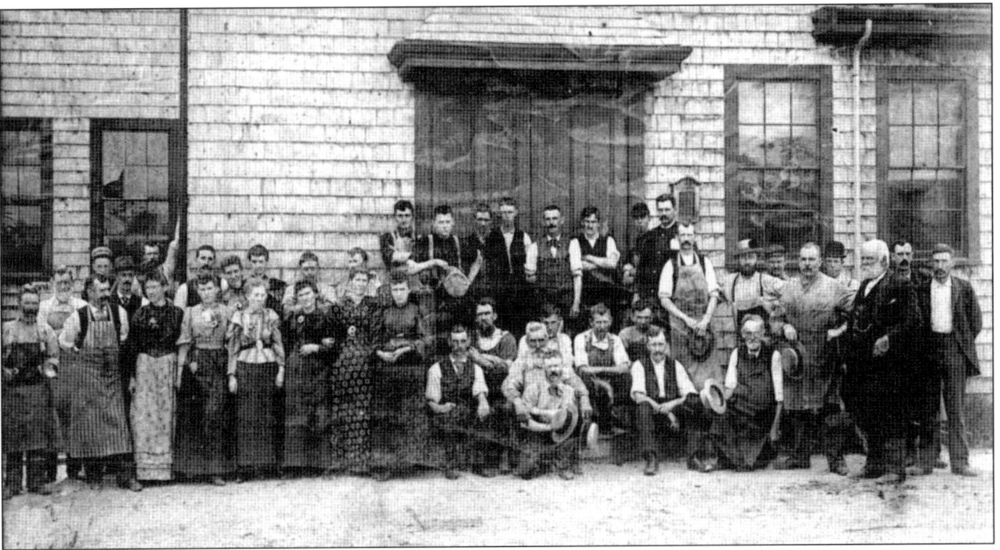

The shoe trade in Hanover developed from a small, cottage industry in which farmers cobbled shoes, to a major manufacturing business with several large factories. This photograph, entitled "the Old Shoe Gang of Mr. Goodrich," shows employees of the Nathan V. Goodrich shoe factory, located on Broadway near the intersection of Cross Street. Shoes were shipped by railroad, and this factory was conveniently located next to the tracks in South Hanover. By the early 1900s, the shoe industry left Hanover, and eventually this factory was razed.

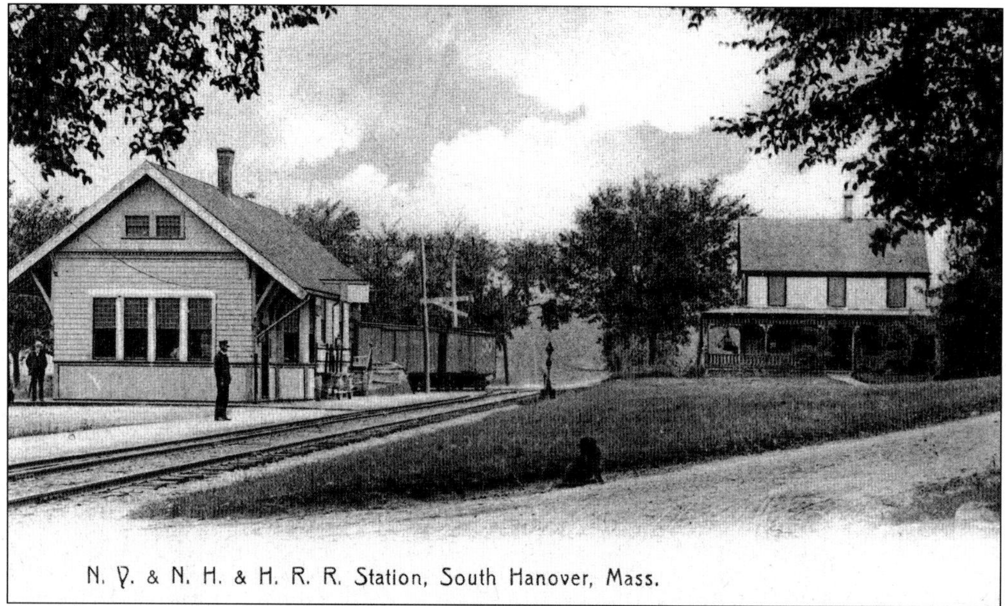

The stationmaster and a faithful dog await the arrival of the next train in South Hanover. Note the proximity of the house to the railroad tracks.

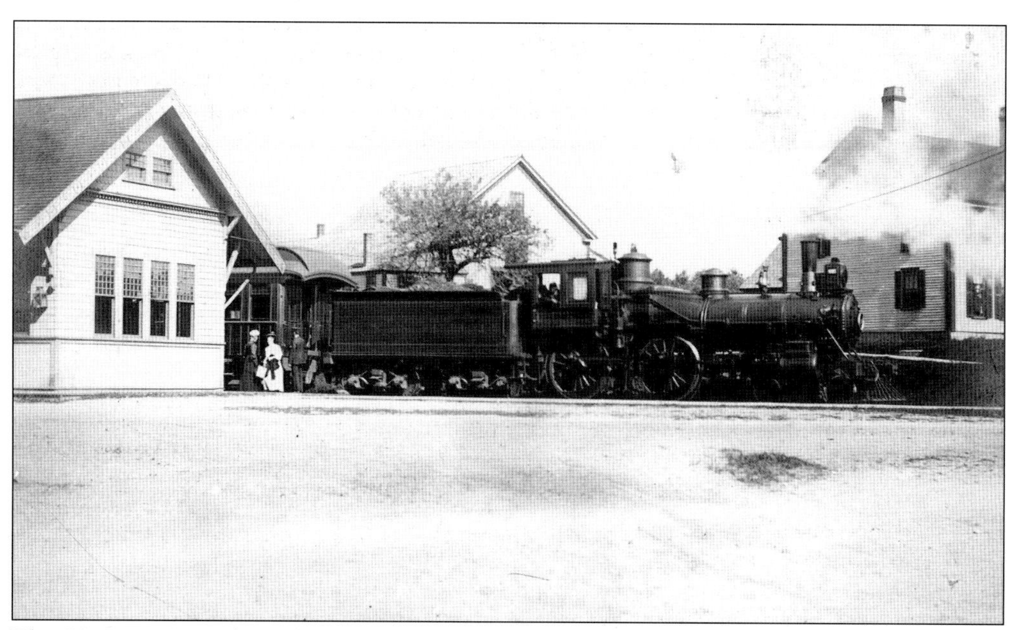

The Hanover Branch Railroad was established to serve businesses in town, as well as to provide commuter rail service to Boston via Abington. South Hanover businesses included the E. Phillips and Sons and Waterman's tack factories, the Nathan V. Goodrich shoe factory, Thomas Drew's store, and I. G. Stetson's store. To proceed to their destinations, train passengers might rent a carriage from the barn pictured in the center background.

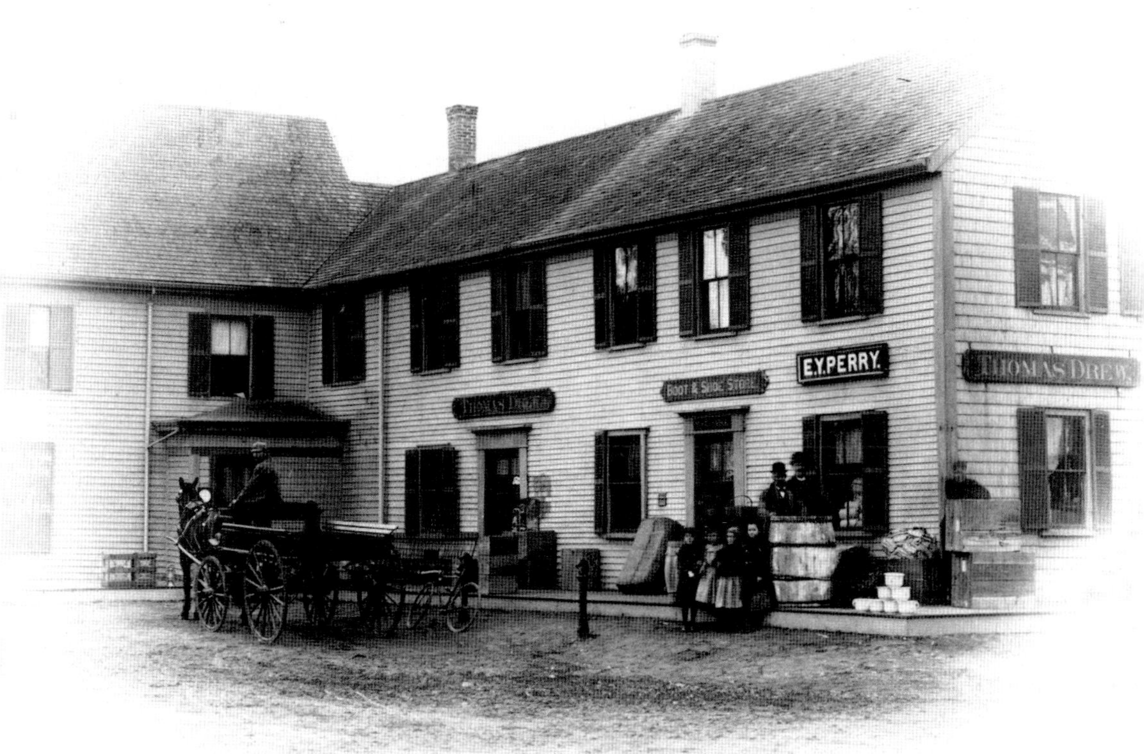

A photographic postcard of the E. Y. Perry store, postmarked August 25, 1909, was sent by Thomas Drew to Lot Phillips, Esq. Drew, an amateur photographer, had created these postcards, and evidently, Phillips, his landlord, was interested in purchasing quantities of them. Note the extension of the building on the left, which was later moved to another South Hanover location.

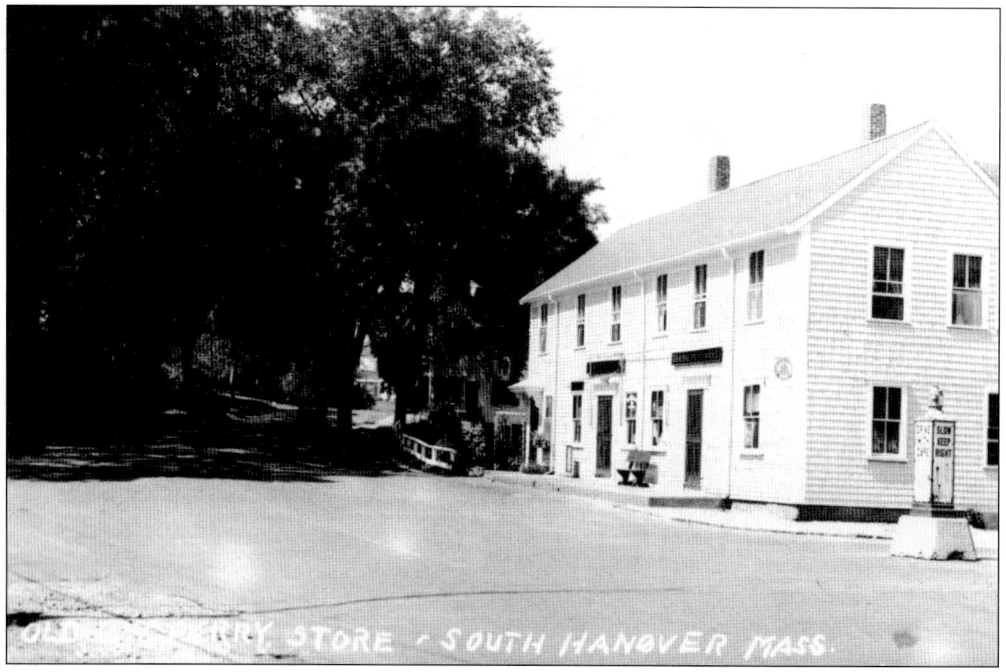

Edward Y. Perry was a vital force in the development of South Hanover businesses, including this general store, a tack factory, shoe factory, box mill, and grain business. Perry was the founder and president of the Hanover Branch Railroad until its incorporation into the Old Colony Railroad. This photographic postcard shows the old E. Y. Perry store at the corner of Broadway and Cross Street in South Hanover, now the site of Myette's Country Store.

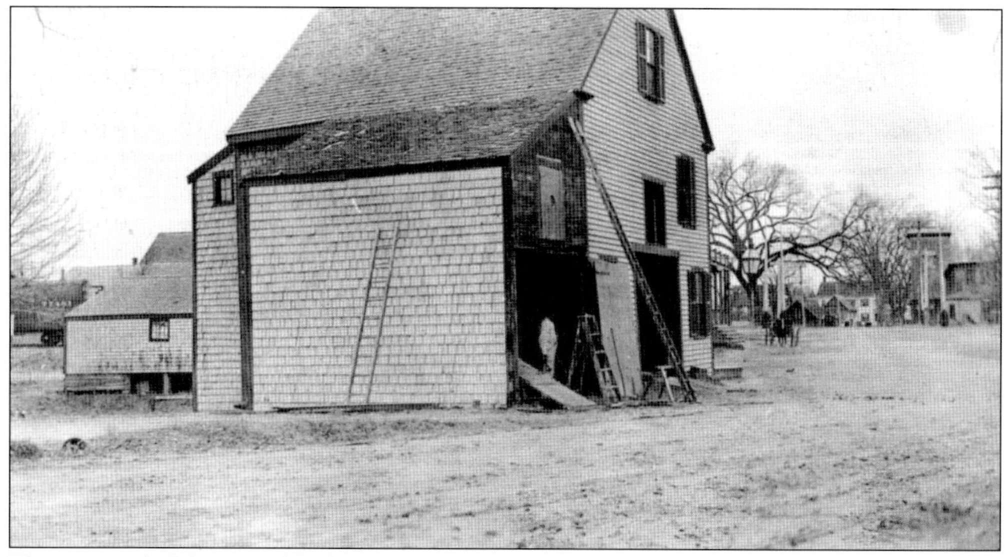

The west end of the Perry block, on Broadway at Cross Street in South Hanover, was moved to another location. This real-photo postcard shows the process under way. The Goodrich shoe factory is visible in the background on the right.

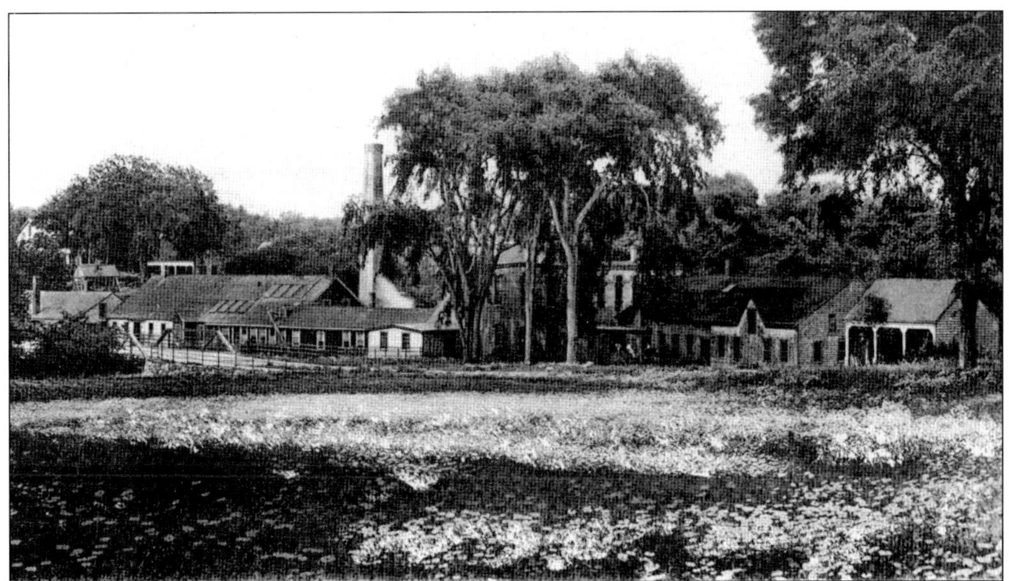

The E. Phillips and Sons tack factory straddled the Indian Head River in South Hanover, with buildings on both the Hanover and Hanson sides of the river. Beginning in 1720, Joseph Barstow Jr.'s forge was located here; it was later a manufacturer of cannonballs for the American Revolution. This view from the Hanson side of the river was published by Thomas Drew. Both hand-colored and black-and-white versions of the German-printed card are found.

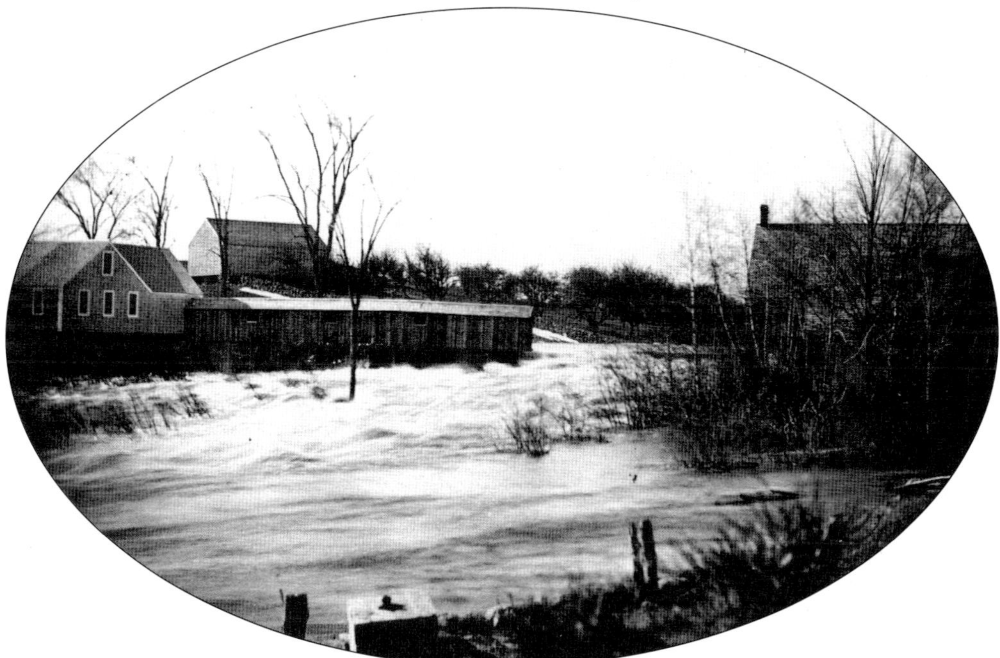

What does a freshet look like? In 1867 Thomas Drew took this photograph of the Phillips tack factory standing amid the rising waters of the Indian Head River in South Hanover. Charles E. Turner described the same event in his diary as, "Great Excitement! Water, Water, Water! Great Freshet! Cushing's Dam gave away. The bridge down by Perry's Factory! Blueing Shop went down stream. Greatest time ever known!" (Diary courtesy of Elsie Nelson.)

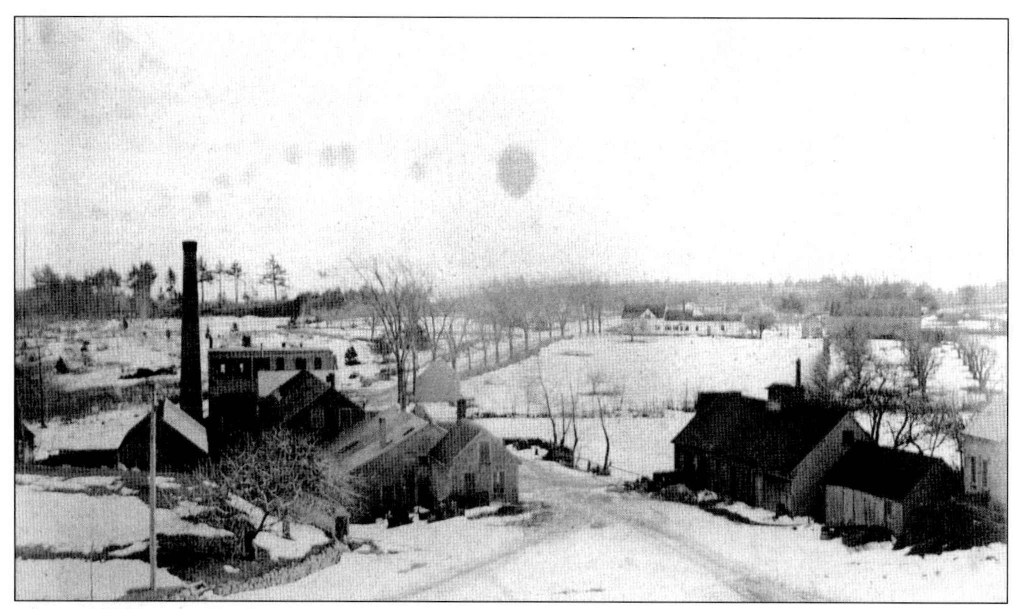

This 19th-century winter scene is viewed southward on Cross Street, toward the frozen Indian Head River and State Street in Hanson. The E. Phillips and Sons tack factory is on the left. The small building on the right, later used as a store, still remains.

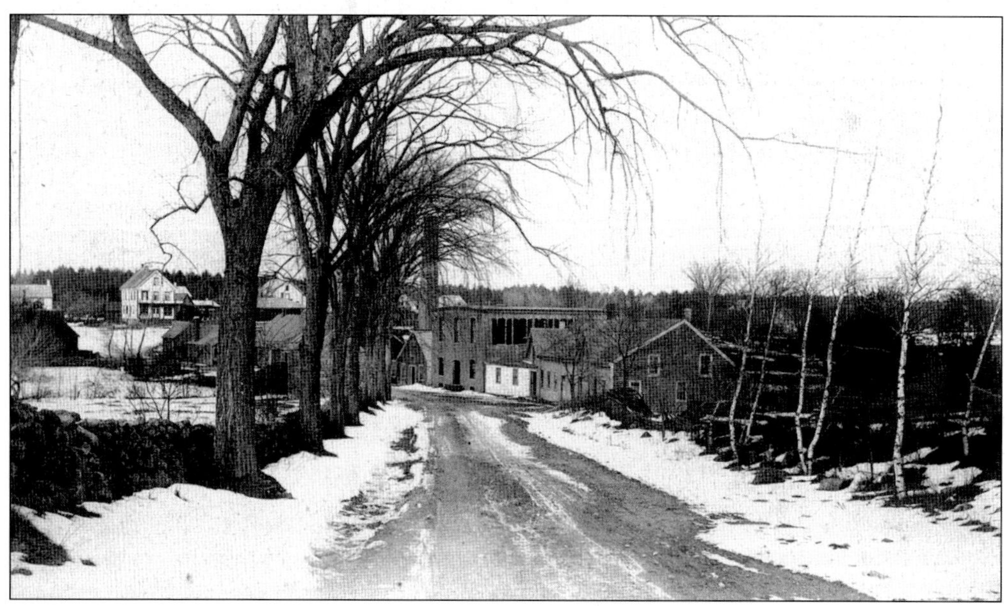

A photograph taken at the same time as the previous image shows the scene as viewed from Hanson looking into Hanover. The E. Phillips and Sons tack factory is on the right, part of Thomas Drew's store can be seen on the extreme left, and part of a railroad car and the South Hanover station can be seen to the right of the I. G. Stetson store.

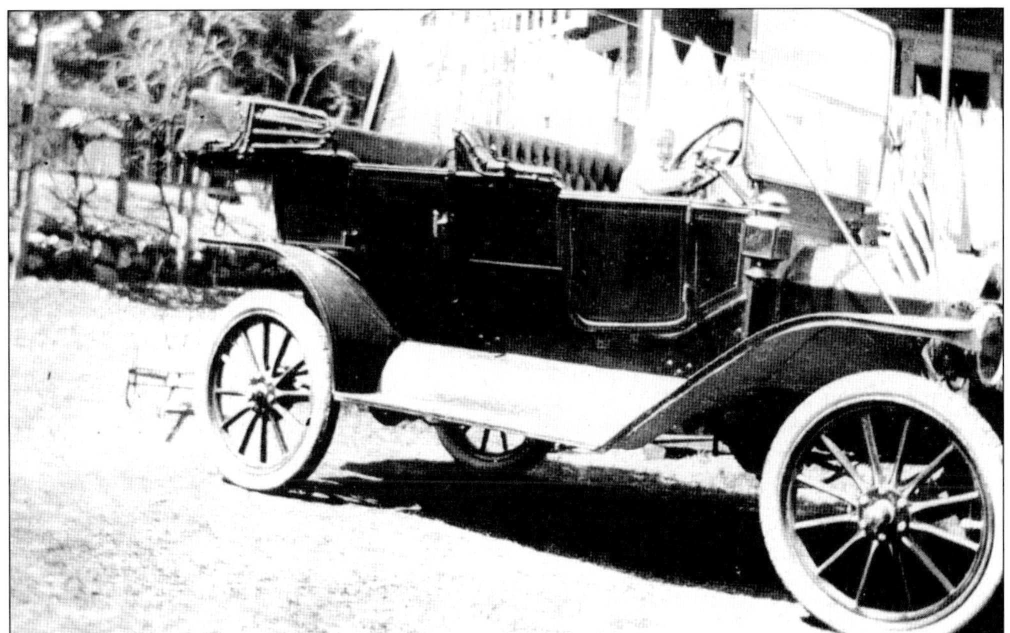

In 1917, T. Drew Bates was already practicing for his future behind the wheel. Bates was always on the go, whether manning a police car, a school vehicle, or the tractor given him upon his retirement from a lifetime of town service.

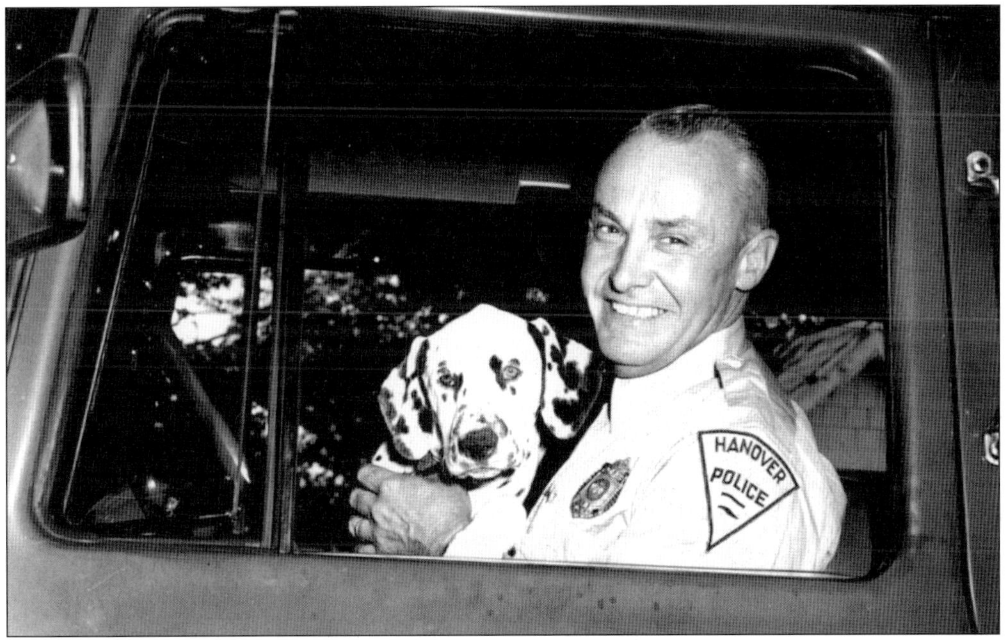

T. Drew Bates, named after his uncle Thomas Drew, amassed a remarkable record of service to the town. He retired from the police department in 1980 after 32 years of service, and served as a member of the fire department for 47 years, including 15 years as chief and forest fire warden. He also headed the school maintenance department for many years. This photograph shows Drew in his policeman's uniform, sitting in the fire rescue truck with the new fire department mascot, Deputy Dog.

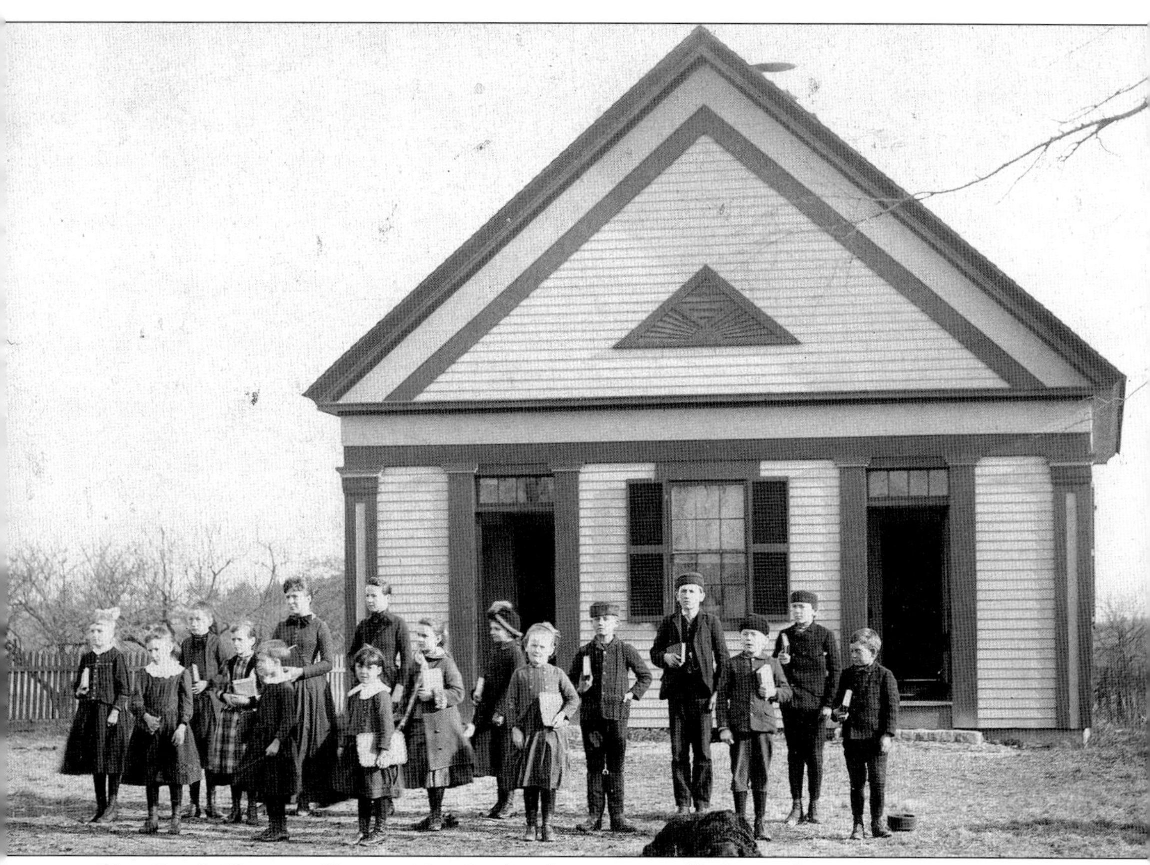

The South Hanover District No. 3 school was originally located on Cross Street, and later was moved to a location opposite 1194 Broadway. After the school was closed down, the building was moved farther down Broadway and was converted for use as a home. (Photograph by Silas Gurney, Rockland.)

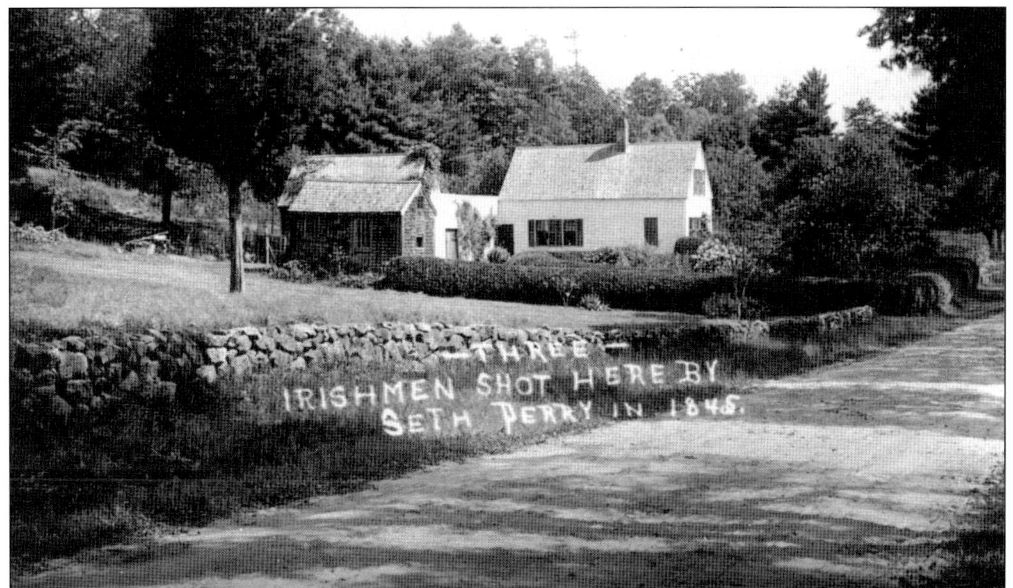

This photographic postcard is titled "Three Irishmen Shot Here by Seth Perry in 1845." In the 1840s many Irish immigrants were employed in the construction of the Old Colony Railroad. A January 1905 Hanover Branch newspaper article reported that on March 17, 1845, four Irish men from North Hanson became involved in a fight with some locals. Seth Perry shot three of them and was sentenced to 14 years in jail.

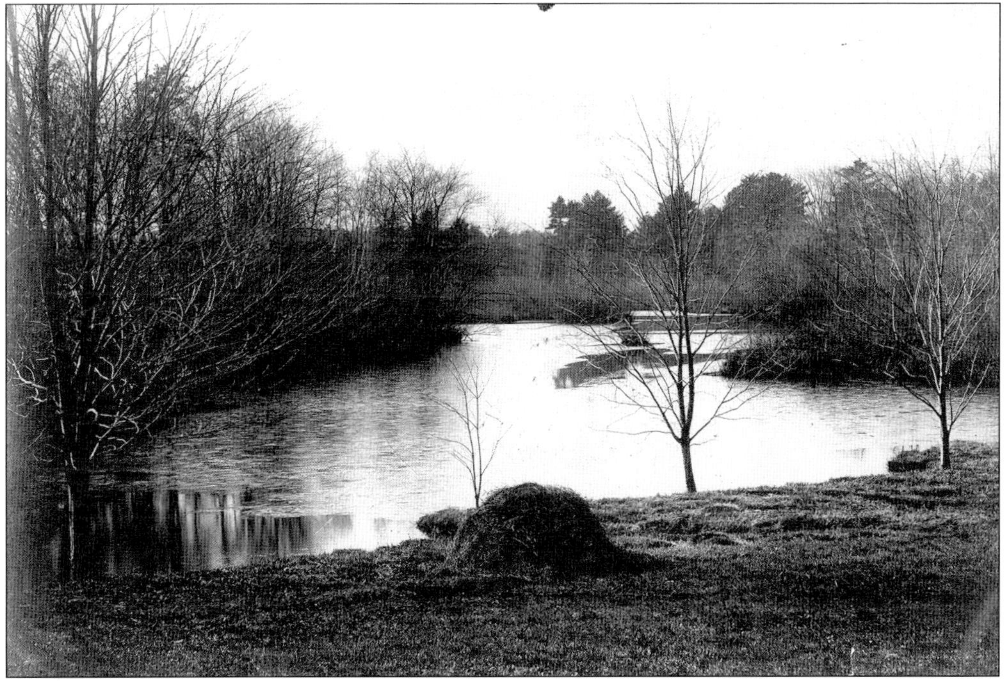

This view of an early winter morning on the Indian Head River looks upstream from Thomas Drew's house, at 1194 Broadway in South Hanover.

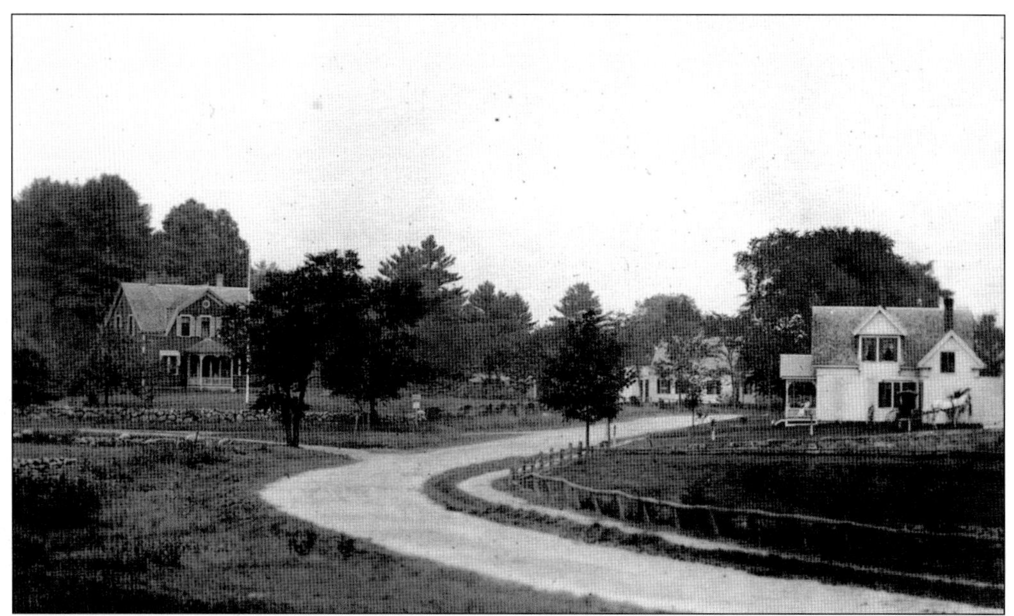

The intersection of Broadway and Winter Street has borne varied names through the years, including Dog Corner and Brighamville. The origin of Dog Corner is unknown, but Brighamville refers to Dr. Edwin Brigham, whose home is seen on the left at the corner of Winter Street.

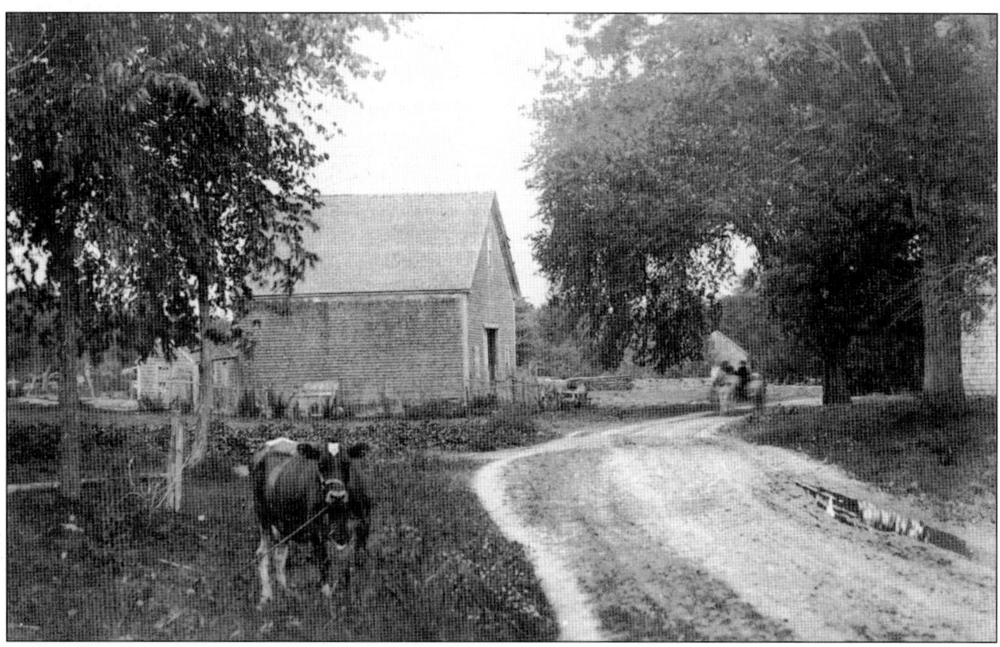

An album of Thomas Drew's photographic postcards yielded this treasure, with a little poem on the reverse: "If you will guarantee to me/ The lovely sights which I long to see/ I will come down with my camera/ And snapper with my/ Tra la Tra la."

Four

West Hanover-Drinkwater

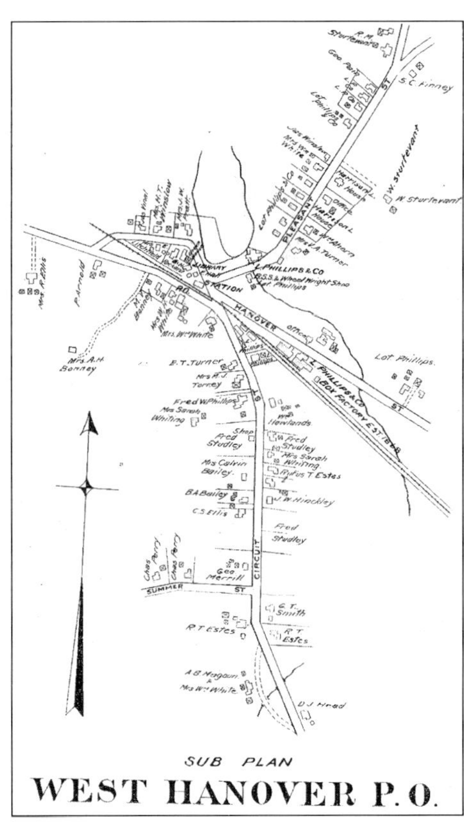

Detail from Plate 14, *Atlas of Plymouth County*, 1903.

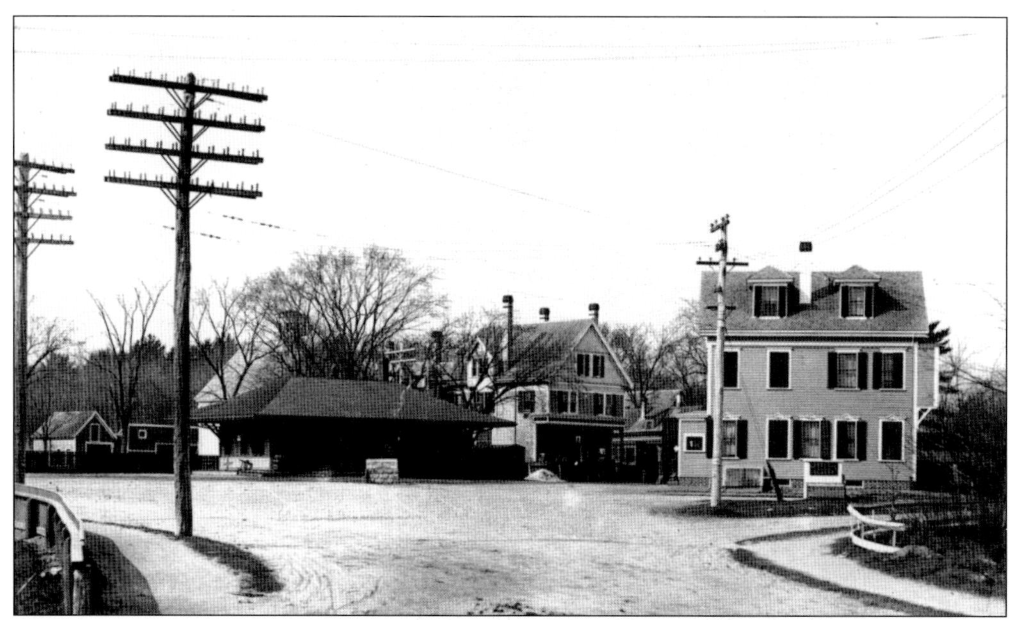

Thomas Drew was standing where the liquor store is today when he captured this West Hanover view, looking south on Pleasant Street. Circuit Street is the sharp turn in front of the two-family house on the right. The West Hanover railroad station is left of center, and the Josselyn store to its right. The Josselyn store, later Lufkin's furniture store, and an antiques shop remain today, as does the two-family house in the right foreground.

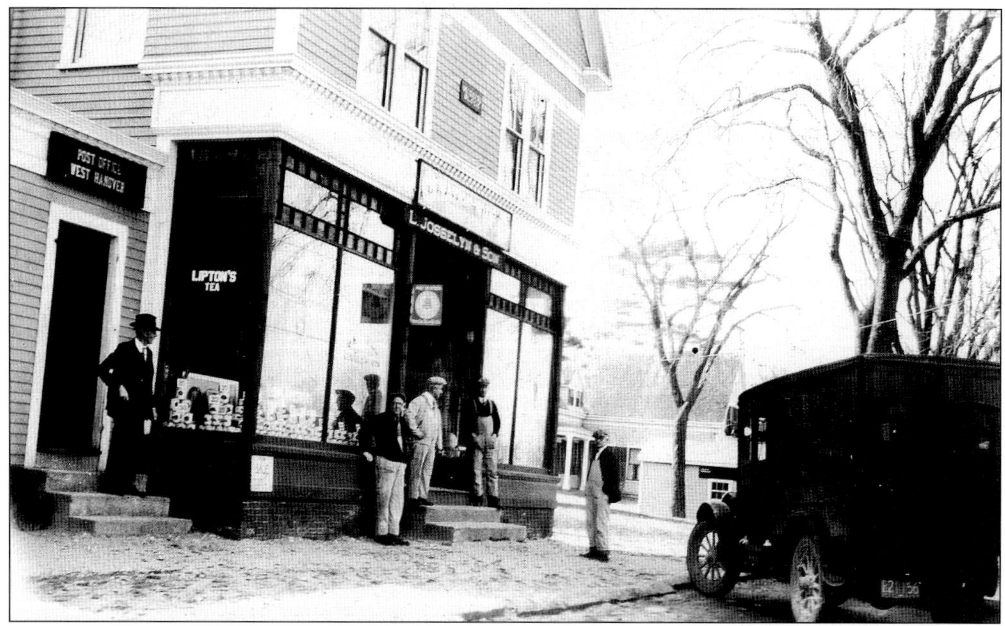

Horatio Magoun established a general store in West Hanover just before the Civil War. William White later conducted the business along with other partners, including Lewis Josselyn. Josselyn eventually assumed complete ownership, and he and his son operated the store until 1946. Here, on the left, Eugene Tobey emerges from the post office to chat with, from left to right, Bob Merrill, Irving Josselyn (storekeeper), Fred Tuck, and Gordon Rogers.

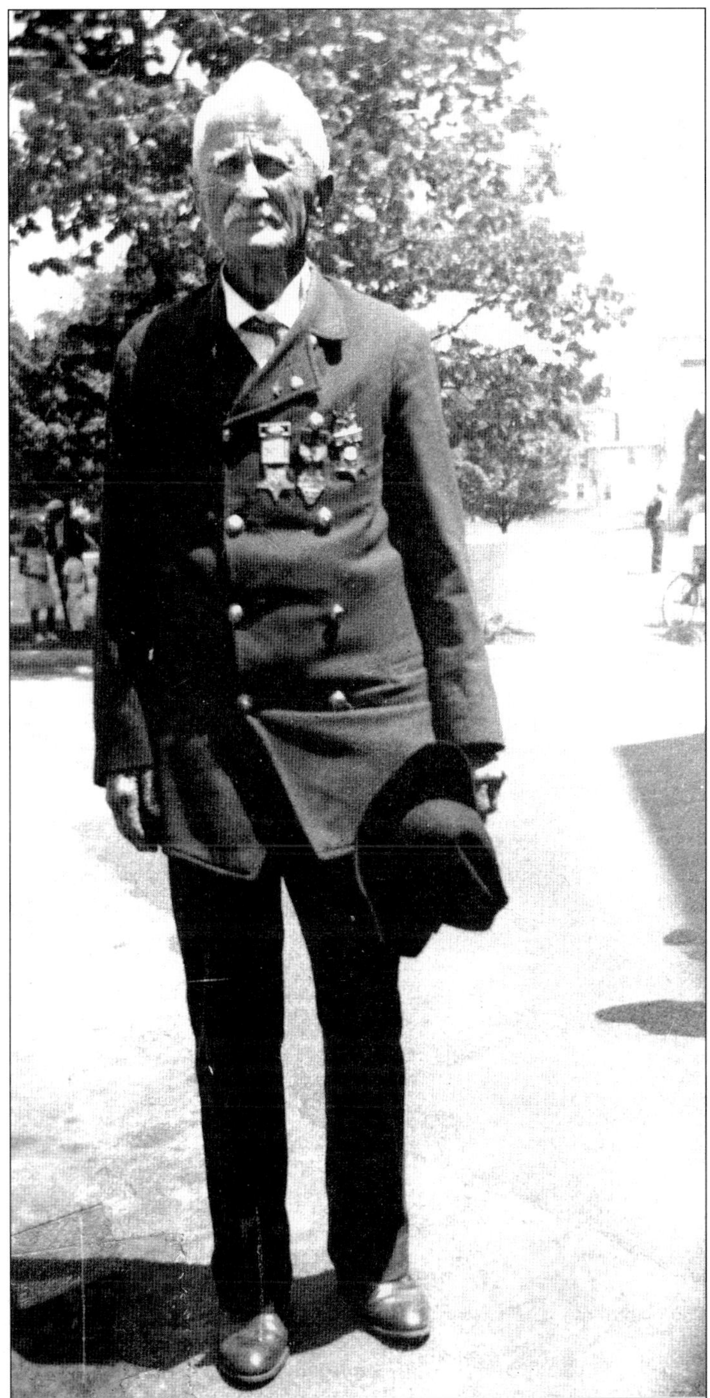

Lewis Josselyn (1842–1944), Hanover's last surviving Civil War veteran, never missed a Memorial Day parade. In 1862 Josselyn and 20 other Hanover men answered President Lincoln's call for volunteers. Josselyn served at Baton Rouge, Fort Hudson, Cane River, Mesura Plains, and other locations. He later ran the West Hanover general store and, in retirement, became a farmer. He had 12 children, and several of his descendants still live in Hanover.

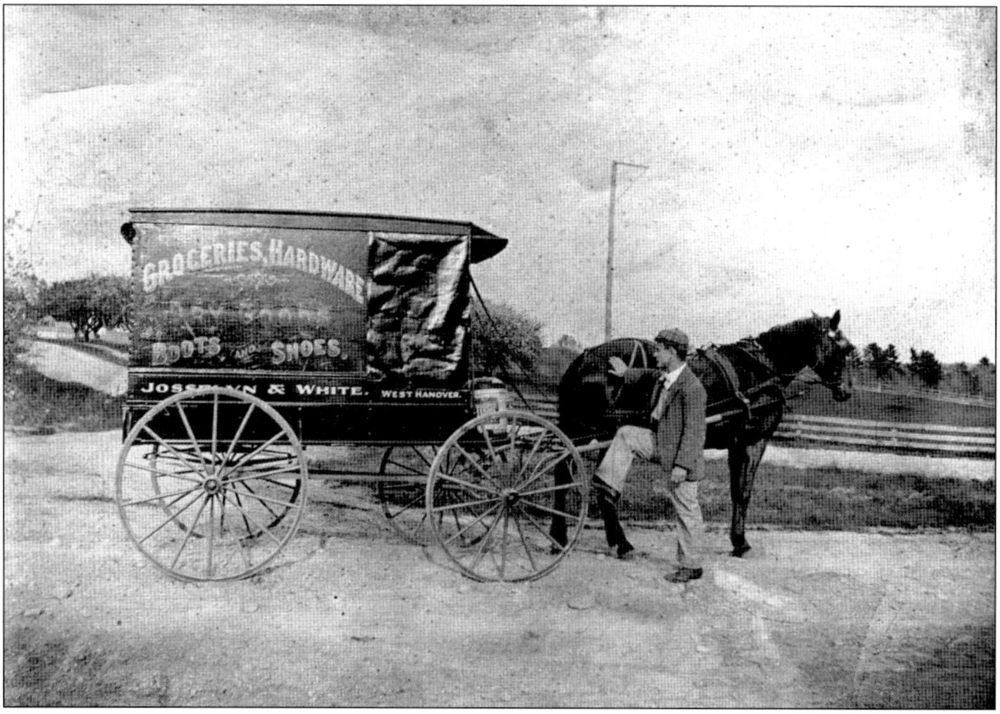

From 1904 to 1946, the West Hanover general store was known as L. Josselyn and Son. Lewis Josselyn began the business with M. V. Bonney, and later ran the shop with the Packards and William White. Lewis's son, Irving, took over the business in 1916. Irving is shown here with the business wagon that still bears the old Josselyn and White sign. Longtime Hanover Historical Society treasurer, Esther Josselyn, told many tales about her father and the general store.

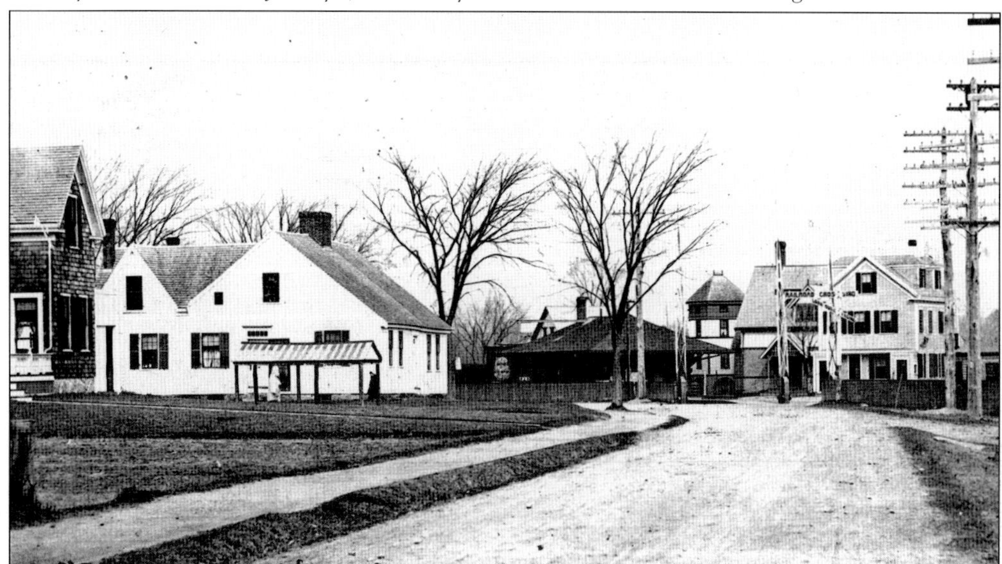

Shown in this *c.* 1915 real-photo postcard is the Hoxie house (left). The house was built in 1735 at the intersection of Hanover and Circuit Streets, and was moved to 119 Center Street in 1955. The West Hanover railroad station (center background) was removed, probably in the 1940s, while the homes to the right remain today.

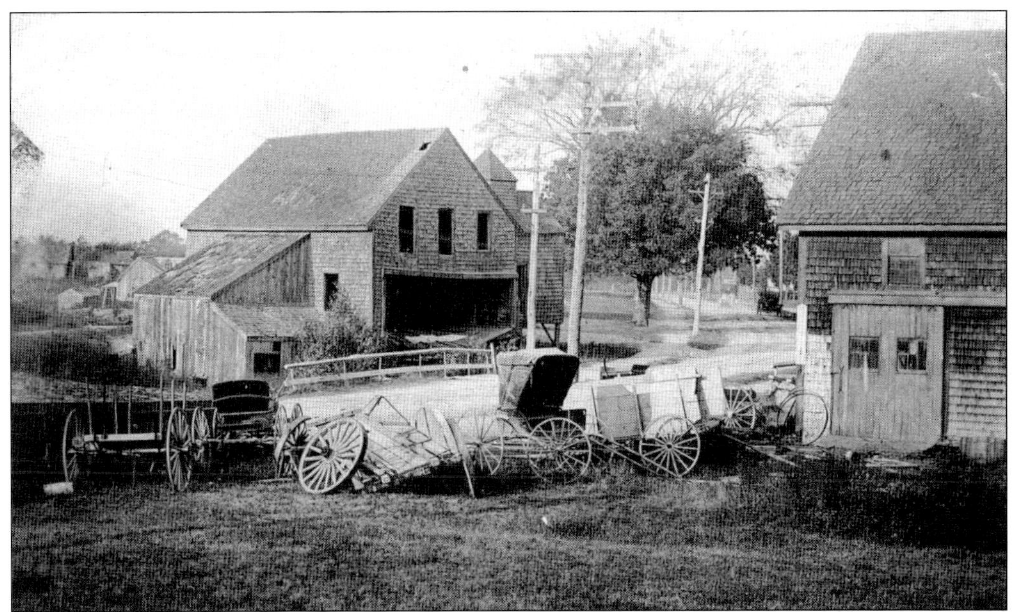

As early as 1724, Nehemiah Cushing built a dam to power a sawmill in West Hanover. Eliab Studley and his family later owned the mill. The brook, a tributary of the Drinkwater River, became known as Eliab's Brook. The mill on the left was used to saw boards, grind grain, and make boxes and buckets. On the right is a blacksmith shop, with an ample supply of wagon wheels stacked outside.

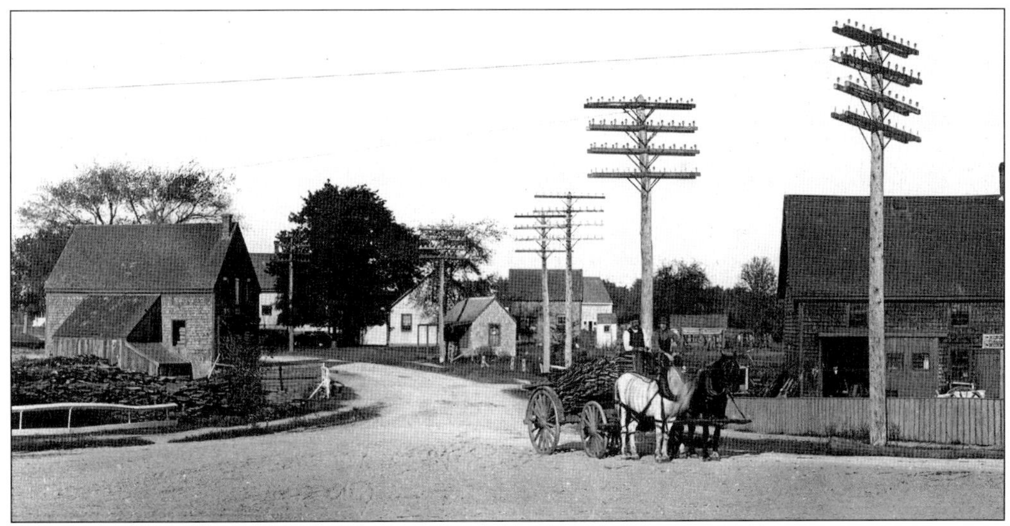

This is a panoramic view of the corner of Pleasant and Hanover Streets in West Hanover Square. The signboard directs the traveler to Hingham and Norwell. William Ahern drives the team, which is carting a load of boards. Florus Josselyn stands in the door of his blacksmith shop on the right.

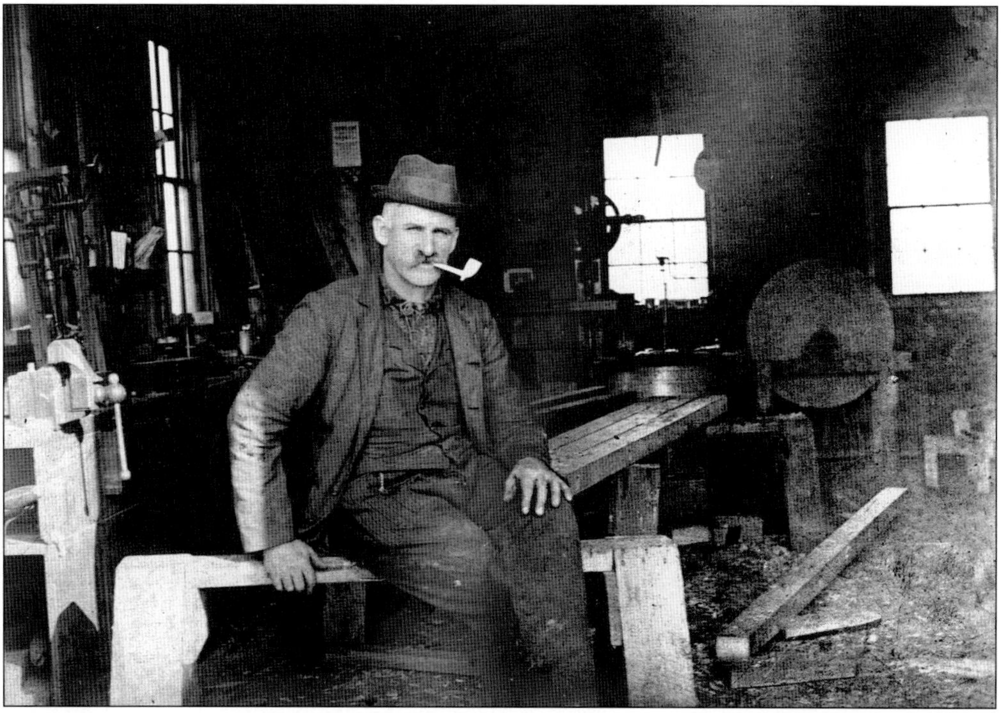

Florus "Flo" Josselyn was a blacksmith with a shop by the mill in West Hanover. He could mend a wagon or shoe a horse, while carrying on a good conversation at the same time.

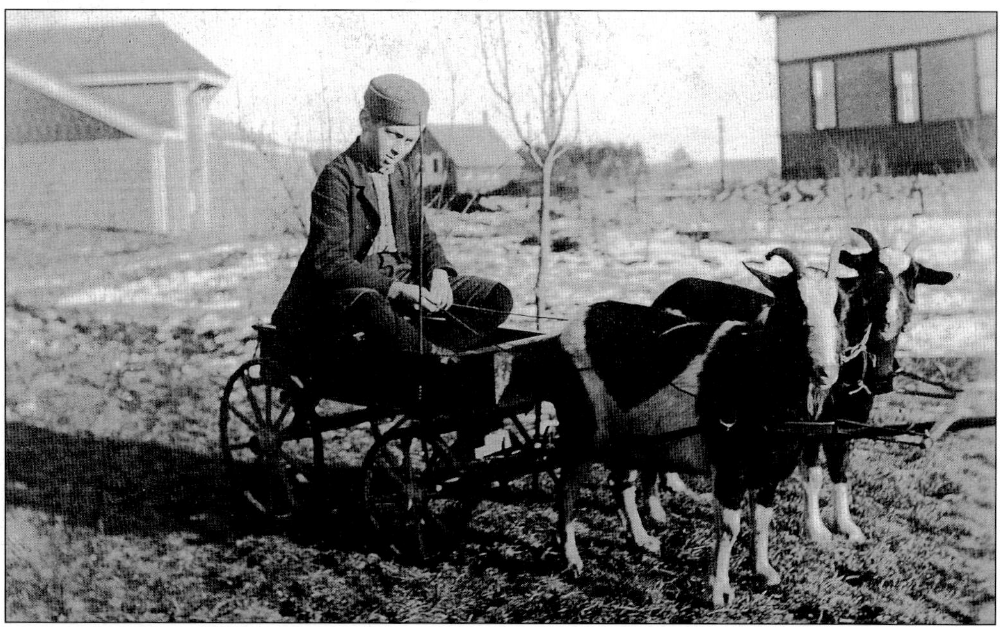

This *c.* 1890 postcard shows Lloyd Packard of West Hanover with a goat team. Library Hall, which was built by the residents of West Hanover, is seen on the right in the background at its original location in West Hanover Center. The structure was later moved a mile up the street and became the Cranberry Cola plant. Flo Josselyn's blacksmith shop is seen in the upper center, and a Packard greenhouse entrance is visible on the extreme left.

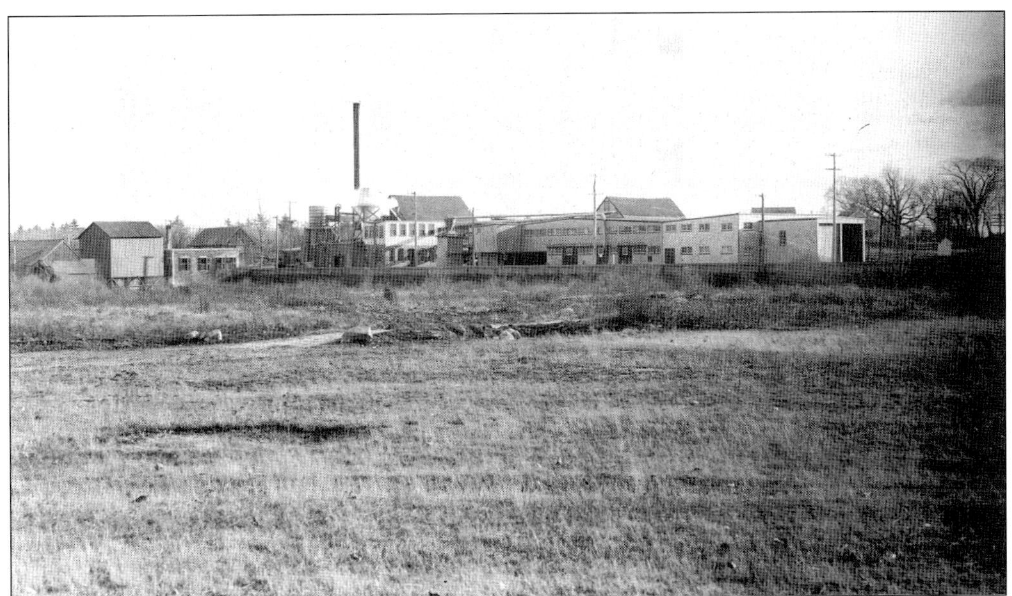

Thomas Drew took this photograph of the Lot Phillips box factory on Hanover Street in West Hanover, from across the Drinkwater River. He was probably standing on Pleasant Street at the time. Hanover Street is behind the fence.

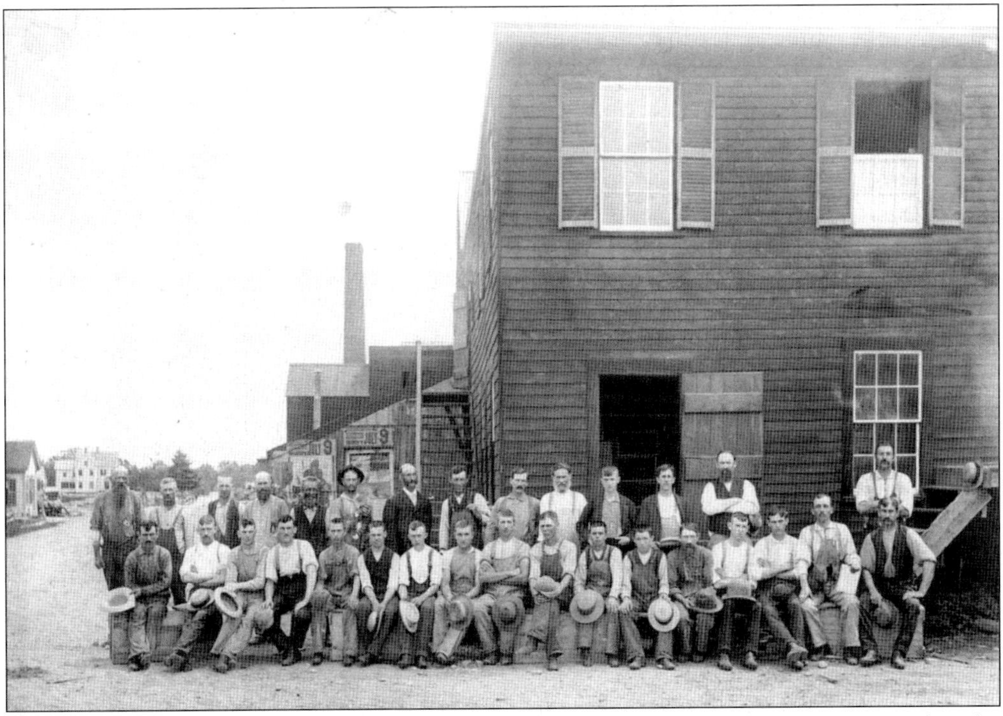

In 1871, encouraged by railroad owner E. Y. Perry, Lot Phillips began manufacturing shingles and boxes in a West Hanover mill next to the railroad tracks. His products were used to pack tacks, shoe nails, shoes, bottles, vegetables, cranberries, and even caskets. Phillips purchased woodlots throughout Plymouth County, from which he harvested timber. He employed many men such as these, and constructed homes in the neighborhood for some of them.

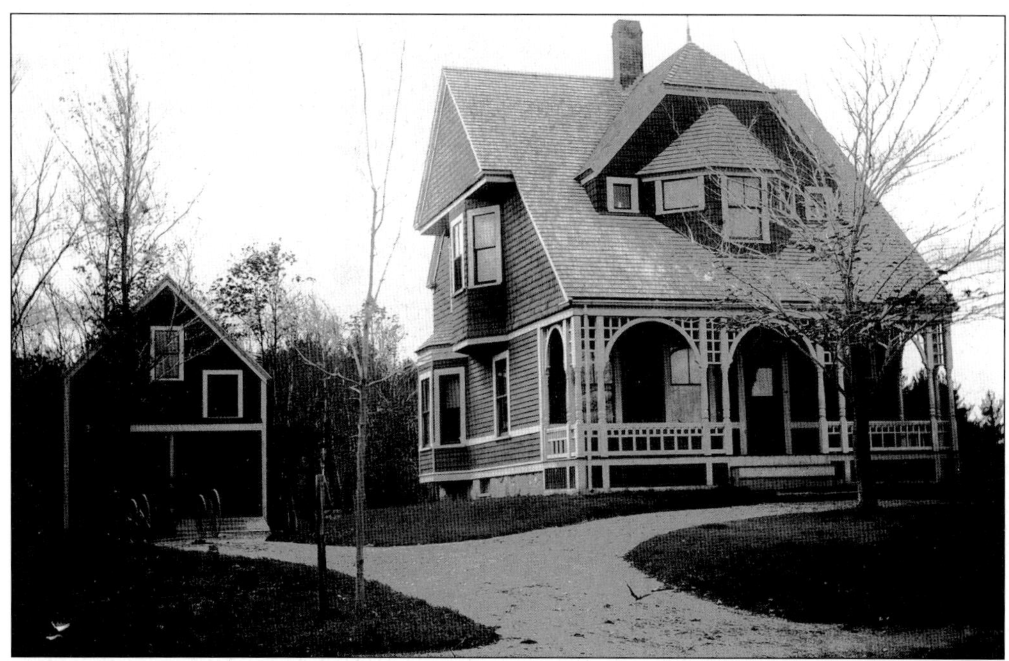

Pearle C. Arnold married Rosabel, the daughter of Alpheus Packard of West Hanover, in 1894 and built this house at 1518 Hanover Street shortly thereafter. It was one of several houses in the town that had a windmill for pumping water. Pearle's son, Harold, one of the authors' sources for West Hanover history, lived here for many years.

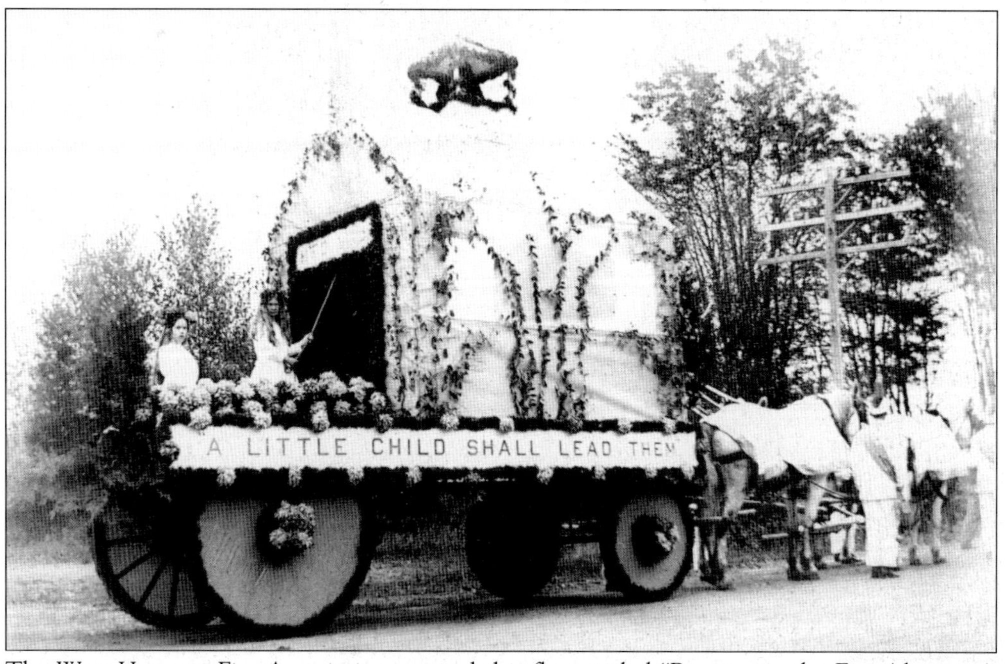

The West Hanover Fire Association entered this float, titled "Ringing in the Fire Alarm—A Little Child Shall Lead Them," in a 1909 Hanover parade. The float depicts an actual event, as recalled by Harold Arnold. One day, a call came in and no men were nearby. Two little girls, Dorothy Studley and a Phillips girl (probably Evelina), pulled the bell rope and rang the alarm.

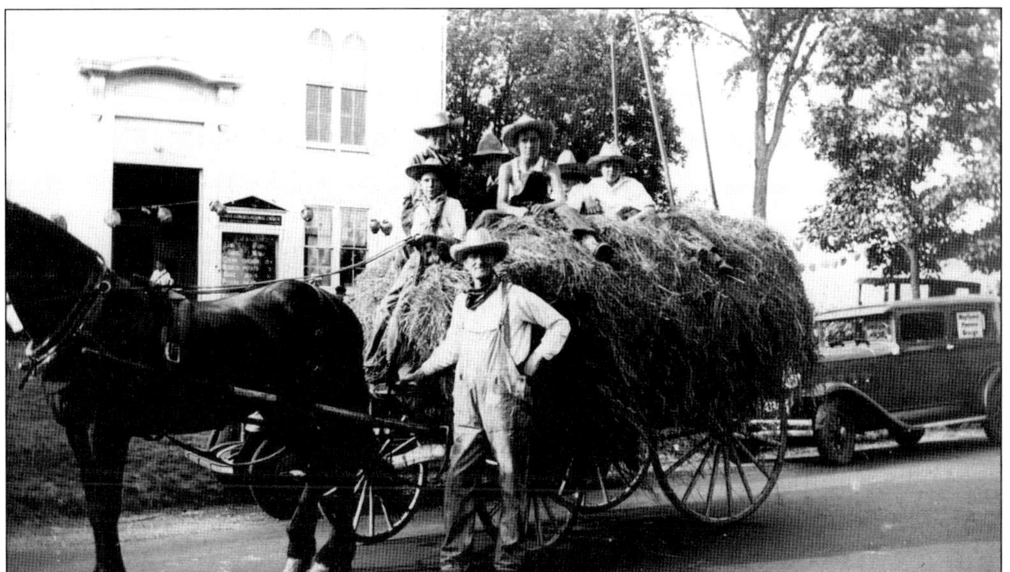

The 300th anniversary of the Massachusetts Bay Colony was celebrated with a parade in 1930. Charles Gleason loaded a wagon with hay, and Boy Scouts from Troop No. 1 piled on board. Gleason, Troop No. 1 Scouts, and faithful horse Nancy Hanks paused for a photograph in front of the First Congregational Church.

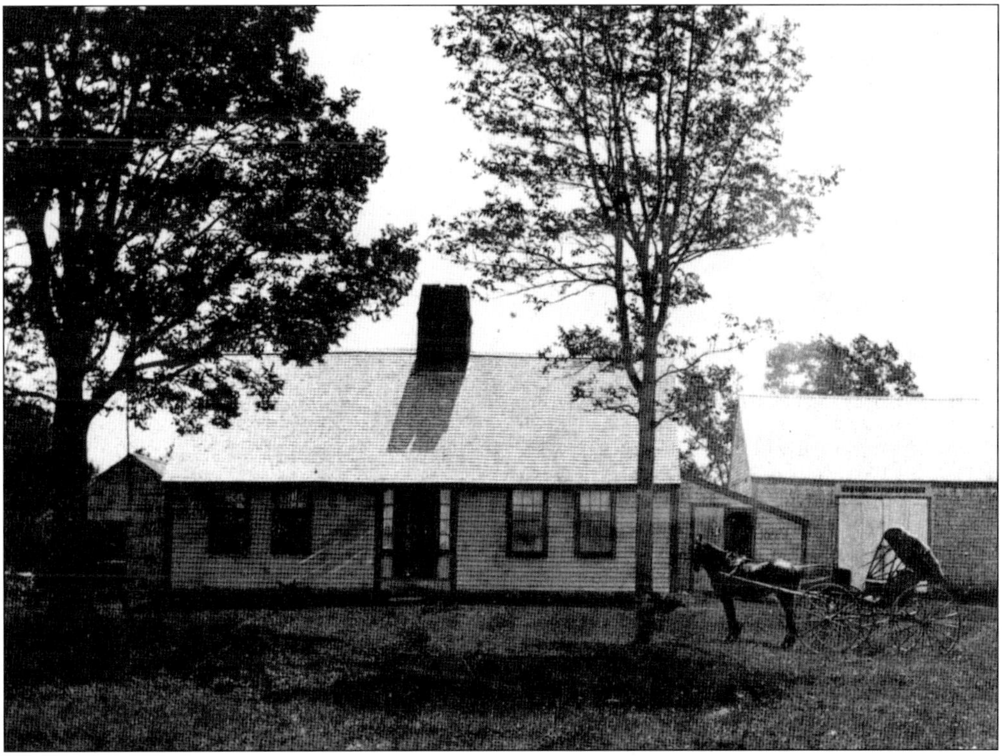

The Otis Ellis farm at 1566 Hanover Street was set back 200 feet to 300 feet from the road, near the Rockland town line. Otis's daughter, Priscilla, married Dr. Henry W. Dudley, of Abington. Dr. Dudley's buggy is seen in this view.

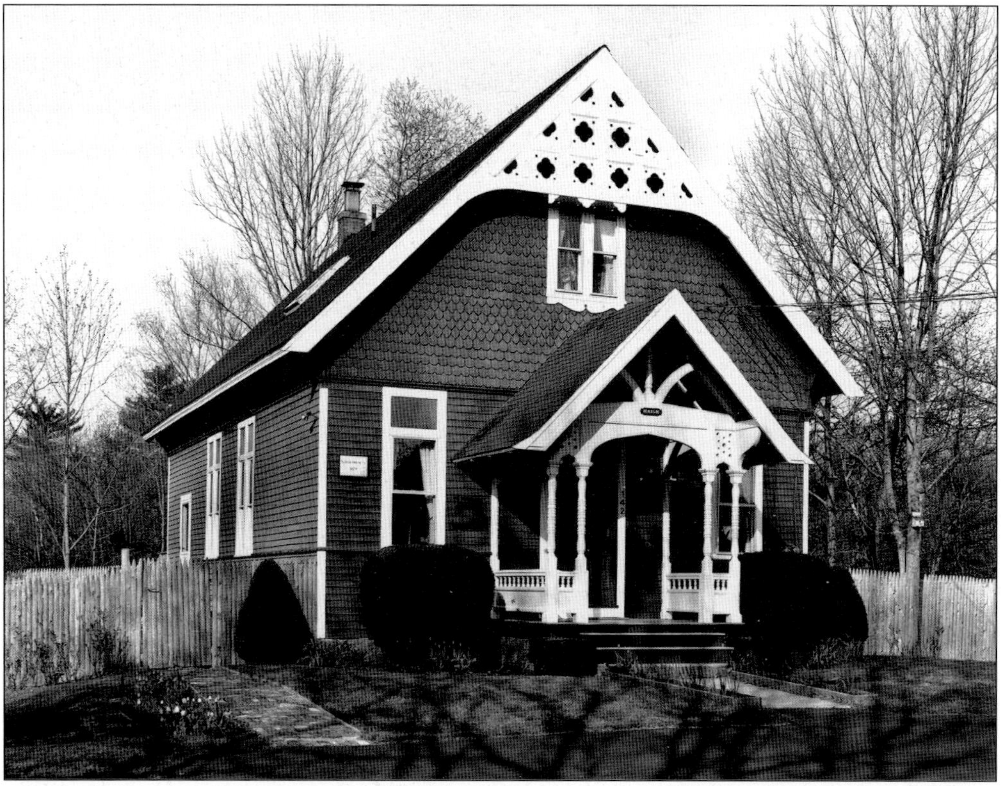

The Little Red Schoolhouse, located at 142 Whiting Street, is the third schoolhouse to stand on this site. Built in 1879 and in use until 1927, it is now a private residence. Tryphena Whiting, who grew up next door, was one of the longtime teachers in this school. (Photograph by Diane Haigh.)

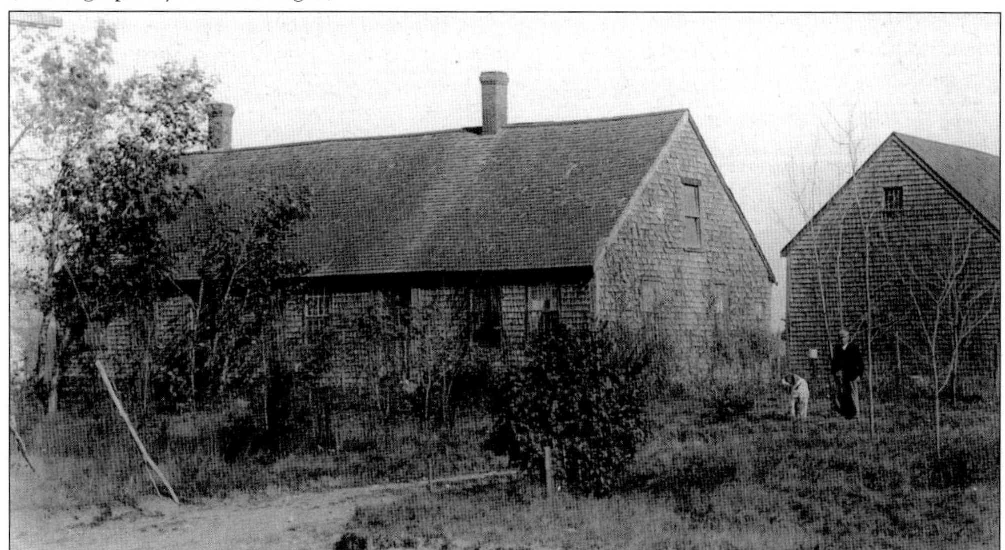

This 1740 dwelling at 301 Pleasant Street was home to the Curtises, Turners, Estes, Baileys, and Campbells prior to its demolition. Referred to as the "Long House," many of its residents were Quakers involved with the West Hanover mill.

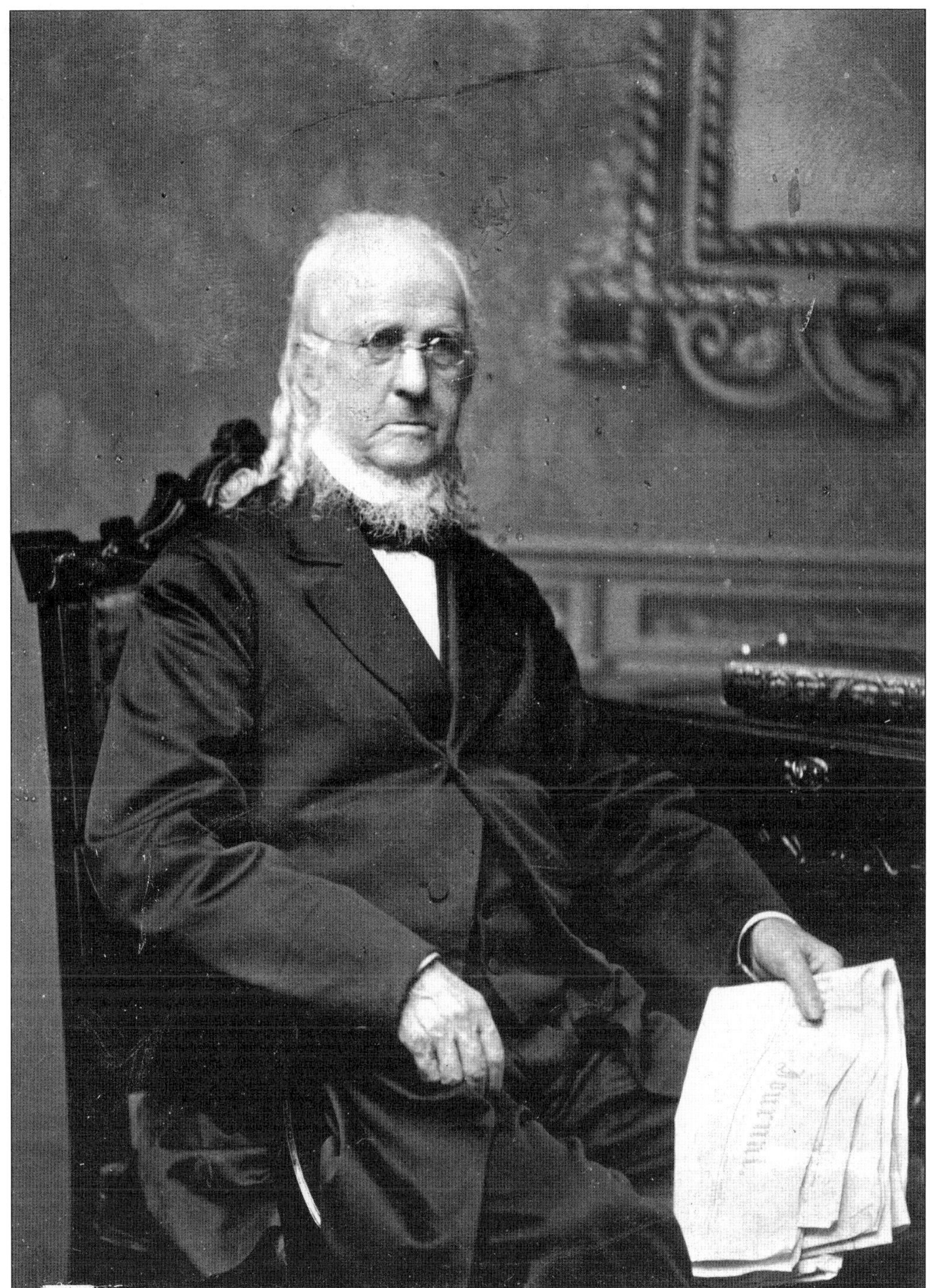

John Bailey Jr., born in Hanover in 1787, was a third-generation clockmaker. He was a Quaker, and lived briefly in the Long House, shown on the previous page. Bailey moved to New Bedford, but after being driven out by proslavery politicians, he relocated to Lynn, a strong antislavery town. Bailey once said, "As long as fish swim in the sea, and clams live in the sea, I'll not sell my principles."

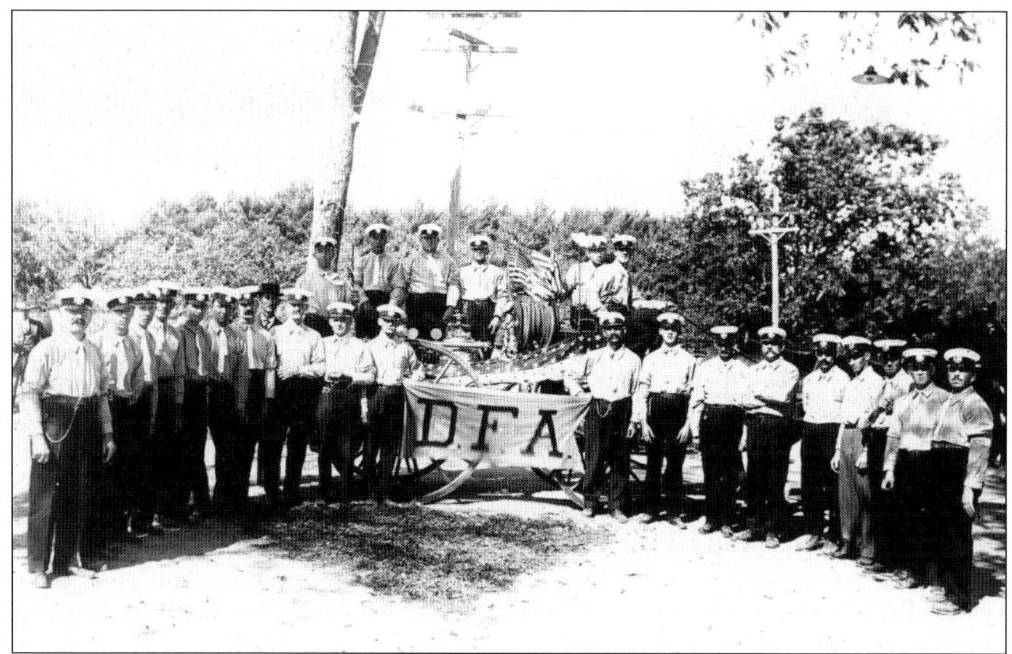

The Drinkwater Fire Association provided fire protection for the village and the National Fireworks Company, which owned much of the area. Officers of the association were president Calvin Ellis (back row, third from the left), secretary Chester W. Kiley (front row, seventh from the right), treasurer Clarence Hill (eighth from the left, in the black hat), and steward Albert H. Slaney (back row, second from the right). George J. J. Clark, president of the National Fireworks Company, is first on the left in the front row.

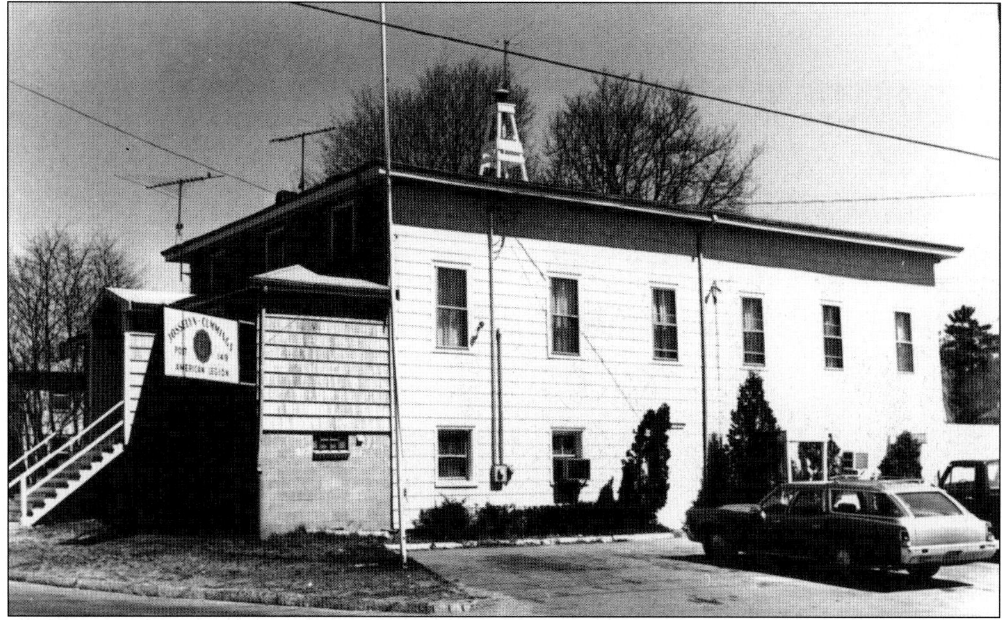

Members of the Drinkwater Fire Association built Drinkwater Hall *c.* 1919. It was a social gathering place and also housed the Drinkwater fire engines. It is now home to American Legion Post No. 149 in Hanover. Earle E. Josselyn organized the Josselyn-Cummings Post in 1920.

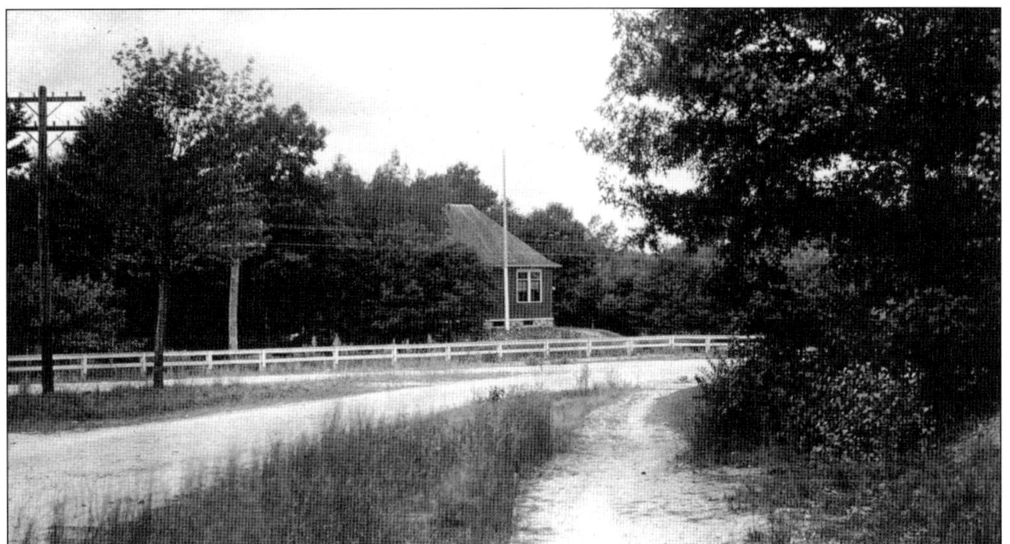

The King Street School peeks out from the woods in this *c.* 1908 photographic postcard by Thomas Drew. Former students of the school remember the separate entrances for boys and girls, and the outhouses behind the school.

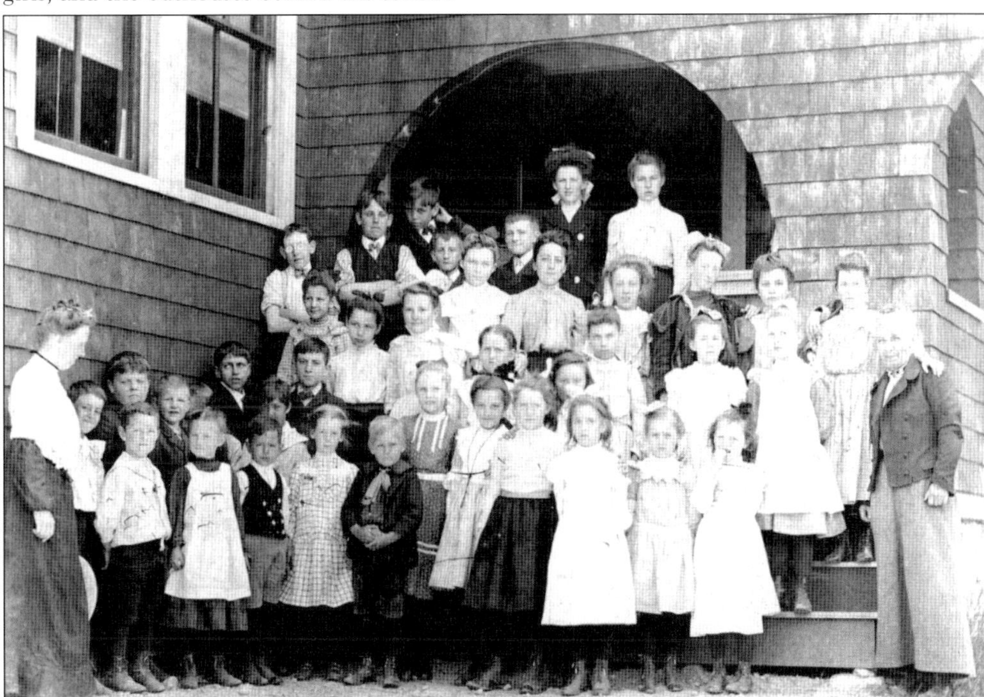

The King Street School, which was actually on Circuit Street, was built in 1899 and replaced an earlier school on School Street. Students in this *c.* 1905 photograph include Elizabeth Phillips and Howard Ellis (front row), Elva Josselyn (Henderson), Annie Cummings (Inglis), Stella Church (Wolfe), and Hazel Winslow. Ella May Stetson Bates was the teacher. The school closed in 1953, and the building now serves as the Hanover Grange Hall and the Hanover Senior Center.

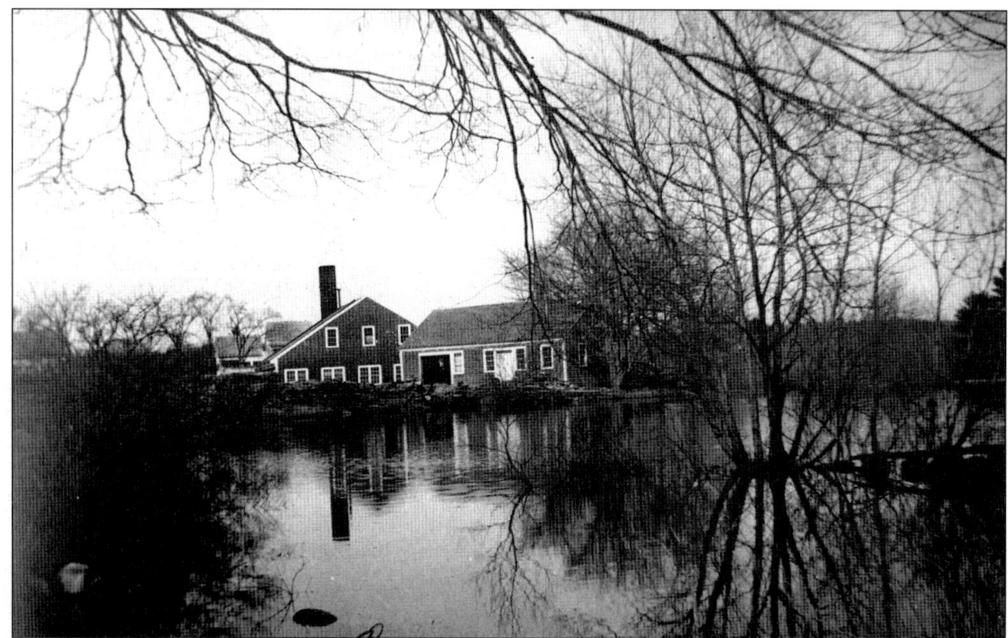

The Drinkwater Iron Works was erected at this site *c*. 1710. Members of the Barker family were probably some of the earliest workers. During the Revolutionary War, cannons were cast here and period cannonballs have been found at the site. The forge shown was working here in 1816, and anchors were produced here by Edwin Barstow, the last anchor maker in town. Shortly after George J. J. Clark purchased the property *c*. 1900, the forge burned to the ground.

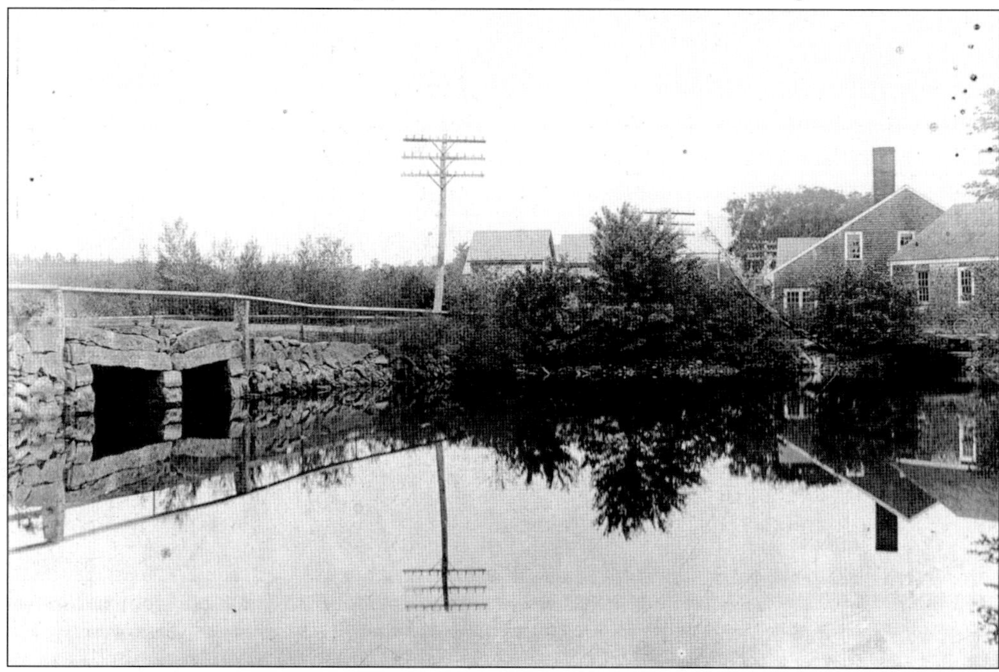

The Drinkwater River flows under King Street at the old anchor forge. Fifty to sixty tons of anchors were produced at the forge annually by the Bates and Holmes company. Edwin Barstow worked here until the late 1800s. Charles Stetson then used the structure as a machine shop.

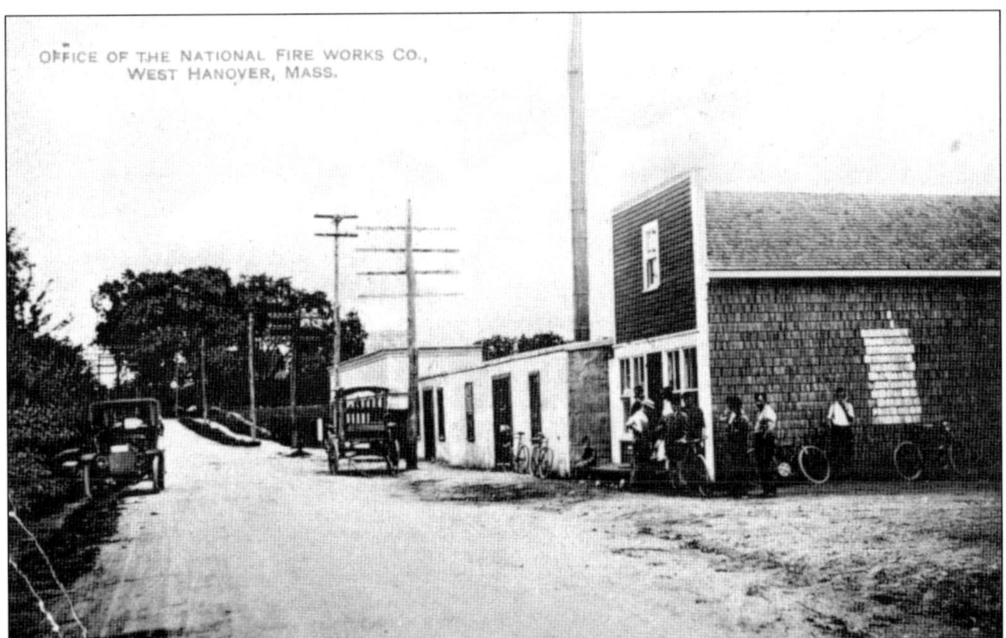

This W. H. White postcard shows the National Fireworks Company office on King Street in West Hanover. Some of these buildings remain today. While this village is on the west side of Hanover, it was commonly known as Drinkwater. The name West Hanover was used to describe the village to the north where the West Hanover railroad station was located.

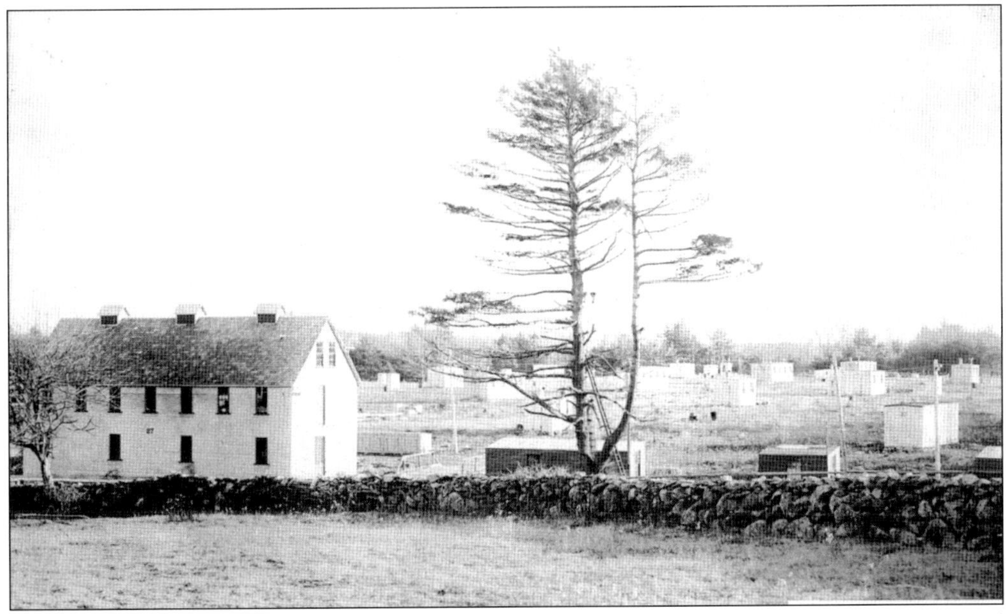

The manufacture of fireworks began in Drinkwater in 1897, when Thomas Archibald moved the Standard Firecracker Company from Rockland to the old anchor forge. George J. J. Clark began the National Fireworks Company at the same site in 1900, eventually replacing Archibald. This photograph from the early 1900s shows the many small structures that were used for manufacturing. In the event of an explosion—and there were many—the amount of damage would be limited and the loss of life reduced.

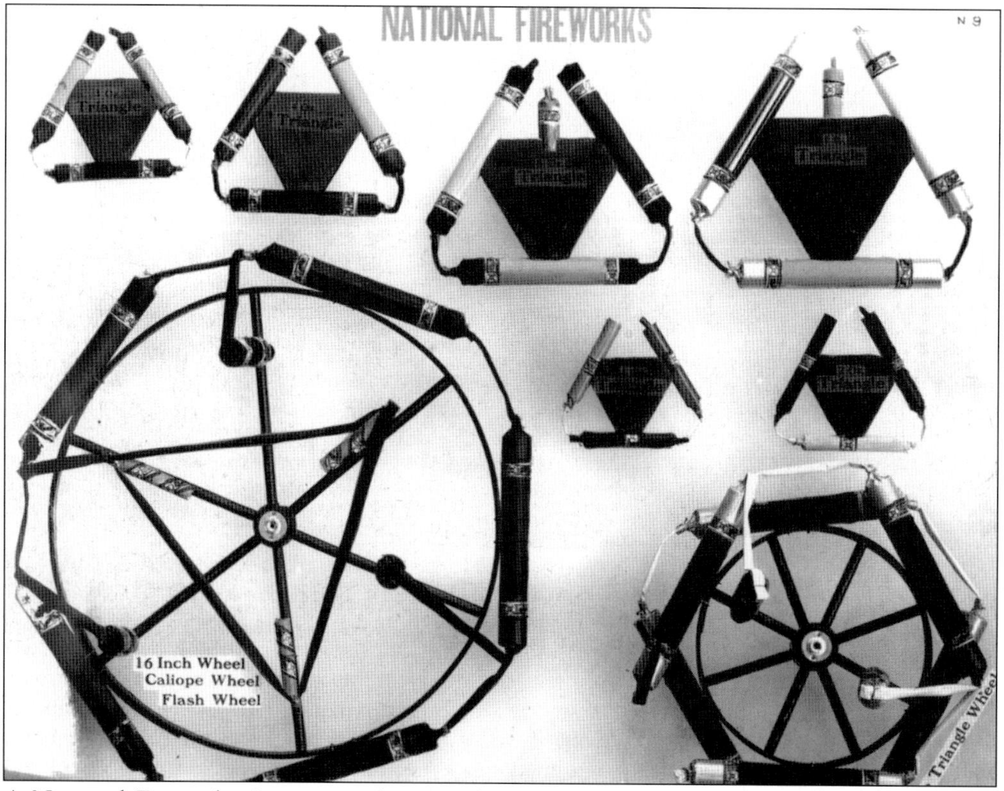

A National Fireworks Company salesman's binder is the source of this photograph showing fireworks pieces, including triangles, a triangle wheel, and a 16-inch calliope wheel. The National Fireworks Company was one of the world's largest pyrotechnic firms. The company made everything from sparklers to ornate set pieces for fireworks shows. During World Wars I and II, the company contributed to the war effort by making munitions.

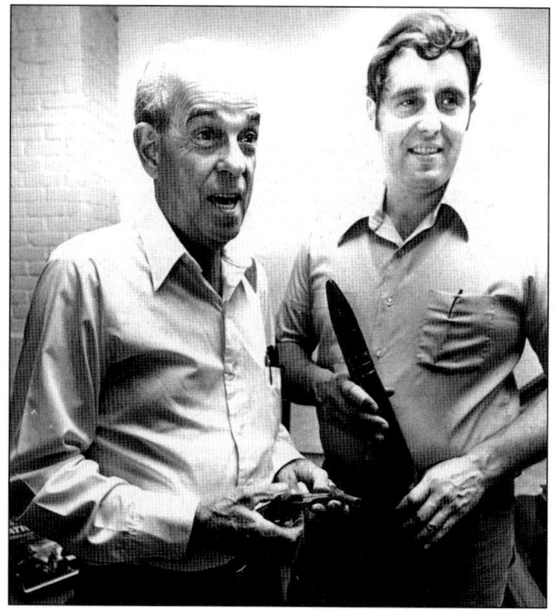

Lawrence Slaney and Leslie Molyneaux plan a 1980s presentation on the National Fireworks Company for the Hanover Historical Society. Slaney (left) holds a cap gun manufactured at the National Foundry in Whitman, while Molyneaux holds a World War II shell manufactured at West Hanover. Slaney worked at the plant for many years, and Molyneaux began collecting information about the National Fireworks Company in the 1970s.

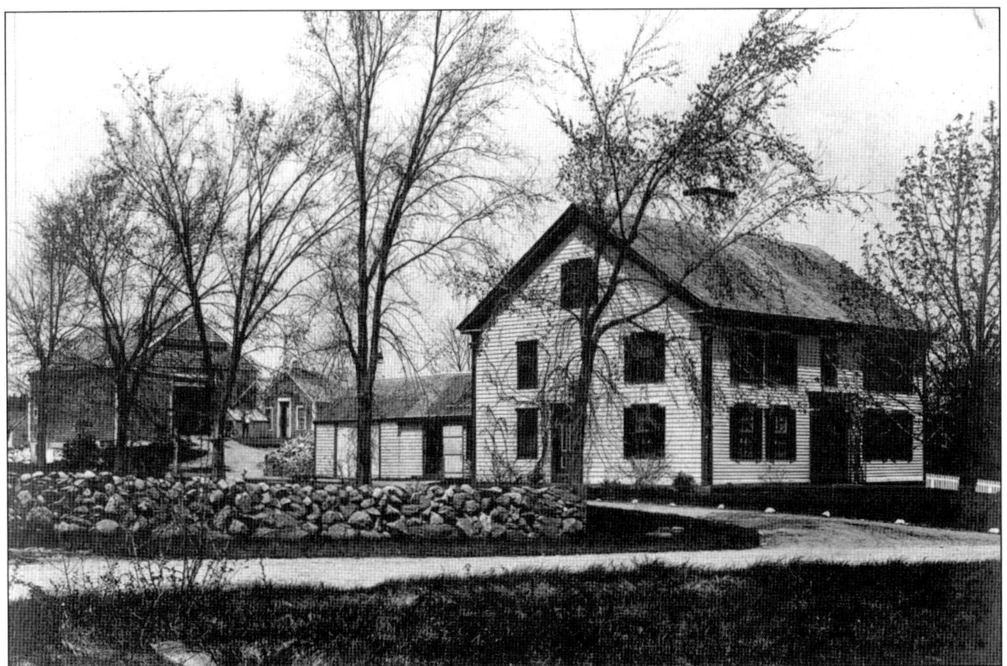

This *c.* 1900 Edgar B. Packard photograph of Drinkwater Farm shows the center-chimney Colonial-style home located at 231 King Street. Built by Samuel Barstow, a descendant of Hanover's first settler, this was the home of Robert Church when he returned from the Civil War with Joseph Washington, an orphaned black boy. Eugene Church, Robert's son and inventor of the Axtel weather strip, lived here as well.

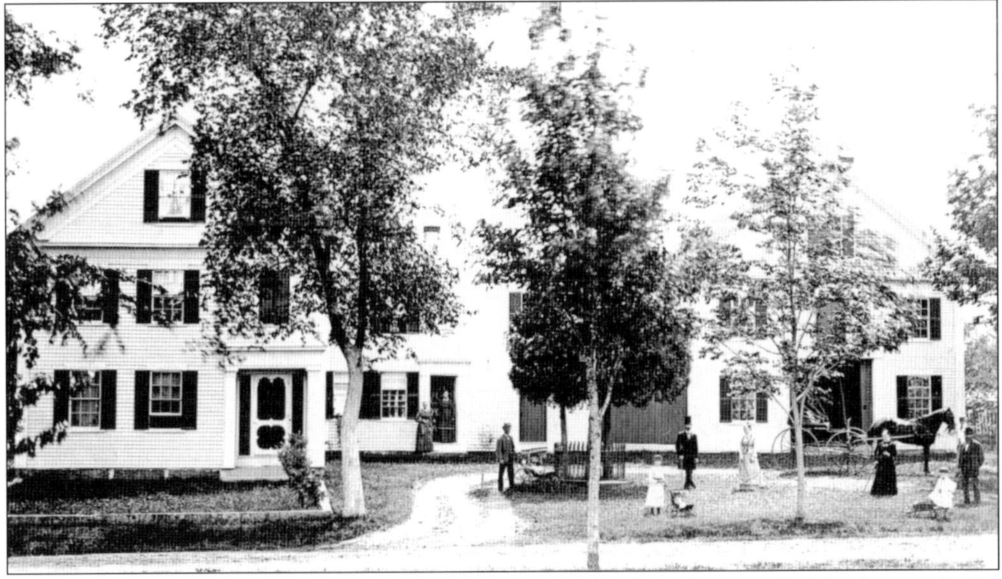

The Ellis family proudly gathered at 334 King Street for this photograph. The boy with the wheelbarrow is Fred R. Ellis. Later called "Hanover House" when it was owned by the National Fireworks Company during World War II, the structure was used as a hotel for visiting dignitaries who were overseeing munitions contracts. After the war, it became a private psychiatric hospital. (Courtesy of Gail Ellis Vincent.)

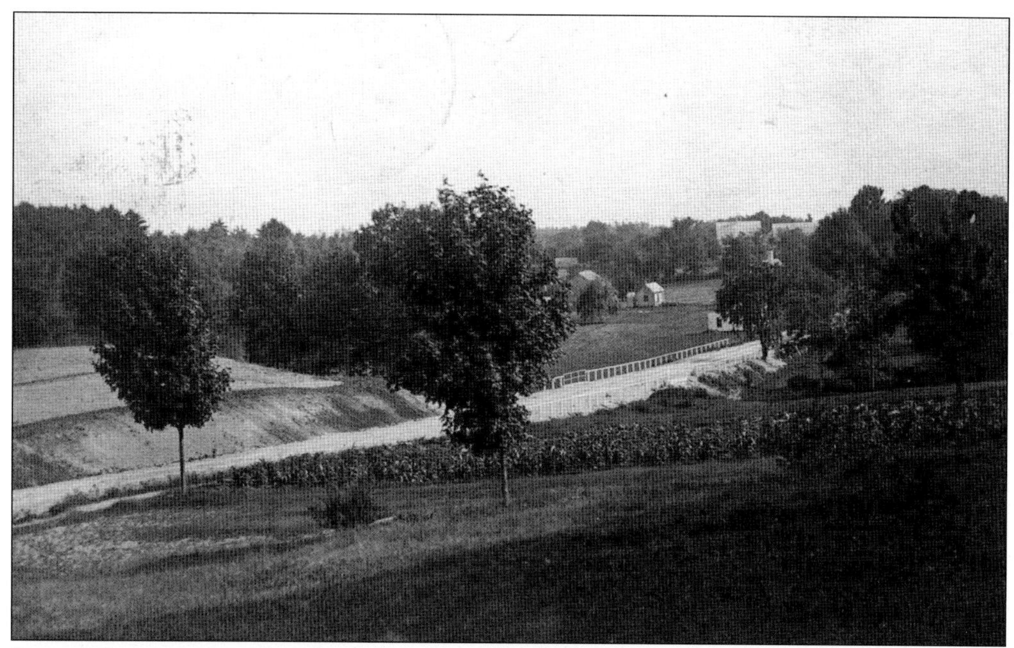

Part of the town boundary between Hanover and Hanson is the Indian Head River. The crossing at the end of Broadway was first spanned by a wooden bridge *c.* 1710. In 1907, a concrete arched bridge, commonly called Teague's Bridge, was constructed by William H. Ward. This view looks across the river to Hanson in the distance.

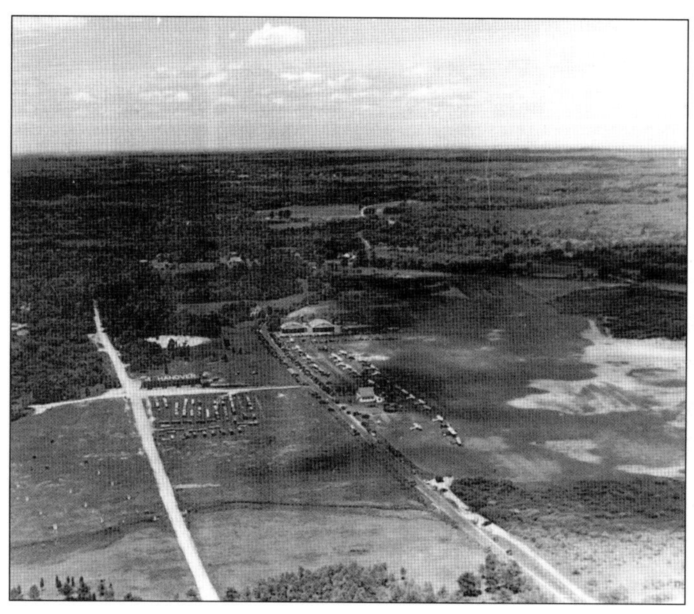

An aerial view of Clark Airport, taken in 1942, shows dozens of planes on the ground in front of the two hangars. Near the center of the photograph, Winter Street runs from the left of the hangars down to the bottom. The wide road on the left, running parallel to Winter Street, is inside the grounds of the National Fireworks Company and would soon be "Mag Row," where magnesium rod was made into powder to make flares for World War II.

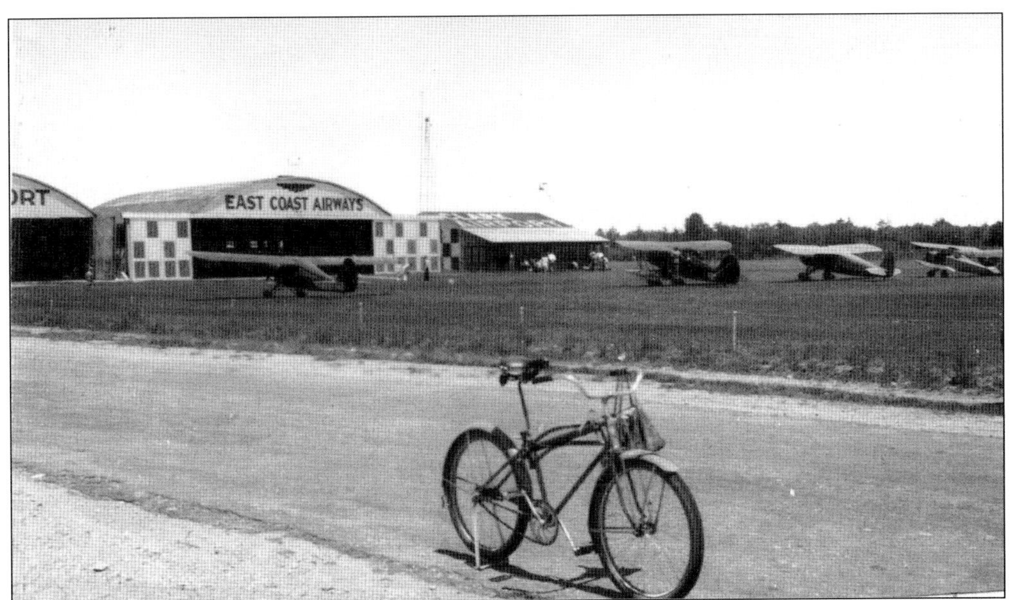

Yes, Hanover once had an airport. Before Clark Airport opened in 1929 in the area between Winter, Myrtle, and Center Streets, hills had to be leveled, power lines moved, and rocks and trees removed. Officially called East Coast Airways, the initial airport consisted of one plane, one hangar, and 35 acres. The airport soon expanded, housing planes from Hanover, Rockland, Marshfield, and Abington. (Note that Charles Gleason placed his bicycle in many of his photographs.)

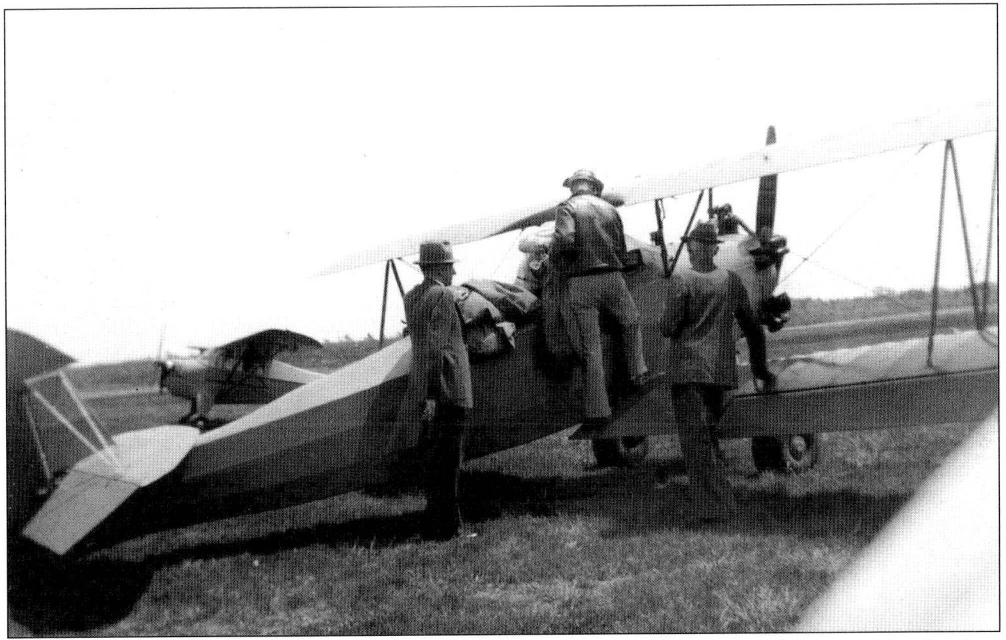

Bartholomew C. Downing, Hanover postmaster, delivers the mail to Clark Airport for the first airmail out of Hanover.

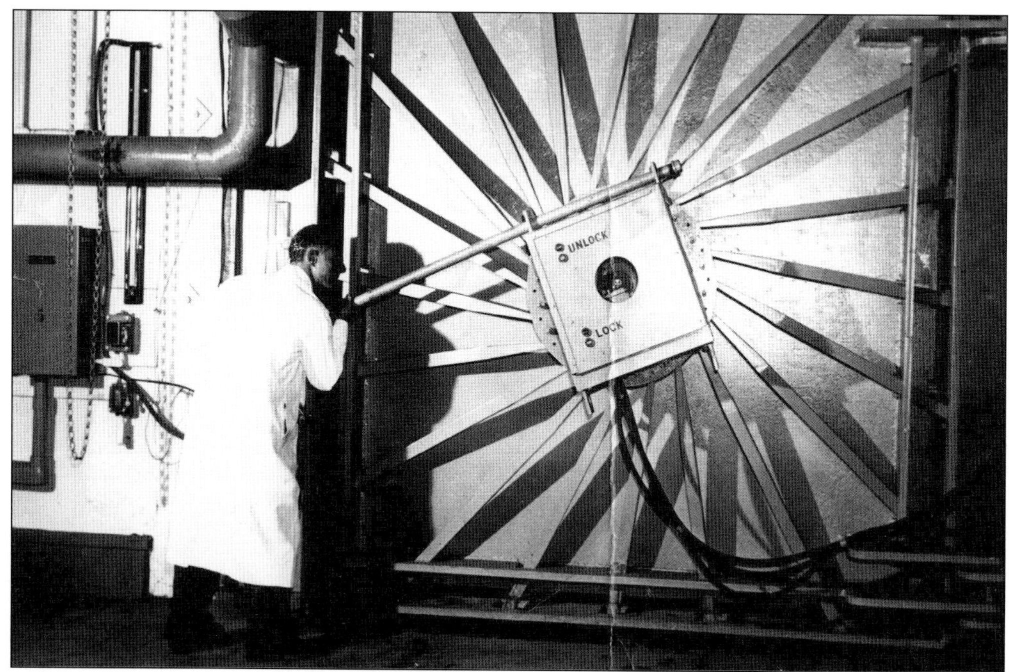

An environmental chamber is pictured at the National Northern plant in West Hanover. Located on the west side of what is now Industrial Way, the chamber allowed scientists to replicate the temperature, humidity, and pressure conditions for any place on earth. National Northern owned 302 acres of the old National Fireworks Company plant in West Hanover and nearly 2,000 acres of former National Fireworks testing grounds in Halifax, on which they developed, evaluated, and tested ordnance.

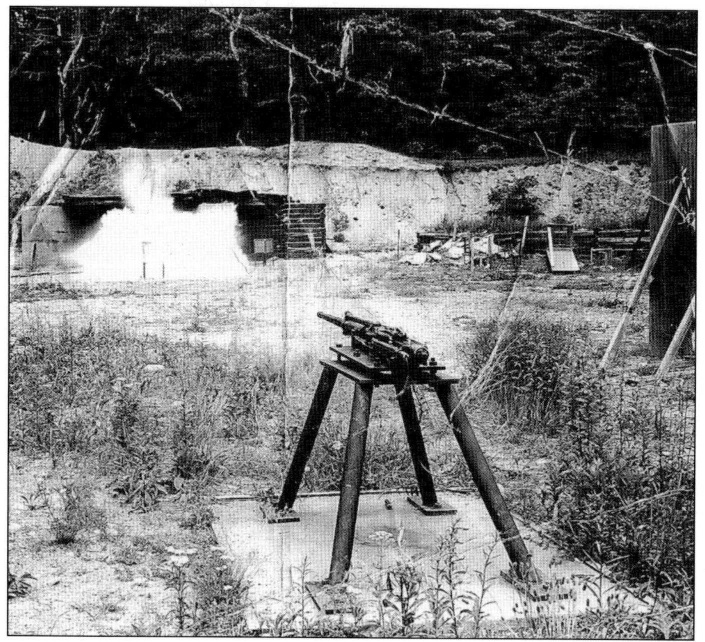

The National Northern gunnery range off Winter Street in West Hanover was located on what is now Hanover conservation land. This photograph of a 20-millimeter gun being fired bears the stamp of the American Potash and Chemical Company, which bought the National Northern plant in 1948. The National Northern division of the American Potash and Chemical Company operated from offices on King Street.

Five

North Hanover

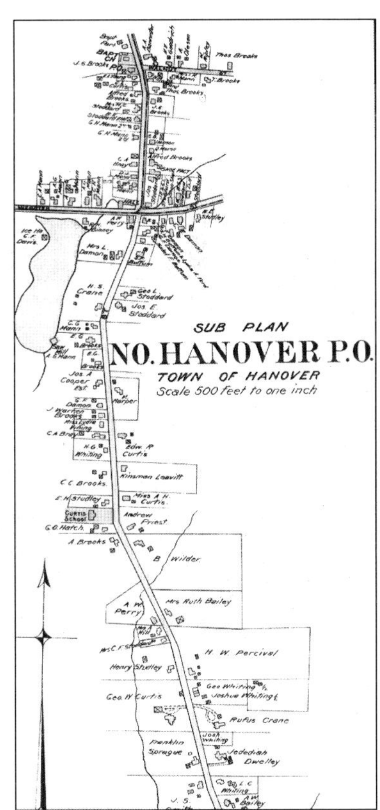

Detail from Plate 14, *Atlas of Plymouth County*, 1903.

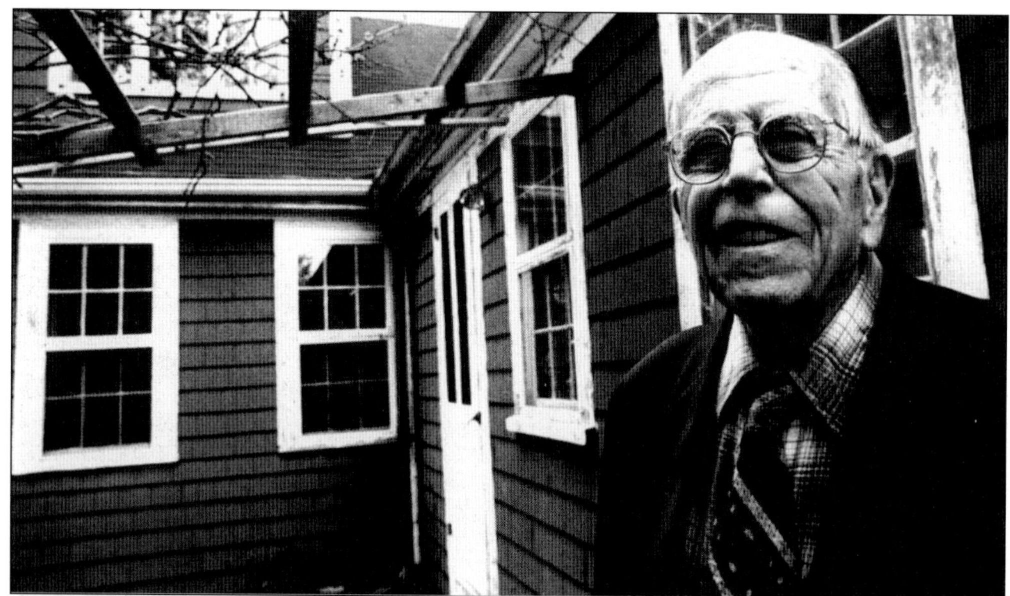

Donnell Brooks Young was born in this 1786 house at 1137 Main Street, and it was his home when he passed away at the age of 101. Dr. Young, an important Hanover historian, is shown with his grape arbor, from which a slip of wild grapevine was taken to Concord and later named the "Concord grape." Among his many accomplishments was his participation in the 1912 Olympics in Stockholm, where he competed in the 440-meter run.

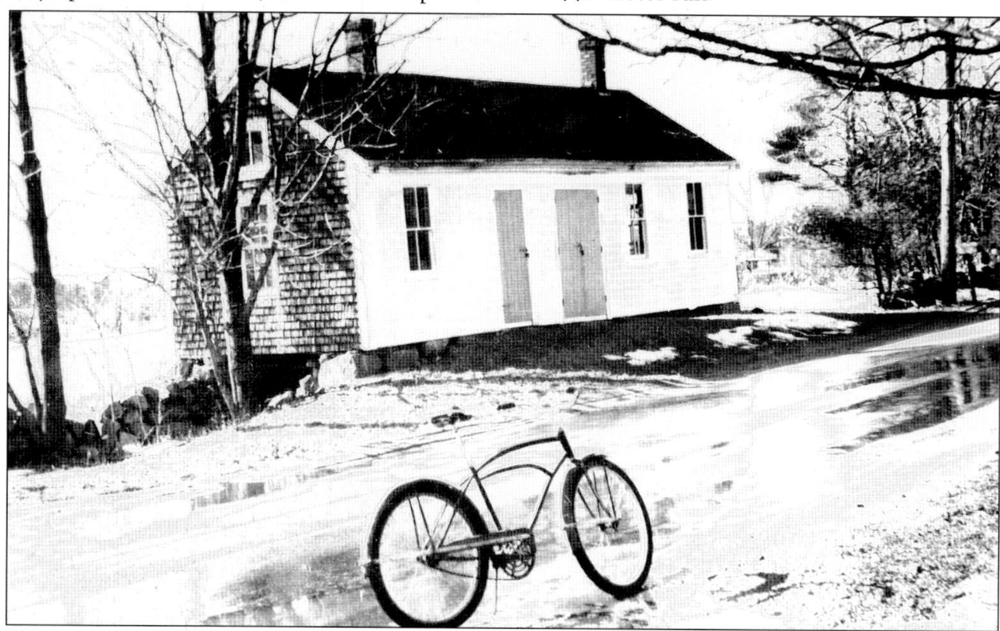

This little shoe shop on Main Street was one of many that once dotted the landscape in Hanover. Before 1800, all shoes were locally made in these small, home-based operations. Later, the shoes were partially made in these shops and then were taken to be finished in larger shops in Abington, Rockland, and Hanover. On Main Street in North Hanover there were as many as 12 shoe shops run by the Brooks, Studley, Curtis, Blanchard, Damon, Crane, Hatch, and Buffam families. (Photograph by Charles Gleason.)

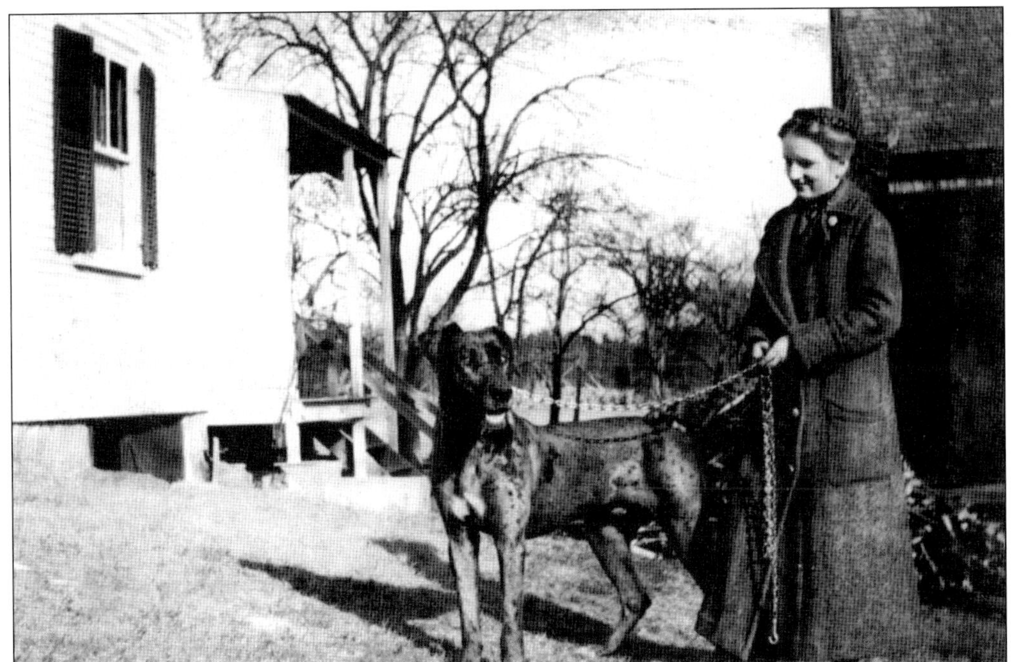

Helen B. Whiting lived all her life in this home at 715 Main Street, built by an ancestor on her mother's side. A Hanover teacher for 43 years, she is remembered by many former students. Roger Leslie remembers that Whiting gave kids a ride to the King Street School in the rumble seat of her car. Alice Sides Shaw recalls a ride to Nantasket Beach and ice cream from Whiting.

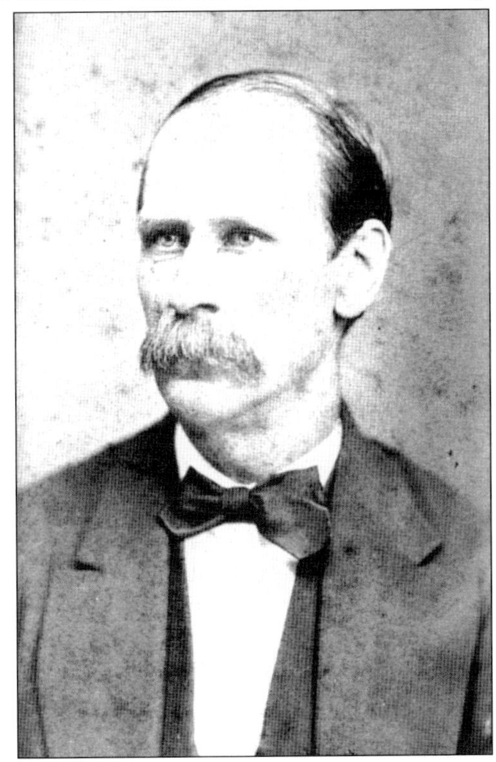

Jedidiah Dwelley was born in Hanover in 1834 and died here in 1912, just two years after the publication of Dwelley and Simmons's *History of Hanover*, which he coauthored with John F. Simmons. A jack-of-all-trades, he was a shoe cutter, surveyor, justice of the peace, insurance agent, auctioneer, selectman, county commissioner, state representative, and a member of the Massachusetts Senate. Above all, he was a historian.

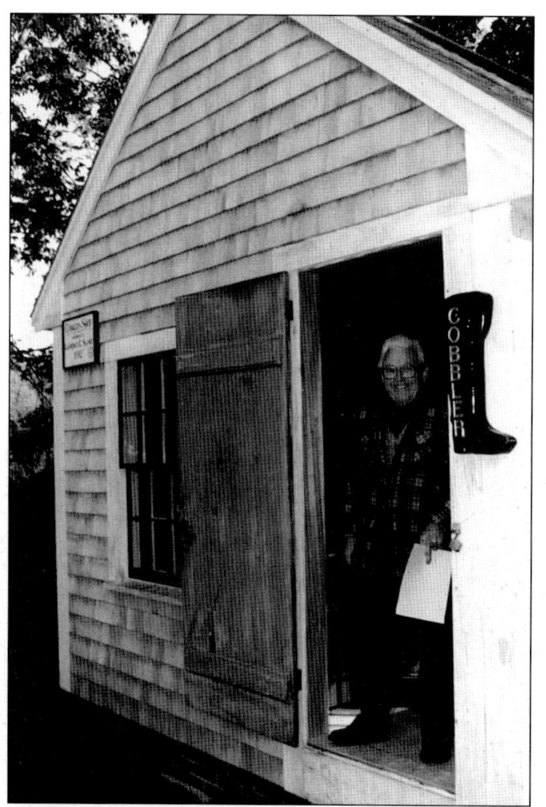

Bill Sides, a Hanover native, served the town well. He was a lifelong member of the First Baptist Church, Sylvester School principal, School Committee member, and Boy Scout leader for many years. A loyal member of the Hanover Historical Society, he gave his services where needed. Here, Sides stands in the doorway of the cobbler's shop, which he and Lawrence Slaney reconstructed behind the Stetson House. The two men also restored Charles Gleason's peddler's wagon.

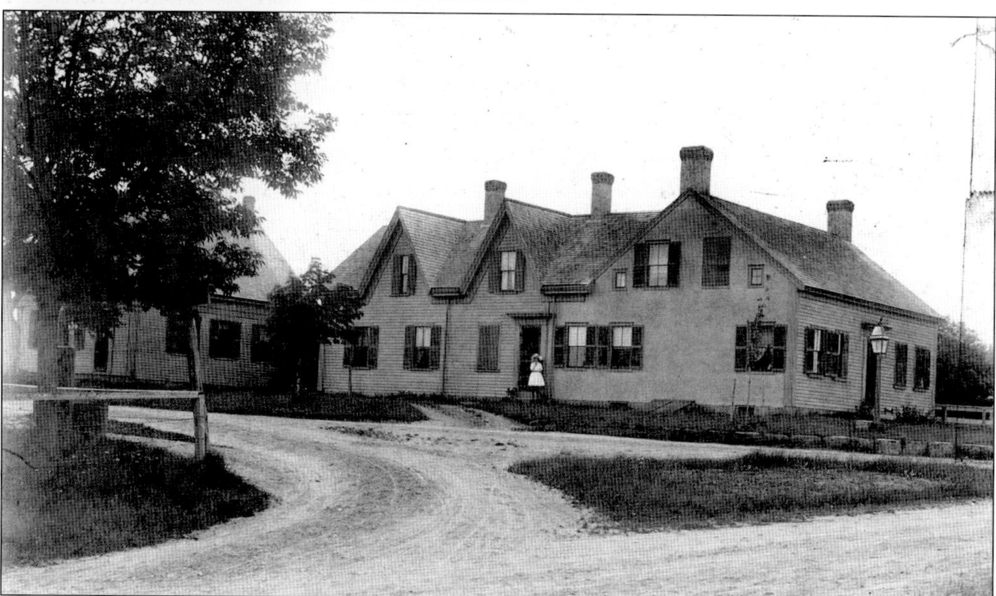

The town's first almshouse was located on Washington Street in Assinippi, but in 1876, due to the increased need of shelter for indigents, the house at 506 Main Street (pictured) was purchased. It was an operating farm where residents worked. An old schoolhouse from the field across the street was relocated next to the house and used as a dormitory for the men. The house was bought by the Amazeen family *c.* 1938 and was converted back to a private residence.

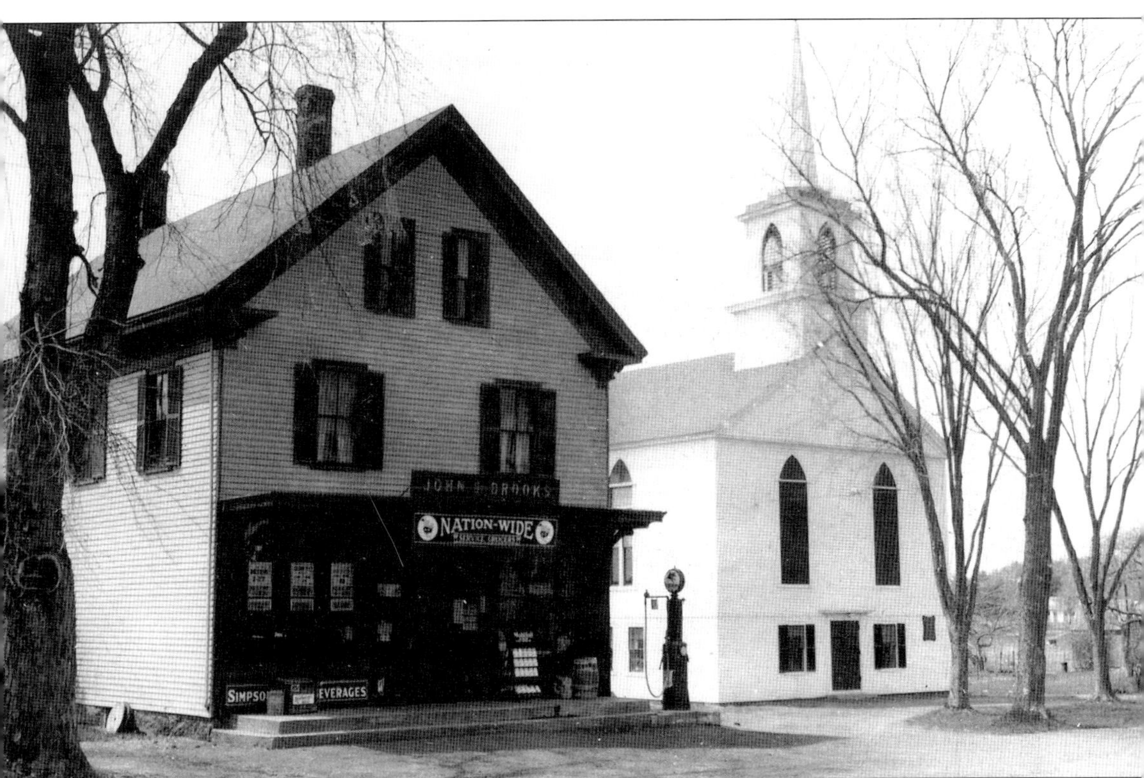

The social, religious, and business center of the village of North Hanover is shown here. The Brooks store is on the left, and the First Baptist church is on the right. The church was erected in 1812. It was remodeled in 1859 by raising the original sanctuary and building a vestry and other rooms underneath. In 1967, the building was torn down. The congregation now worships in a sanctuary at the corner of Main and Webster Streets.

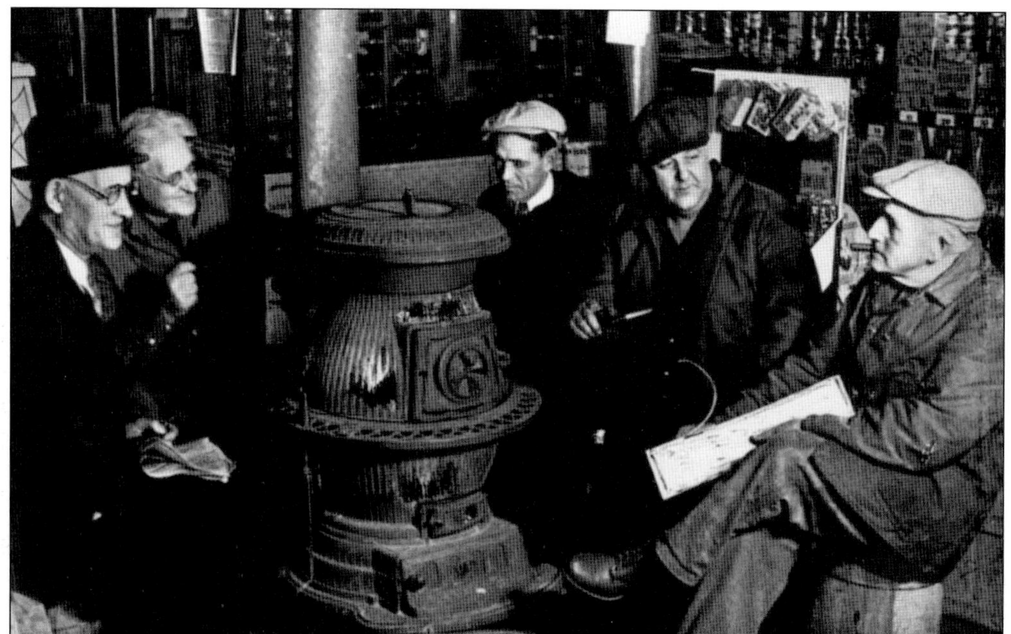

The Brooks store was the gathering place in North Hanover, as this *c.* 1940 view shows. Founded in 1854 by John S. Brooks, the store was continued by family members until *c.* 1965. Shown around the wood stove are, from left to right, Bob Brown, John F. Brooks (proprietor), an unidentified truck driver, Ed "Tub" Dwelley, and Charlie Prindle. Brooks wrote more than 100 poems, some of which were used as advertisements for his store.

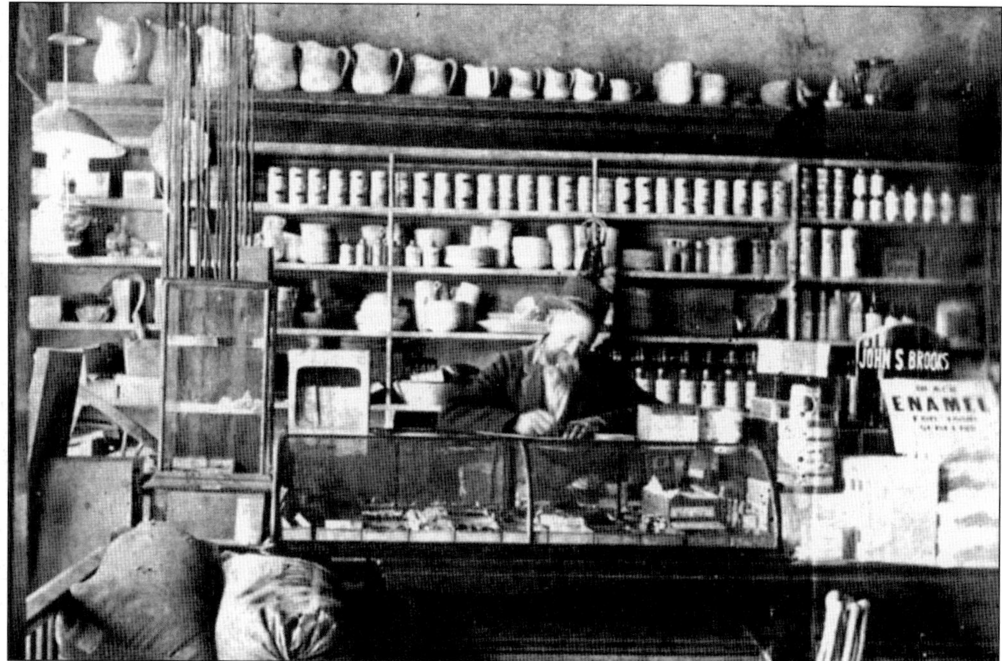

A 1937 Brooks store calendar photograph shows storekeeper Thomas Brooks in 1897. The store was a vital part of the village. In the case is penny candy for the children, and the shelves are amply stocked with everything families might need, including 12 graduated pitchers on the top shelf.

In 1904, North Hanover was the first village to organize and raise subscription money that was matched by the town for the purchase of fire apparatus. North Hanover thus earned the title of Station No. 1.

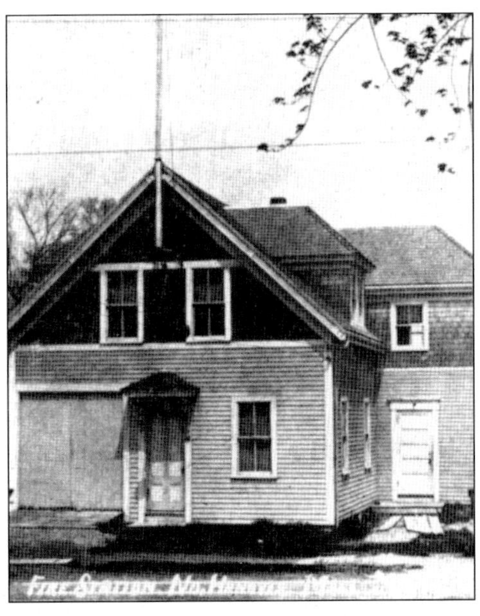

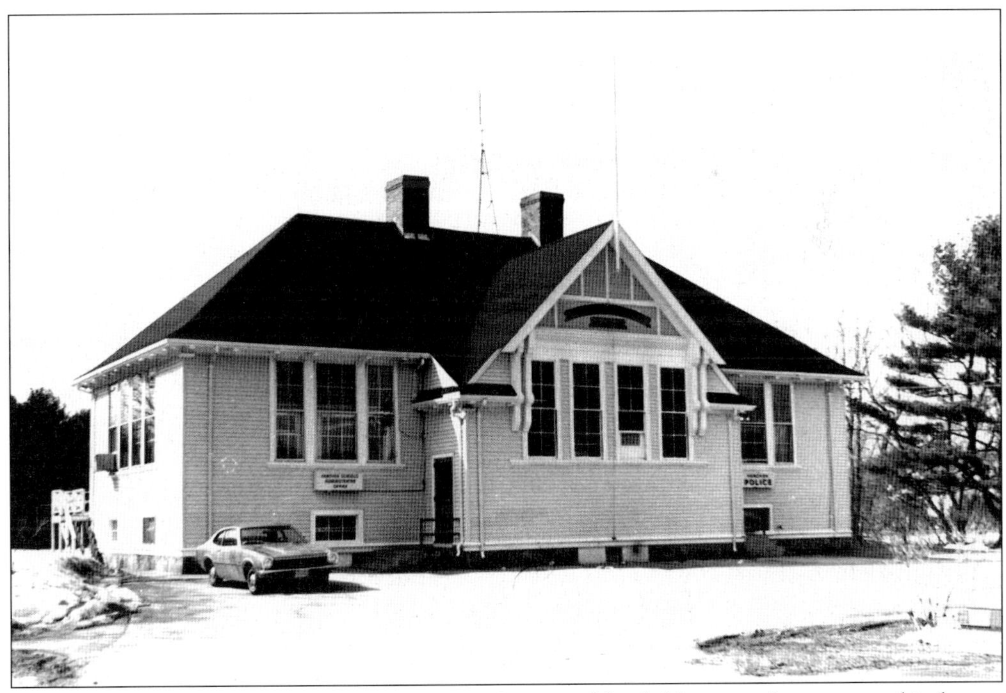

The Curtis School was built in 1896 on Main Street in North Hanover. It was named in honor of native John Curtis, who made a liberal contribution toward the purchase of the land and furnishings for the building. The structure served the community for many years as a school and later as a school administration building and police station.

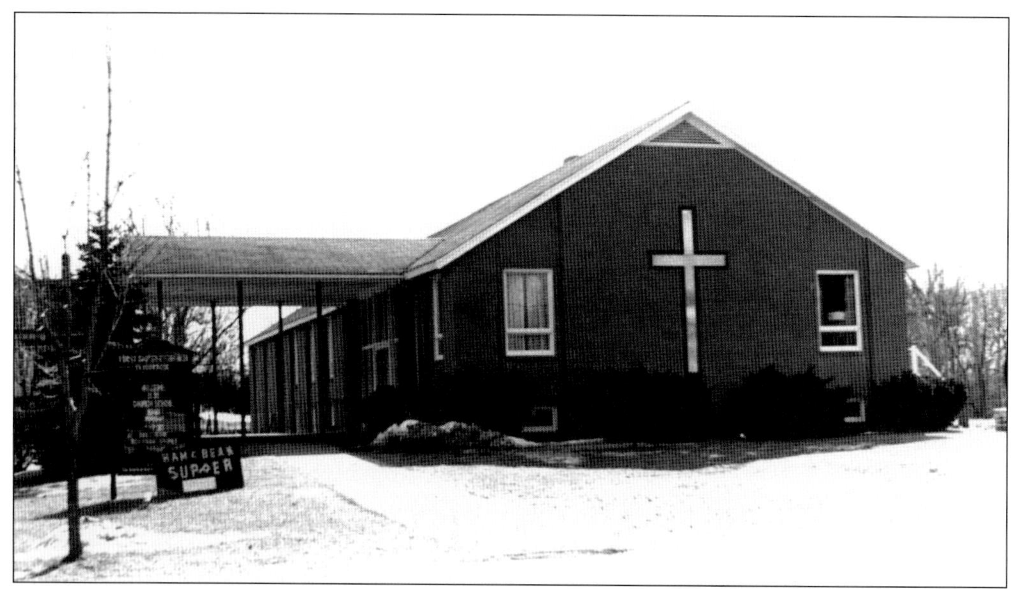

In 1960, the First Baptist Church in North Hanover broke ground for a Christian education building. When it became apparent that the old church on Main Street was unsafe and too expensive to repair, it was torn down and services were held in the new building (pictured). The parish is active in the community, and the town food pantry is located here.

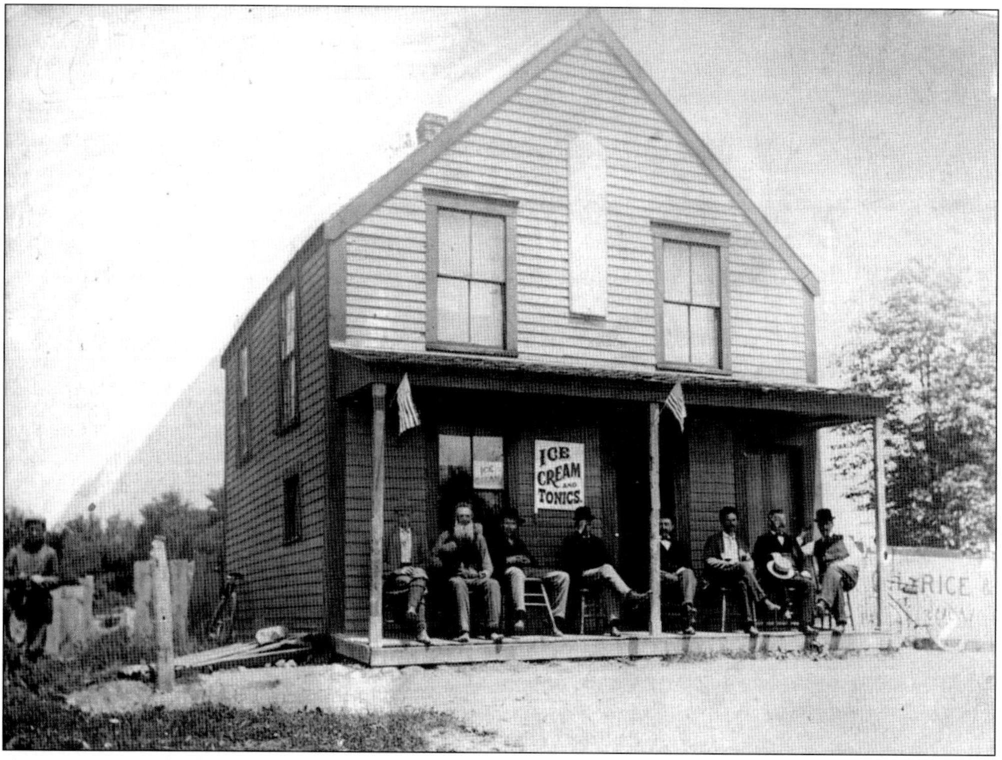

At one time, a barber shop operated in this building at 1079 Webster Street, on the corner of Whiting Street. By 1893, the trolley from Rockland to Assinippi and Queen Anne's Corner made stops on the opposite corner. This structure has been a private residence since 1939.

Six
Assinippi

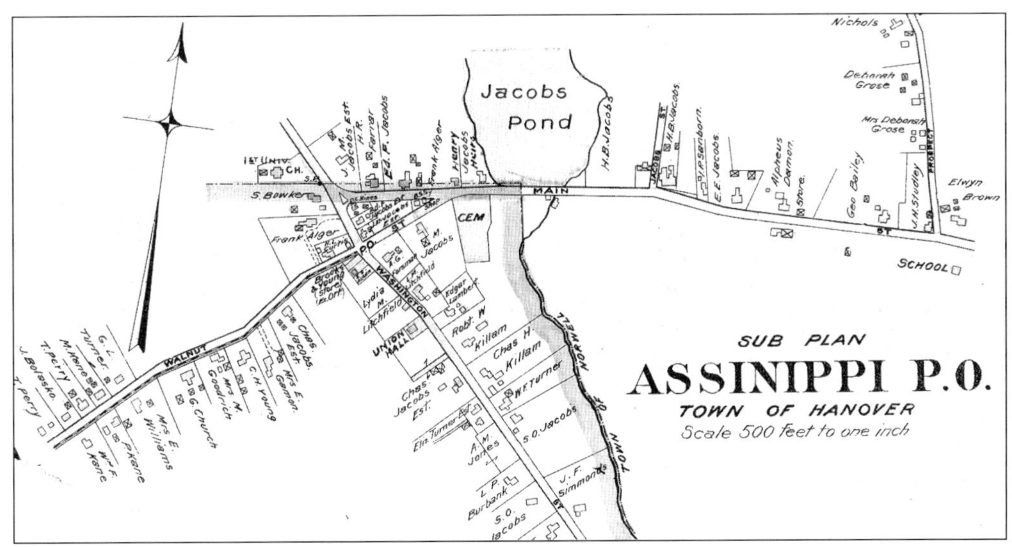

Detail from Plate 14, *Atlas of Plymouth County*, 1903.

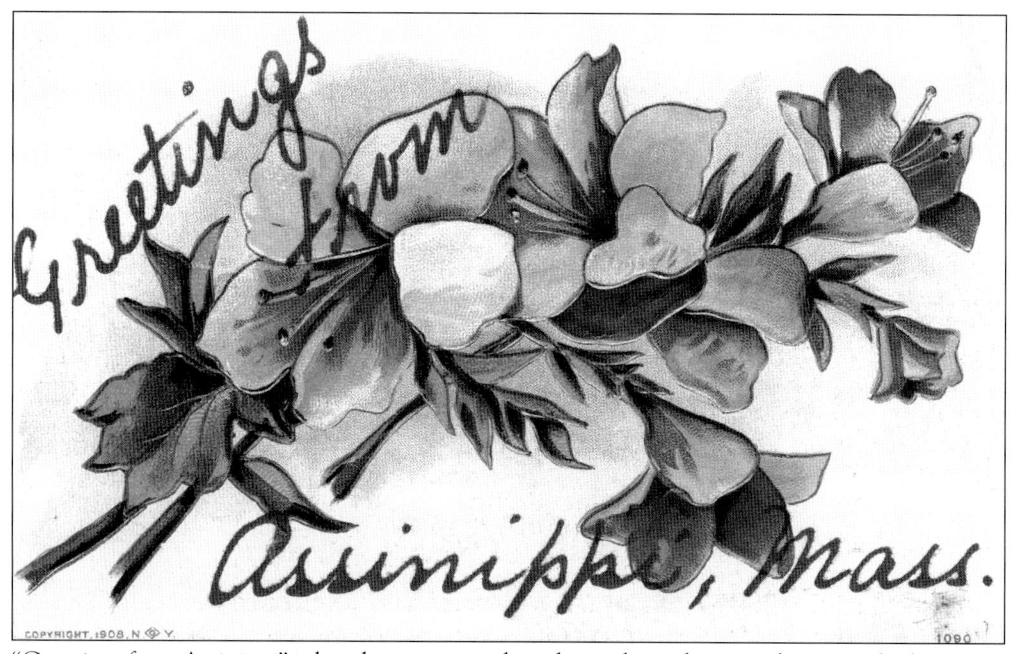

"Greetings from Assinippi" is handwritten in red on this embossed postcard, postmarked in 1909.

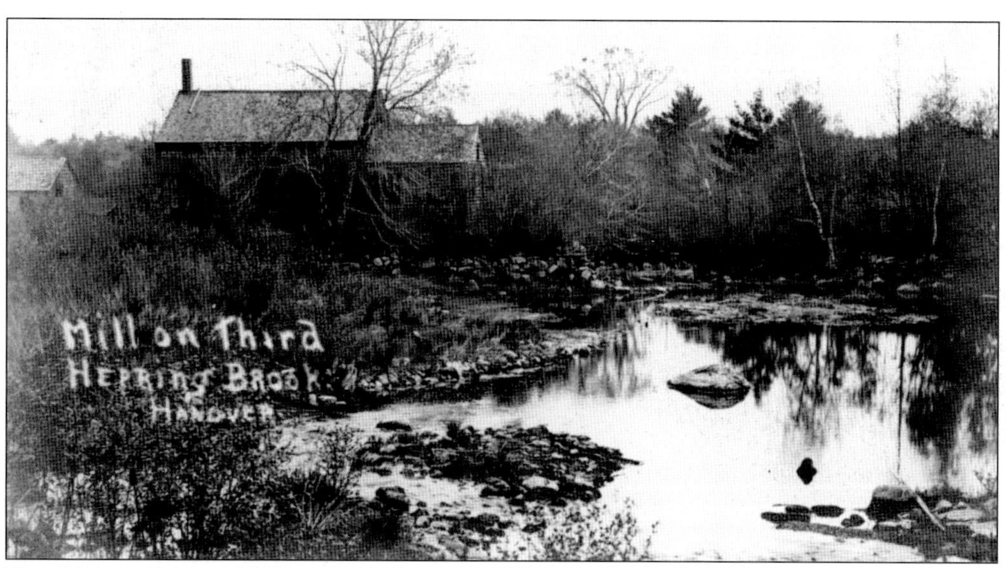

This Thomas Drew *c.* 1900 postcard shows a mill on Third Herring Brook. Which mill is it? At that time, a number of mills were still operating: Jacob's mill in Assinippi, and, farther downstream, Clapp's mill, Church's mill, Simmons mill, and Tiffany mill.

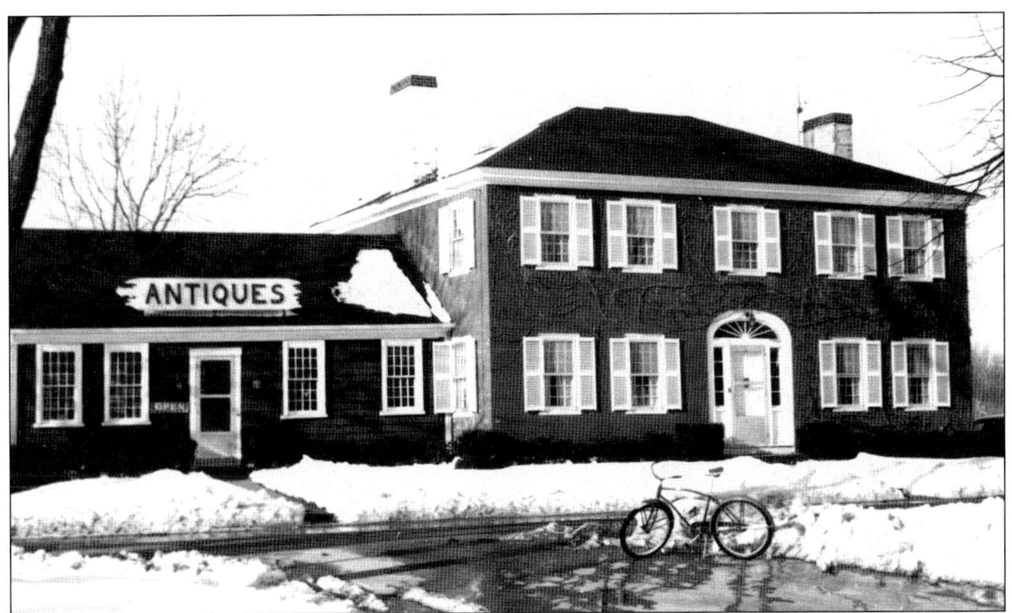

In the early 1700s, David Jacobs and sons Joshua and Joseph dammed Third Herring Brook, creating Jacobs Pond to power a sawmill and gristmill. Grandson Elisha later built a brick factory, and the Line House (shown here). Through the years, this Federal Colonial–style home has served as a residence, meat market, and antique shop. When this photograph was taken, the Bowles family was selling sandwich glass and other antiques. It currently serves as a bank and law offices.

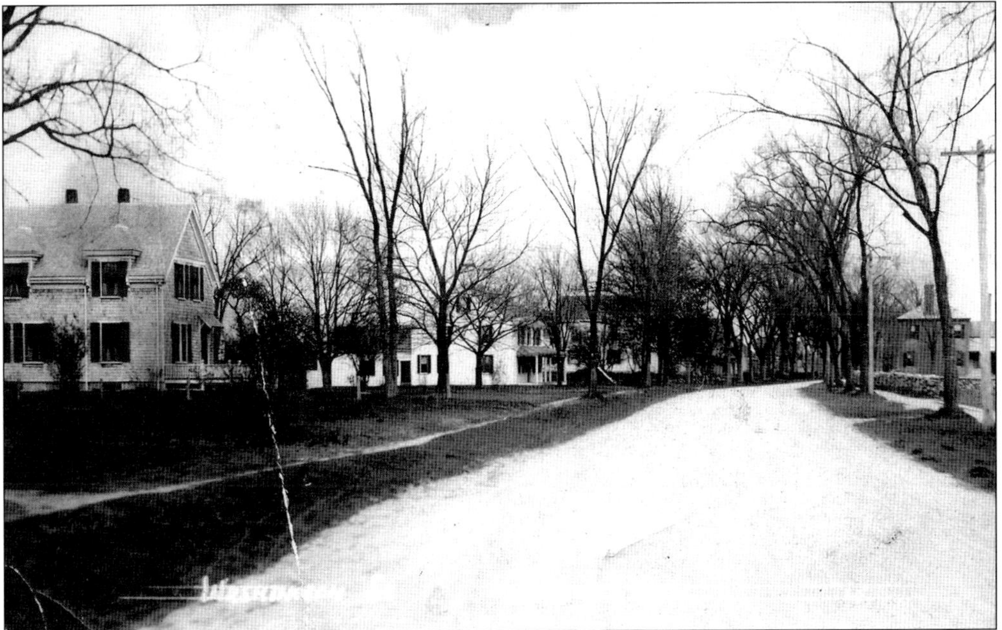

This photographic postcard shows Washington Street in Assinippi c. 1924, with its old houses, sidewalks, and elm trees. The first house on the left was incorporated into the Barnside Restaurant. The large Colonial-style house on the left was demolished for the Barnside. The brick house across the street, known as the Stephen Jacobs house, is still standing.

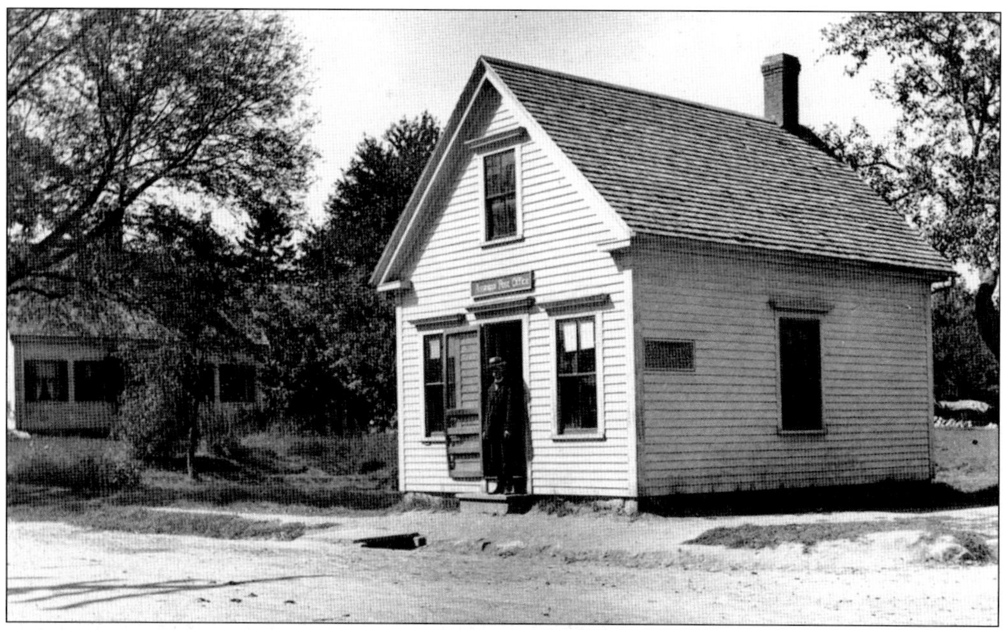

Is the well-dressed gentleman in the doorway of the Assinippi post office the postmaster? The Goulding Spring Tonic sign on the building advertises a Whitman, Massachusetts, bottling company.

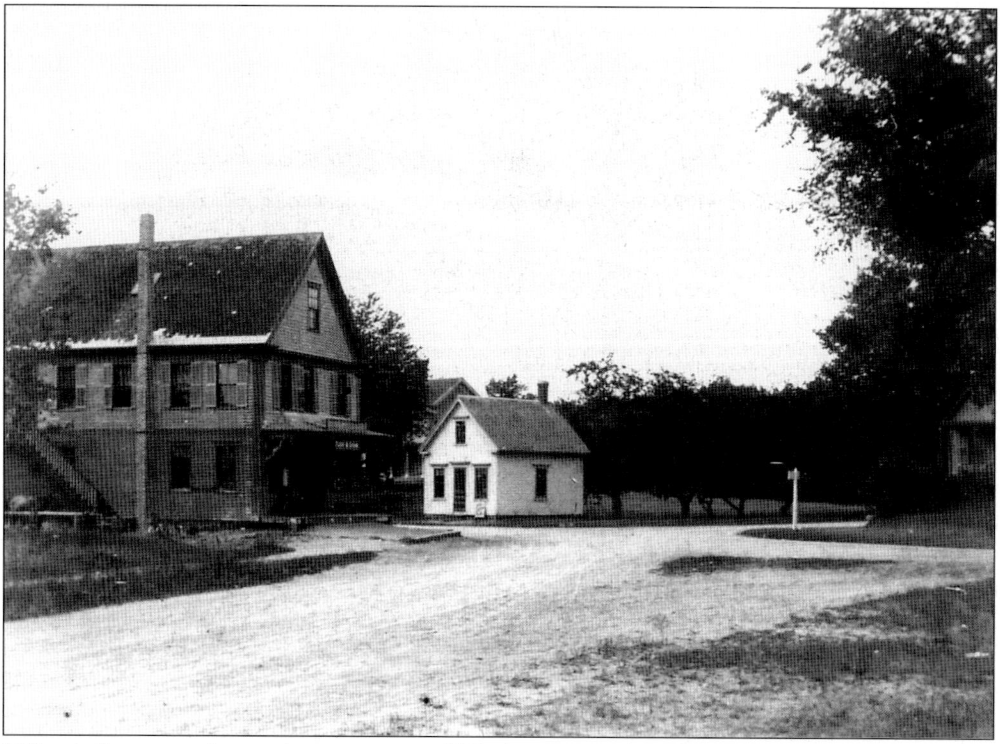

Killam's Store, on the southwest corner of Washington and Webster Streets, is shown on the left in this real-photo postcard. The small white building across Webster Street was the Assinippi post office.

The first meetinghouse of the Universalists in this area was built in 1792. It was replaced in 1832 by a new structure that had a steeple and bell to draw worshippers to services. Following a fire that destroyed the church in 1893, the congregation, led by Rev. Melvin Nash, built the present church on the Hanover-Norwell town line in Assinippi. This postcard was mailed from Assinippi in 1907.

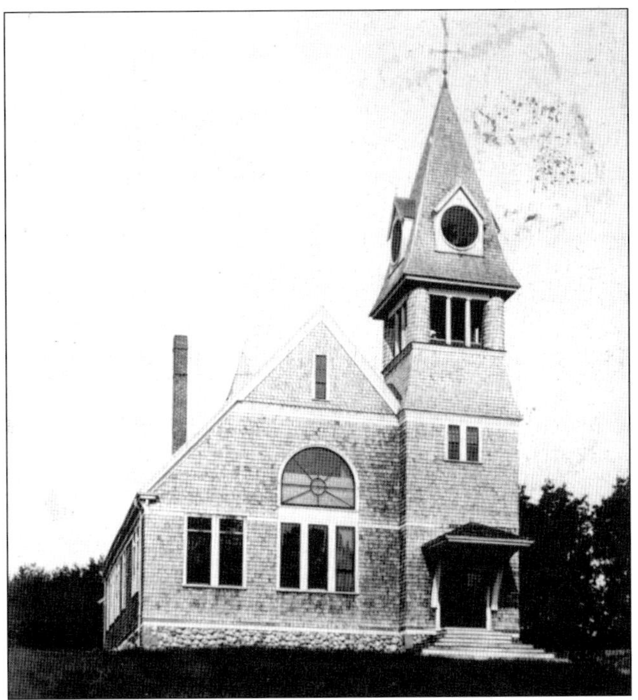

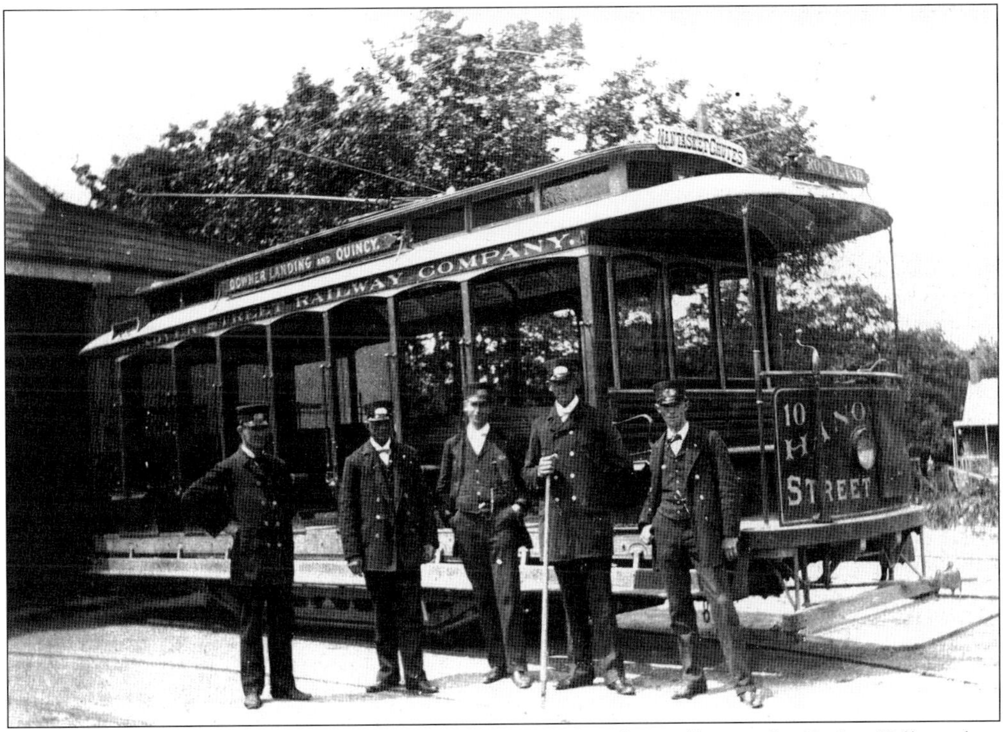

Five Hanover Street Railway employees stand in front of a trolley at the Ridge Hill yard in Norwell. Completed in 1893, the trolley line ran from Union Street in Rockland, down Webster Street into Hanover, up Main Street into Norwell, and into Queen Anne's Corner in Hingham. A spur continued up Webster Street to Assinippi.

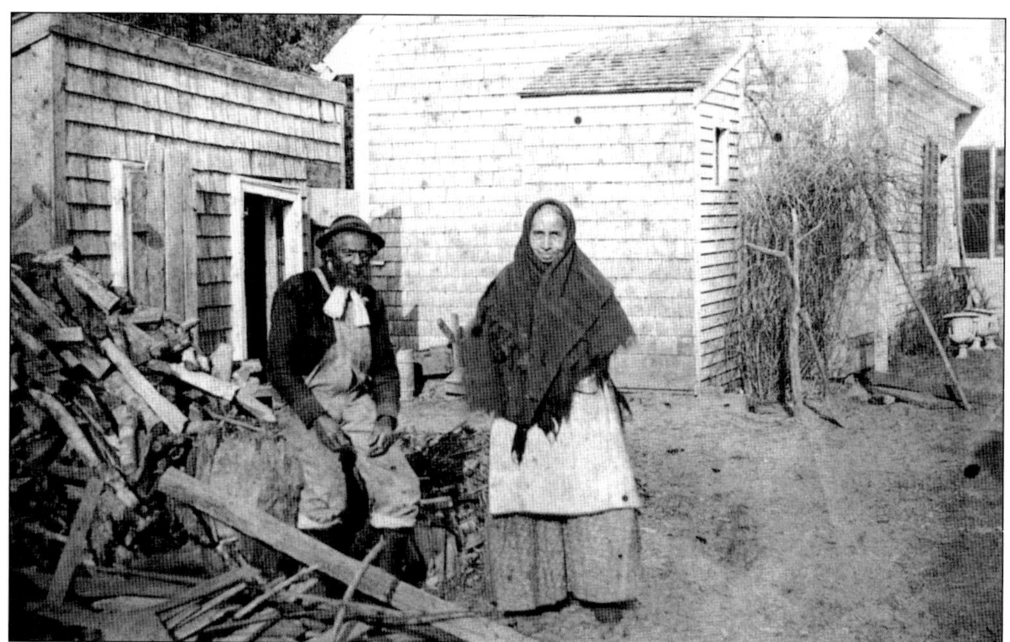

"R. B. Sylvester, photographer, Hanover, Mass." reads the stamp on the reverse of this photograph of Diana Freeman Pierce and her husband. According to the 1910 *History of Hanover*, Diana was born in 1828, and was the great-granddaughter of a slave. Diana married twice; her first husband, Lemuel, died in the Civil War, and she later married Parmenas Pierce. Her family home was on Henry's Lane, and she and Parmenas lived on the corner of Mill and Pond Streets.

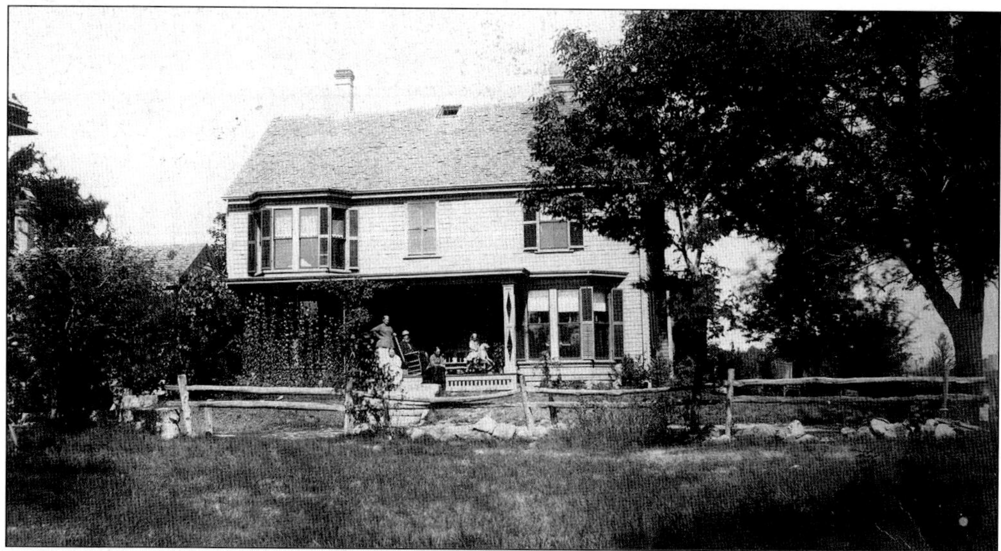

John Simmons (1851–1908), coauthor of the Dwelley and Simmons *History of Hanover*, lived in this Washington Street home in Assinippi. The house, constructed in 1750, was enlarged to two stories by his grandfather, Ebenezer Simmons. Shown in the photograph are "Ma" and "Pa" Simmons, John's wife Fanny, and their young son Henry. The family has played an important role in recording the town's history, and has donated many items to the Hanover Historical Society. The house was demolished *c.* 1960.

Seven
The Bicentennial and Beyond

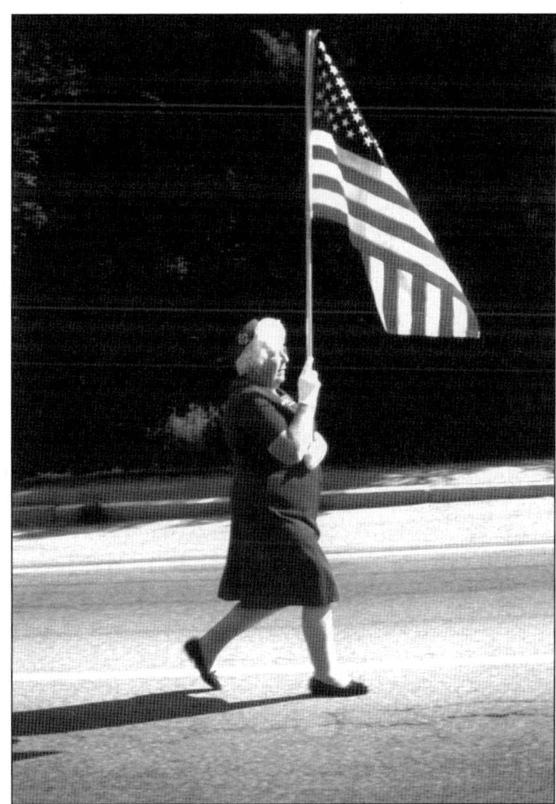

Virginia Szejnar holds a place of honor in Hanover's town parades. Her mother was postmaster at Assinippi for many years, and her father served as a town constable. Szejnar graduated from Sylvester High School in 1938, married, and raised her daughter here. She has been a volunteer extraordinaire for many organizations in town, and was the first to receive the Spirit of Hanover award in 2002.

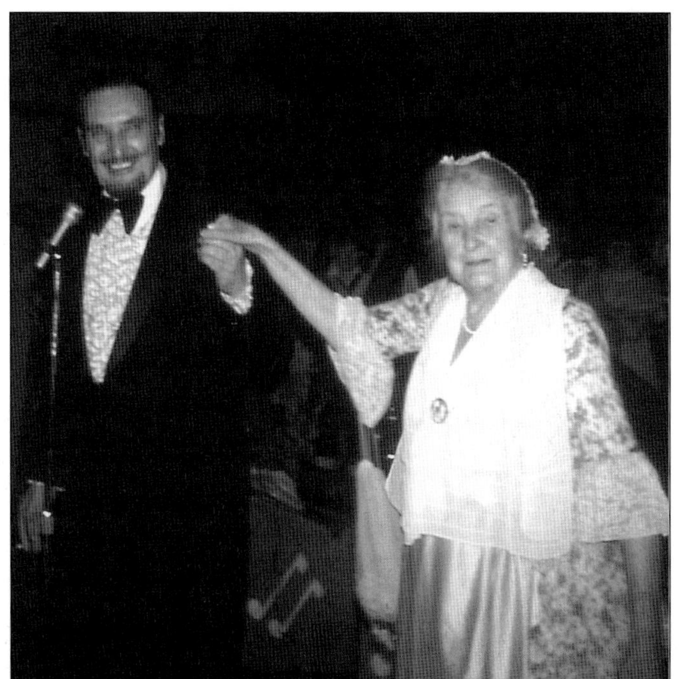

John Libertine and Fanny Phillips are seen in costume at the 1975 Patriots Ball. Libertine, a longtime member of the Hanover Planning Board and chairman of Hanover's Bicentennial Committee, was a past president and active supporter of the Hanover Historical Society. Phillips was honorary chairman of the Bicentennial Committee and a founding member of the historical society. (Photograph by Jean Migre.)

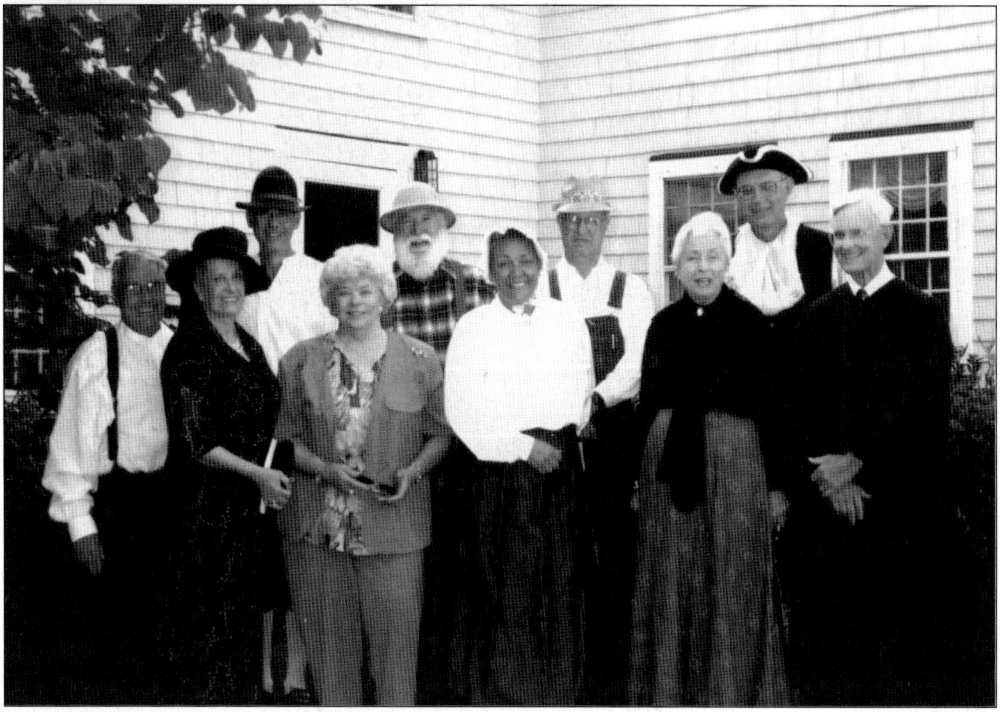

Members of the historical society enjoy playing roles from the past. Annual performances that portray people prominent in Hanover's history have been held for the past seven years. Pictured from left to right are Don Deluse, Janet O'Brien, Hal Thomas, Carol Franzosa, Bob Shea, Hannah Coffey, Kenton Greene, Barbara Barker, Jim Hunt, and Roscoe Riley. (Photograph by Jean Migre.)

George Lewald plays the role of the judge in a re-creation of the trial of the British soldiers involved in the Boston Massacre. The role was a good match for Lewald, an attorney, who served the town through 30 years as a member of the Advisory Committee, Moderator, and Selectman. The Town of Hanover is a better town because of George Lewald and others like him. He was a gentleman and a scholar. (Photograph by Jean Migre.)

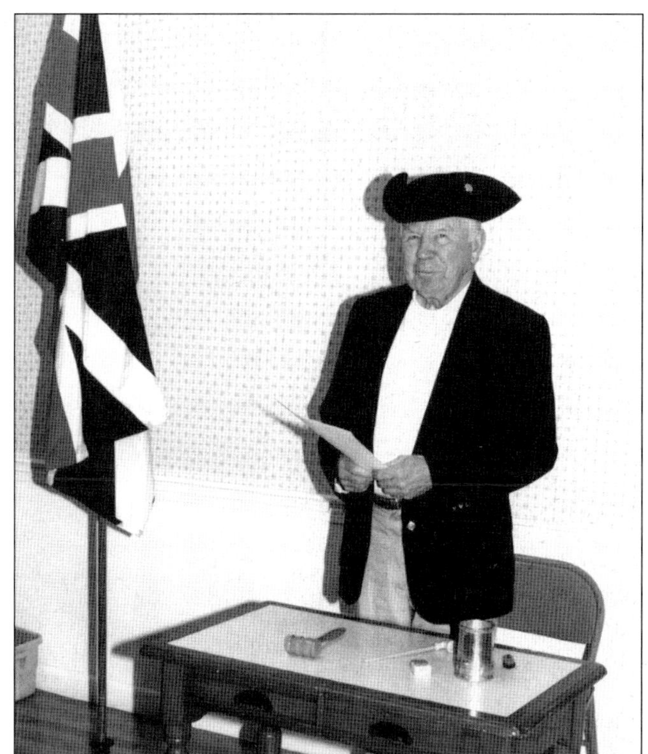

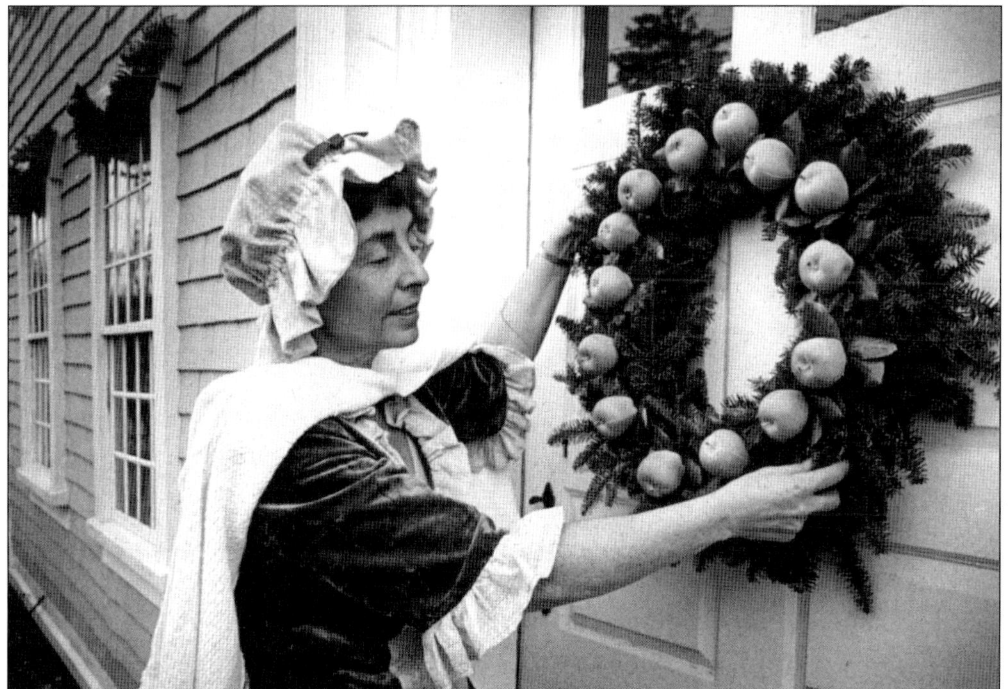

Barbara Barker has spent all of her 40 years in Hanover immersing herself in its history. A teacher in town for 30 years, she has been chairman of the Hanover Historical Commission since its inception in 1983. Here, she places a wreath on the historic Stetson House.

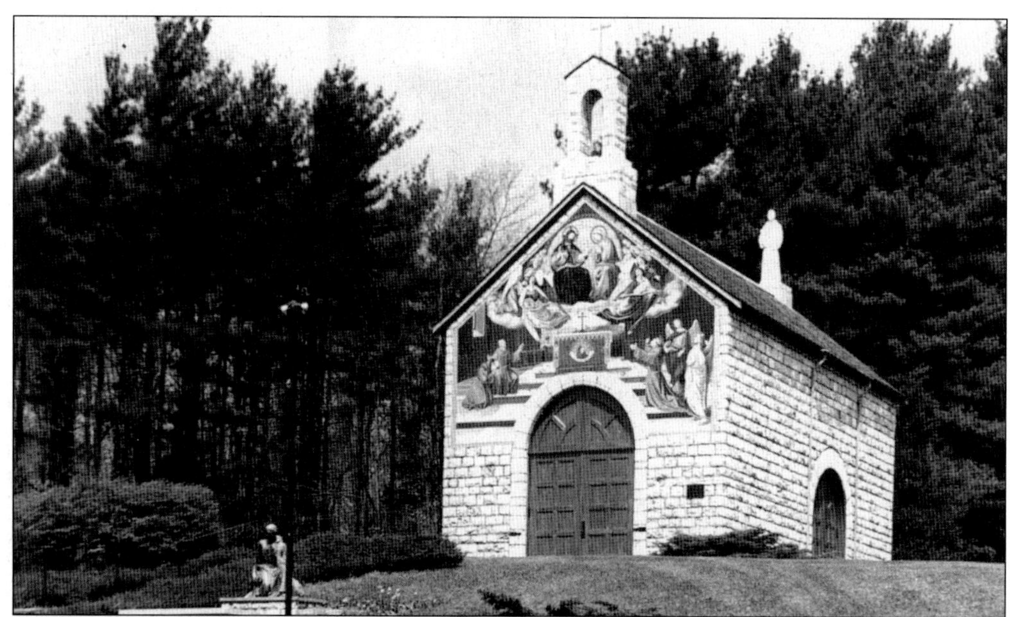

Portiuncula Chapel, a replica of a 13th-century chapel in Italy, was built on the grounds of St. Coletta's School (now Cardinal Cushing School). When it was dedicated in 1953 by Archbishop Richard J. Cushing, he said, "It is fitting that the chapel should be placed in the midst of little children, exceptional children whose hearts are closest to God himself." The chapel is the final resting place for Cardinal Cushing. (1977 photograph by Tony Acampora.)

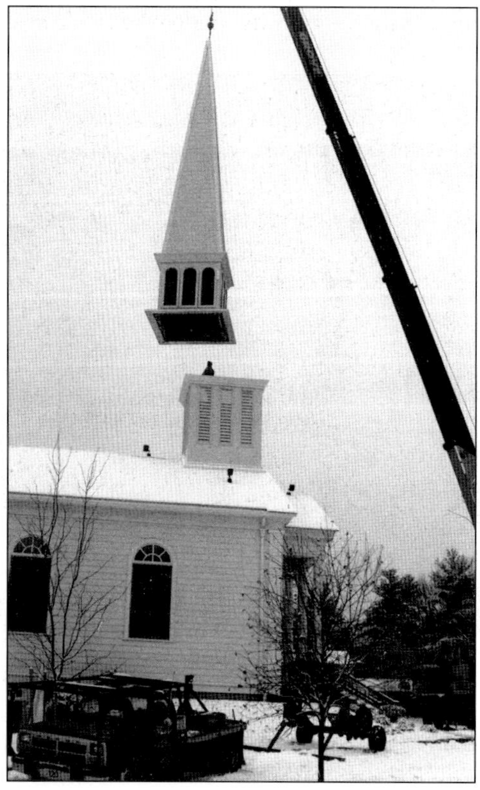

St. Mary's of the Sacred Heart Church installed a new steeple as part of its renovation and expansion. (Photograph by Jean Migre.)

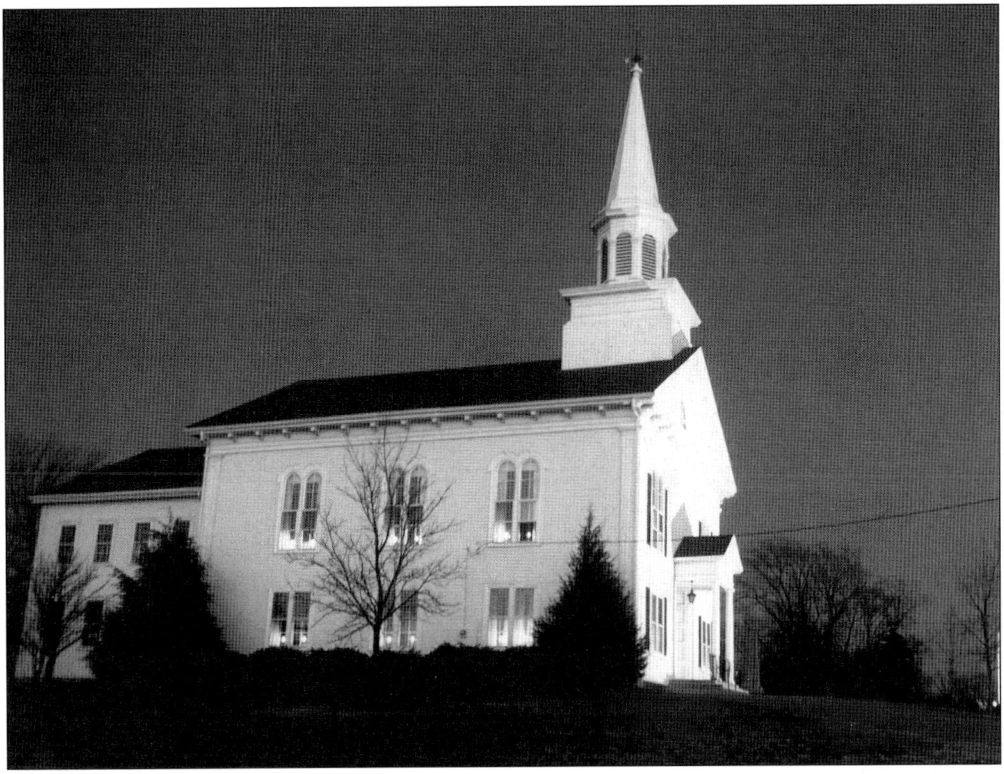

The First Congregational Church in Hanover Center is shown with its window lights glowing on Christmas Eve. (Photograph by Jean Migre.)

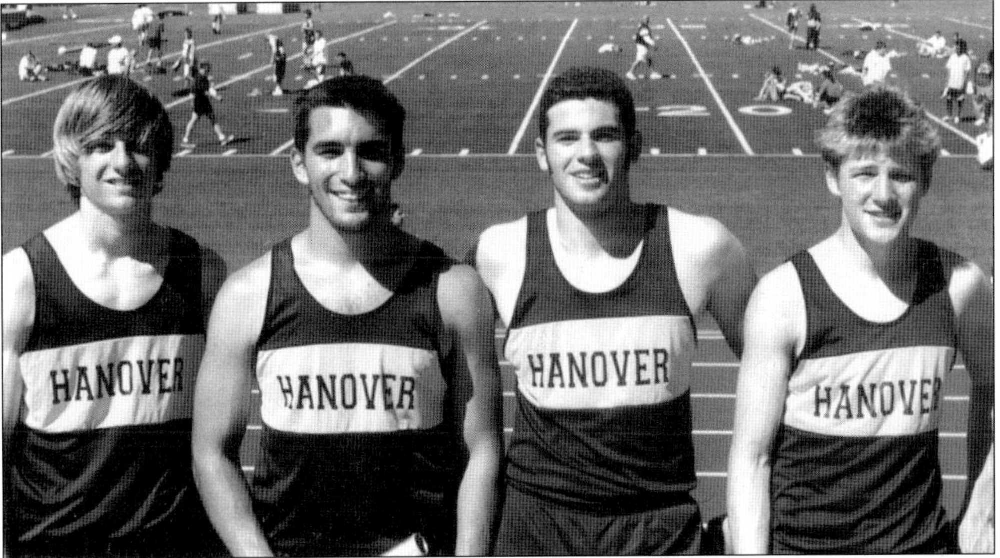

Several longstanding school track records were broken during the 2004 Hanover High School track season. Shown here is the 4-by-100-meter relay team, which ran a record-setting time of 44.72 seconds at the All-State Championships. From left to right are Rob Boyle, Alex Weiss, Paul Maniscalco, and James Wheeler. Other record-setters on the squad included Alex Cook in the mile and Salay Stannard in the long jump.

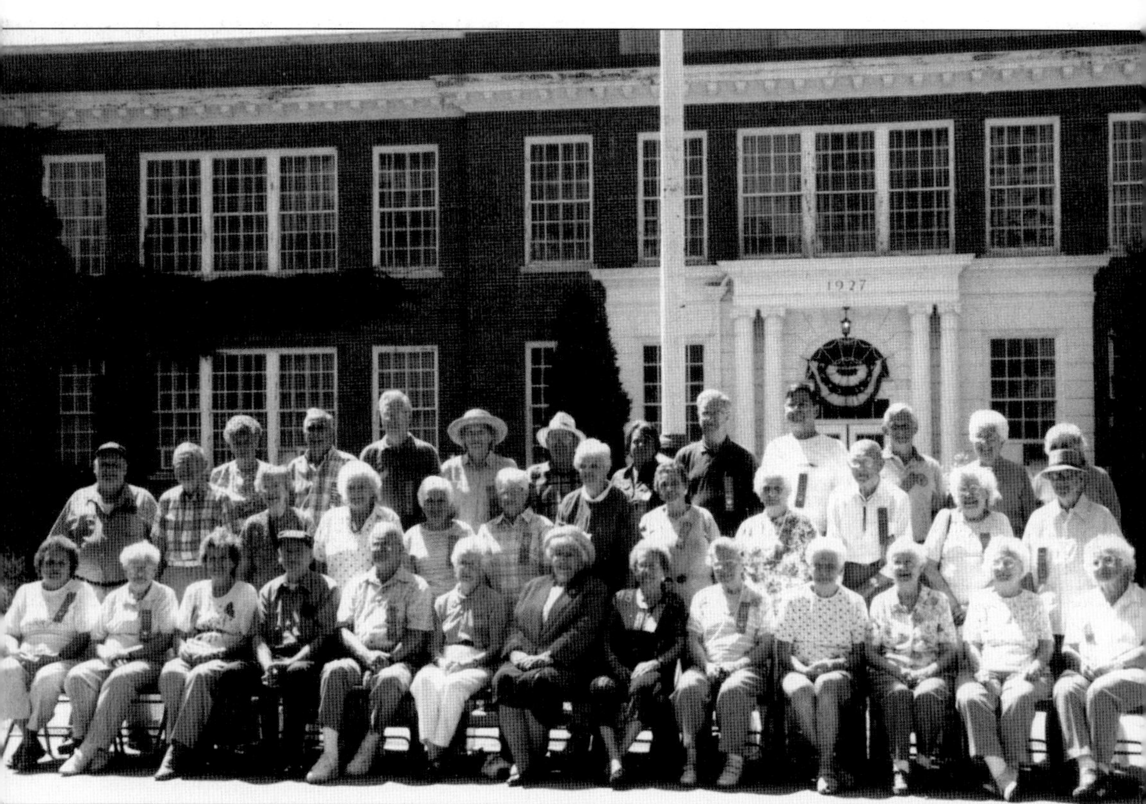

In 2002, a number of graduates of Sylvester High School gathered for the 75th anniversary of the school's opening. Many remembered the school song, written by Esther Hansen and Edna Sangster: "Sylvester High, we're proud of you/ Our own school of the gold and blue/ From North to South/ And East to West/ We know you are the best/ H-A-N-O-V-E-R/ All together let us sing/ Hail! Hail!/ Make the rafters ring/ H-A-N-O-V-E-R! RAH! RAH! RAH!"

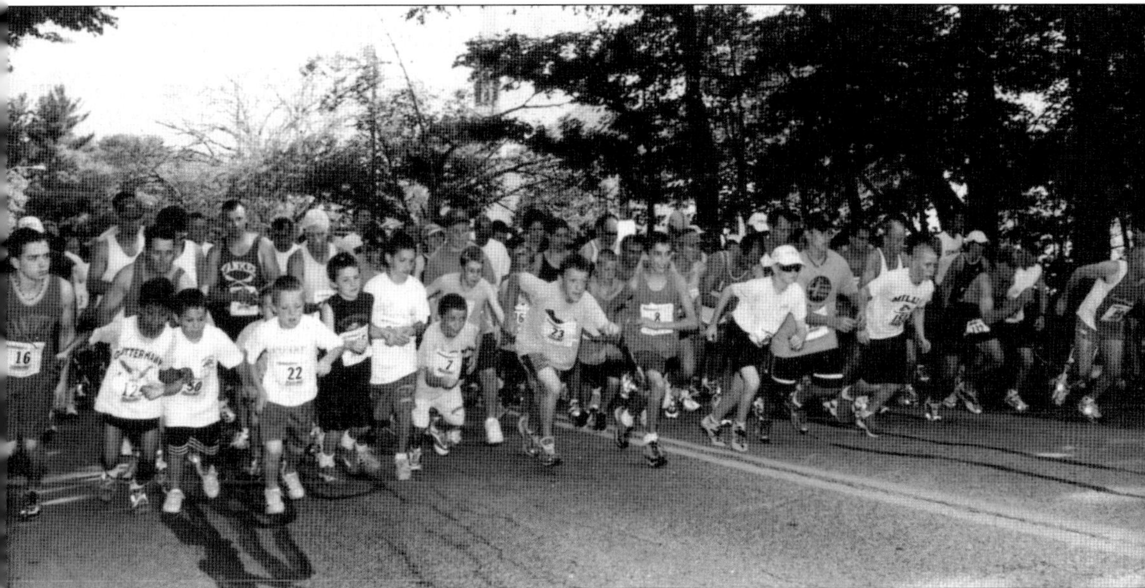

Hanover celebrated its 275th anniversary on June 29, 2002, with a 10-kilometer road race, parade, bandstand performances, and tours of historic sites. The celebration was capped off with an evening bonfire. As seen here at the start of the race, runners of all ages participated. The winner was Alex Cook, No. 16 on the left.

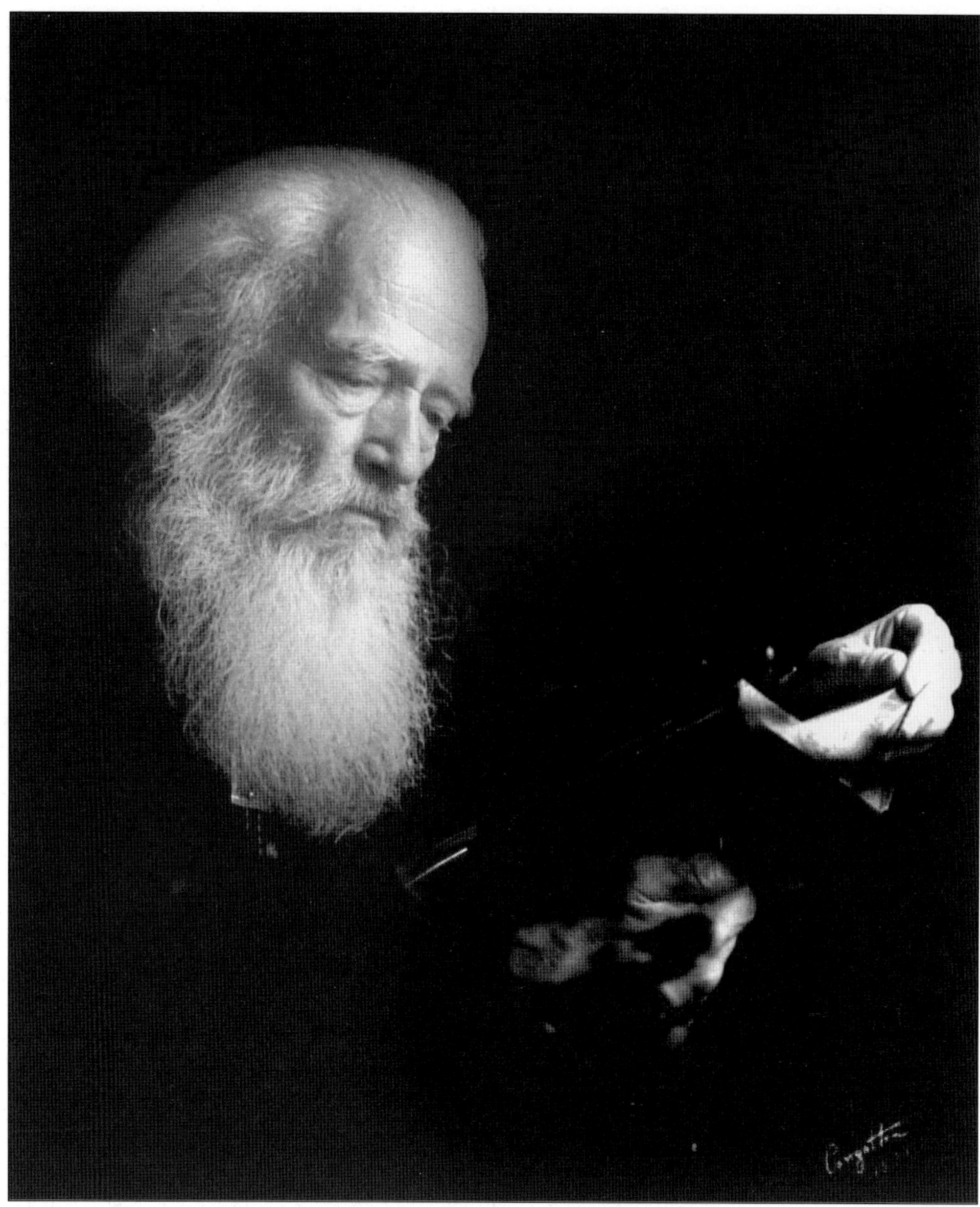

This timeless masterpiece is a portrait of Thomas K. Tindale (1909–1980) taken by J. David Congalton. Tindale, a South Hanover native and government consultant, visited every country in the world, with the exception of Albania and Laos. He and his wife, Harriet, authored the book *The Handmade Papers of Japan* in 1952. Congalton operated Congalton Studios in Pembroke for many years, until his retirement in 2004. Congalton was a Hanover High School teacher for eight years before he became a portrait and commercial photographer. He has earned many awards, including the Professional Photographers of America award.